Putting the EYFS Curriculum into Practice

Sara Miller McCune founded SAGE Publishing in 1965 to support the dissemination of usable knowledge and educate a global community. SAGE publishes more than 1000 journals and over 800 new books each year, spanning a wide range of subject areas. Our growing selection of library products includes archives, data, case studies and video. SAGE remains majority owned by our founder and after her lifetime will become owned by a charitable trust that secures the company's continued independence.

Los Angeles | London | New Delhi | Singapore | Washington DC | Melbourne

Putting the EYFS Curriculum into Practice

Julian Grenier & Caroline Vollans

SSAGE

Los Angeles | London | New Delhi
Singapore | Washington DC | Melbourne

Los Angeles | London | New Delhi
Singapore | Washington DC | Melbourne

SAGE Publications Ltd
1 Oliver's Yard
55 City Road
London EC1Y 1SP

SAGE Publications Inc.
2455 Teller Road
Thousand Oaks, California 91320

SAGE Publications India Pvt Ltd
B 1/I 1 Mohan Cooperative Industrial Area
Mathura Road
New Delhi 110 044

SAGE Publications Asia-Pacific Pte Ltd
3 Church Street
#10-04 Samsung Hub
Singapore 049483

Editor: Delayna Spencer
Editorial assistant: Bali BirchLee
Production editor: Victoria Nicholas
Marketing manager: Dilhara Attygalle
Cover design: Wendy Scott
Typeset by C&M Digitals (P) Ltd, Chennai, India
Printed in the UK

Library of Congress Control Number: 2022939613

British Library Cataloguing in Publication data

A catalogue record for this book is available from the British Library

ISBN 978-1-5297-9917-0
ISBN 978-1-5297-9916-3 (pbk)

At SAGE we take sustainability seriously. Most of our products are printed in the UK using responsibly sourced papers and boards. When we print overseas we ensure sustainable papers are used as measured by the PREPS grading system. We undertake an annual audit to monitor our sustainability.

Dedicated to our mothers:

Janet Grenier, proud Canadian and teacher

Josie Vollans, proud Yorkshire woman who prized education

Contents

About the contributors

Aaron Bradbury is an Early Childhood academic, paying close attention to all aspects of Early Years and Child Centred Practice, Workforce Development, Child Development and Early Help. Aaron's current role is Principal Lecturer for Early Years and Childhood at Nottingham Trent University. He is also the Chair of the LGBTQ+ Early Years working group and manages his own website and community called Early Years Review. Aaron has published texts on apprenticeships and Early Years research.

Matilda Browne is currently the Primary Headteacher at Reach Academy Feltham, an all-through free school for 2- to 18-year-olds in West London. As a Primary Head, she passionately believes that a carefully laid out EYFS curriculum and highly trained staff are vital to a child's success throughout their education and that, therefore, the Early Years should be a priority in all primary schools. Alongside this, Matilda regularly leads training in instructional coaching and was the Primary Curriculum Lead for Humanities, English, Science and RSE for Oak National Academy during the pandemic.

Cassie Buchanan is the CEO of Charter Schools Educational Trust, a cross-phase Trust in South London. Until 2020, Cassie was the headteacher of Charles Dickens Primary School. Under Cassie's leadership, the school became a teaching school, EEF research school, behaviour hub and flexible working ambassador school. Cassie's initial training was as an early years specialist and this has continued to be a passion. Cassie has represented schools on DfE advisory committees, including IELS (International Early Learning Study) and teacher retention and wellbeing. She also represents schools, nurseries and colleges for one of London's Health and Wellbeing Boards. Cassie was awarded an OBE for services to education in January 2021.

Siobhan Campbell was formerly the headteacher of a new, outstanding primary school in Hackney. Most recently, she has worked as a curriculum advisor to schools and as an Evidence Lead in Education for the East London Research School. Siobhan trained as a mathematics specialist teacher and has previously worked as a teacher and school leader in a number of London boroughs.

Tania Choudhury is an accredited SENDCO and Early Years Teacher. She has completed a Master's in Special and Inclusive Education with a particular focus on Autism studies and parental engagement of the BAME community. Tania has contributed towards writings for the Chartered College of Teaching, the Education Endowment Foundation and other institutes on a range of issues related to Early Years. She currently sits on the Editorial Board for the Chartered College's Early Years Hub. Previously, Tania worked with the University of Oxford to learn more about how Bangladeshi children talk and play at home.

Fliss Dewsbery has been studying and working in the field of Early Years for 29 years and has worked in a variety of roles. Facilitating and supporting Early Years Professional Development has threaded throughout her career. She passionately believes that outcomes for children and their families can be improved through robust professional development opportunities, particularly opportunities that facilitate Early Years educators to take a systemic lead on their own learning and the learning of others. Currently, as the Deputy Head of Pen Green, Fliss leads the Research, Training and Development Base where she is responsible for 300 Early Years students.

Jan Dubiel is the Director of Early Years at AISL Harrow International Schools and is a nationally and internationally recognised specialist in Early Childhood Education. He was recently identified by the *Times Educational Supplement* as one of the 10 most influential people in British education and was previously Head of National and International Development at Early Excellence. He has worked as a YN, YR and Y1 teacher, senior leader, consultant and advisor and national lead on the management of the (Early Years) Foundation Stage Profile with QCA. Jan has written widely on different aspects of Early Years policy, pedagogy and practice.

Lindsey Foster is an experienced SENDCo and Deputy Head teacher. She is based at Sheringham Nursery School and Children's Centre. She has a postgraduate diploma in co-ordinating special educational needs and recently achieved the National Professional Qualification for Headship. During her years at Sheringham, Lindsey has had varied experiences and roles as a teacher, SENDCo, Forest School leader, mentor and tutor for school-based initial teacher training. She is passionate about inclusive education and working in partnership with parents. She has a particular interest in play-based learning and Forest School for young children.

Dr Julian Grenier is the headteacher of Sheringham Nursery School and Children's Centre in Newham, London. Julian has worked in the Early Years for the last three decades. He has a doctorate in education (EdD) from the UCL Institute of Education. Julian is a regular columnist for the *Times Educational Supplement*. He has also contributed regularly to *Nursery World* and has written and co-written several bestselling books about early childhood education. Julian has advised the Department for Education on Early Years under Conservative, coalition and Labour administrations. He is the director of the East London Research School. Julian was awarded a CBE in 2022 for his services to Early Years education.

Dr Sinéad Harmey is an Associate Professor in Literacy Education based at the International Literacy Centre at the Institute of Education, UCL's Faculty of Education and Society. Sinéad's research and teaching focus on three interdependent and complementary fields: literacy development and instruction, review methodologies to ensure the successful translation of research to practice, and early literacy intervention.

Dr Alex Hodgkiss is a post-doctoral researcher in the Department of Education, University of Oxford. His research interests focus on the home language environment for monolingual and multilingual families. He also recently led a programme of research on the development and evaluation of programmes to support families in relation to the home language environment.

Fliss James is an experienced Early Years teacher. She is based at Sheringham Nursery School and Children's Centre and is an Evidence Lead in Education for the East London Research School. Alongside this role, Fliss is the EEF Content Specialist for Early Years. During her 19 years in education, Fliss has had varied experiences across the breadth of the Early Years sector as a teacher, trainer, deputy head and tutor for school-based initial teacher training. She has a particular interest in play-based learning, how children learn early mathematics, language development and Forest School for young children.

Professor Eunice Lumsden is Professor of Child Advocacy at the University of Northampton. She is a Route Panel Member for the Institute of Apprenticeships and Technical Education and has advised the government on Early Years qualifications and health inequalities. She led the development of the Early Childhood Graduate Competencies and has contributed to workforce development internationally. Her research interests include the professionalisation of the children's workforce, child maltreatment, social justice, poverty and adoption.

Dr Lala Manners has enjoyed a long and varied career in the field of Early Years Physical Development and Movement studies as a writer, researcher, mentor, practitioner, broadcaster, presenter and consultant. She is currently absorbed in a range of post-pandemic initiatives to support children's overall health and wellbeing. Lala continues to advocate for all things physical in children's lives.

Dr Sandra Mathers is a Senior Researcher and Lecturer at the Department of Education, University of Oxford. She began her career as a primary school teacher and her work remains strongly practice- and policy-relevant. Sandra's research explores how we can best promote high-quality interactions between adults and children, including large-scale longitudinal studies (Millennium Cohort Study, Children of the 2020s), evaluations of government Early Years initiatives (Graduate Leader Fund, Early Education Pilot for Two-Year-Olds), developing and evaluating early language and professional development programmes (URLEY, Talking Time) and studying, and quality and inequality in early education provision.

Anni McTavish worked as a practitioner and manager of an under-fives pre-school in Camden, North London. She is now an Early Years creative arts consultant and trainer. Underlying all her work is an emphasis on children's emotional health and wellbeing. She is currently working on a book about Expressive Arts and Design and facilitates a range of creative projects.

June O'Sullivan MBE is Chief Executive of the award-winning London Early Years Foundation (LEYF), one of the UK's most successful charitable childcare social enterprises.

An inspiring, outspoken speaker, author, podcaster and regular media commentator and advisor to governments, academics and business on all things Early Years, Social Business and Child Poverty, June is a tireless 'disruptor', seeking new ways to influence policy and make society a better place for all children and their families.

Professor Dame Alison Peacock is Chief Executive of the Chartered College of Teaching, a new professional body that seeks to raise our status through celebrating, supporting and connecting teachers to provide expert teaching and leadership. Prior to joining the Chartered College, Dame Alison was Executive Headteacher of The Wroxham School in Hertfordshire. Her career to date has spanned primary, secondary and advisory roles. She is an Honorary Fellow of Queens College and Hughes Hall, Cambridge, and UCL. She is a Visiting Professor of both the University of Hertfordshire and Glyndŵr University and a trustee for Big Change. Her research is published in a series of books about Learning without Limits, offering an alternative approach to inclusive school improvement.

Liz Pemberton (she/her) is the Director of The Black Nursery Manager Ltd – a training and consultancy company which focuses on anti-racist practice within Early Years. With 16 years in the education sector, Liz's roles have included secondary school teacher, public speaker and up until 2020, nursery manager, allowing her to teach, manage, support and educate Early Years students, educators and professionals in a variety of forums. Her mission is to promote inclusive practice in the Early Years education sector, with a particular focus on how race, culture and ethnicity should be considered in this practice.

Sarah Porter is the headteacher at Kay Rowe Nursery School and Children's Centre in East London. She grew up in the countryside but has worked in Early Years for many years in urban areas of London, Bristol and Dorset. Learning outdoors has been a passion for Sarah since the start of her teaching career. She has built wildlife ponds in almost every school she has worked in and really enjoyed seeing the delight and excitement experienced by young children watching tadpoles develop into frogs.

Melissa Prendergast is an experienced Early Years teacher and leader. She is currently Assistant Director of the East London Research School. Melissa is also undertaking a three-year secondment with the charity Peeple, where she is developing a programme to support children's early STEM learning. Her first degree in Ecology influenced her passion for early STEM. Melissa's career in teaching was inspired by her son's experience in a maintained nursery school. The impact of the high-quality education and support her son received was profound. Evidence-informed practice is at the heart of all her work.

Jemima Rhys-Evans is Director of Charles Dickens Research School and London South Teaching School Hub. Before that, she was Deputy Head at Charles Dickens Primary and Nursery School where she led on curriculum design and development. Jemima has led two Department for Education-funded research projects around teacher workload: the Workload Challenge in 2016 and the Teacher Workload Toolkit project in 2020.

Iram Siraj is Professor of Child Development and Education, Department of Education at the University of Oxford. She has directed a number of influential longitudinal studies on the impact of preschool and primary education. Her current studies focus on process quality and key domains of learning, including interventions on the impact of evidence-based professional development promoting physical, language and mathematics learning. She has over 250 publications, including three widely-used rating scales which measure the quality of pedagogy in ECEC that promote child outcomes in the cognitive (ECERS-E 4th Ed. 2010), social-emotional (SSTEW, 2015) and physical (MOVERS, 2017) domains. She was awarded an OBE for her services to ECEC in the Queen's honours in 2015.

Ed Vainker OBE is the CEO of the Reach Foundation and co-founder of the Reach Academy Feltham. Ed co-founded the Reach Children's Hub, building a 'cradle to career' model in Feltham, and is now supporting schools and Trusts around the country to develop their own models. He was in the first cohort of Teach First in 2003 and was awarded an OBE in 2019.

Caroline Vollans was a primary school teacher, specialising in language and literacy development. She then studied and trained in Freudian-Lacanian psychoanalysis. Caroline worked in a hospital as a psychotherapist and a secondary school as a counsellor. She is now a freelance writer and editor, especially interested in topics that combine themes of education and psychoanalysis. Caroline's underlying interest is in giving voice to the unspoken and unheard.

Foreword
Iram Siraj

Two big questions have shaped my thinking and enquiry since I became an early years teacher back in 1983. Why do some children succeed socially, physically and/or academically while others fail? And, how can we help more children fulfil their potential regardless of their background? This book begins to address these questions with leading professionals describing the best early-education, evidence-informed, practice.

My first years of teaching helped me to appreciate the role of those proximal factors which influence children's lives through their early experiences with significant others: parents, carers, siblings, health practitioners, pre-school staff and their immediate community. Similarly, background characteristics and contextual factors (such as poverty, class, developmental issues, ethnicity and gender) also shape children's experiences.

I learned later that these early experiences, from birth to 5, lay the foundations for all future development. My research shows that the life-course trajectories of all future learning are set early, and rarely change during primary and secondary education. It is much easier to change trajectories in the early years.

Every child's life is part lottery, as none can determine their gender, ethnicity, parents or place of birth. These random, and often cruel, factors are the strongest determinants of life prospects, which is precisely why early education is so important. It is during the early years of rapid physical growth and brain development that children benefit the most from high-quality education and schooling – which then becomes a protective factor, ameliorating the risks from the birth lottery.

Despite this, it is only in the last two decades that Early Childhood Education and Care (ECEC) has been offered to all 3- and 4-year-olds (and to most 2-year-olds from families living with disadvantage). Although society has welcomed this provision, it has not been matched with an equal investment in the quality and coherence of the ECEC system, which remains fragmented and with some poorly qualified staff. There have been attempts to strengthen the sector because of the clear research evidence; but there is still a long way to go, and this is recognised by the number of All-Party Parliamentary Groups (APPGs) and House of Commons select committees which have taken evidence over the last three decades.

In the absence of rapid progress in legislation and policy, it is gratifying to see how some leadership in the sector now supports staff in a variety of settings, and this book, edited by Dr Julian Grenier and Caroline Vollans, is an excellent example of this. It is also refreshing to see the ECEC sector starting to think seriously about context, curriculum, pedagogy and assessment in early education. In the heated debates between early years specialists, it is encouraging to find a book which is both broad and balanced, and which supports ECEC educators to improve their understanding of knowledge domains, pedagogical skills, curriculum design and how young children learn.

The book resonates well, and extends the Early Years Foundation Stage (EYFS) and *Development Matters*. The authors of the chapters respect educators' ability to understand and appreciate the importance of solid research on important topics like inclusion, early language, literacy and maths development.

The examples and case studies of practice bring the book to life, and include babies, toddlers, pre-schoolers and reception-class children. They also draw on a variety of providers, including childminders and pre- and primary school provision. The 14 chapters provide a comprehensive guide to an early education curriculum for ECEC educators and leaders. It will help them to design and implement a strong curriculum supported by appropriate pedagogy and effective assessment.

In particular, this book helps every early educator to dampen the effects of the birth lottery and provides them with tools and knowledge to give children from the most disadvantaged backgrounds the start they deserve to fulfil their potential.

Iram Siraj OBE
Professor of Child Development and Education at the University of Oxford

1

Introduction: The importance of curriculum in the early years

Julian Grenier

In December 1999, I was sitting in a grand office overlooking the River Thames. I should have been concentrating on a meeting. Instead, I was looking out of the window, watching the construction teams as they failed to lift the Millennium Wheel into place. The focus of the meeting was putting the finishing touches on an exciting new document: *Curriculum Guidance for the Foundation Stage* (QCA, 2000). But it was proving as difficult to get the document into shape, as it was to get the big wheel standing up straight.

Nearly a quarter of a century later, both have stood the test of time well. *Curriculum Guidance* remains an important milestone in the history of the early years in England. It was the first time the government acknowledged the importance of early learning. Its scope was ambitious, and its tone was friendly. Like *Birth to Three Matters* (DfES, 2002) which followed on, it was practical. Like many practitioners, I referred to these documents all the time.

After 2000, the term 'curriculum' got rarer and rarer in discussions about Early Childhood Education and Care. By the time we got to the 2012 revision of *Development Matters* (Early Education, 2012), 'curriculum' had completely vanished. What does this tell us?

History matters

The story is important, because it explains some of the rationale behind the 2021 changes to the Early Years Foundation Stage.

Going back to 2012: this was the year that assessment, outcomes and tracking triumphed over curriculum. Why did this happen? Firstly, there was a desire to think about 'personalised learning' for every child. Once a child had accomplished something, the educator would plan their individual 'next steps'. Secondly, there was a desire to ensure that every child thrived in the early years. We could track each child, and then analyse the outcomes of different groups of children (by gender, for example, or by ethnicity). By acting quickly if a group fell behind, we could promote more equal outcomes.

These intentions were admirable. They were underpinned by the best of motives – that every child mattered, and no child should be left behind. However, in practice, there were unintended and negative consequences.

Firstly, many of us put our main emphasis on helping children to move from one age-band to the next. We tried to demonstrate, through our data, that every child was making strong progress. But the pressure to show progress in this way was at the expense of children's secure learning. Instead of giving children plenty of time to gain a deep understanding of counting to five, for example, the pressure was to move them to the next level by getting them counting with bigger numbers. The 'best-fit' approach to assessment compounded this problem. It meant that a child might be assessed as 'secure' in an age-band, yet still have major gaps in their understanding.

The focus on outcomes ultimately narrowed the experiences many children had in the early years. The Reception year came to be all about the 17 Early Learning Goals. It also created a workload crisis. Imagine that you have 30 children in your group, and each child has two or three personalised 'next steps'. That means you need to hold 60 to 90 'next steps' in mind at the same time, and plan for them all. Evidencing that children had achieved those next steps became a huge task.

When children experience a narrow education, focused on achieving good outcomes in exams, tests or assessments, they experience an impoverished curriculum. The evidence from a range of studies, by Ofsted and the Sutton Trust, for example, shows that this is especially bad for disadvantaged children (Allen and Thomson, 2016; Ofsted, 2019a). The source of those problems is in the early years. Where, for example, there is pressure to 'get children writing' in Reception, this can be at the expense of their speaking and listening. Without well-developed early language and a rich vocabulary, children will struggle to read and write well. What happens when we make children write sentences, when they do not yet have the physical dexterity they need? The children end up ploughing their pencils miserably through exercise books, achieving little and losing all motivation to write.

Disadvantaged children are already well behind all children by the end of the early years. That 4.6 month gap doubles by the end of primary school, and doubles again by the end of secondary. Similar gaps affect many children from ethnic minority backgrounds, most notably children of Gypsy/Roma, Black Caribbean and Pakistani heritage.

This is an unacceptable state of affairs.

The importance of curriculum

Curriculum Guidance for the Foundation Stage suggested that children learn in two major ways:

- when they play freely in well-resourced environments, with adults sometimes intervening sensitively
- when adults show children how to do things, by modelling

Shortly afterwards, the important EPPE (Effective Pre-School Education) study began reporting its findings. Together, the introduction of a statutory phase, and the dissemination of research findings, brought about a radical improvement in early childhood education in England (Siraj-Blatchford et al., 2008). Findings from the linked REPEY (Researching Effective Pedagogy in the Early Years) study showed which practices in early education were effective in promoting children's learning. Notably, this included 'Sustained Shared Thinking', defined as:

> … an episode in which two or more individuals 'work together' in an intellectual way to solve a problem, clarify a concept, evaluate activities, extend a narrative etc. Both parties must contribute to the thinking and it must develop and extend.

> (Siraj-Blatchford et al., 2002, p. 8)

Here, we see how sophisticated understanding of both curriculum and pedagogy are necessary. As practitioners, we are 'scaffolding' children's learning. We give children just enough help to achieve something they could not do on their own. We are constantly mindful of children's emergent development: what they are learning to do, but can't quite do yet. This is a deeper and richer understanding of the adult role than the useful but limited suggestions in *Curriculum Guidance for the Foundation Stage*: 'intervening sensitively' whilst children play, and 'modelling'.

This means that we need a wide-ranging pedagogical repertoire. Sometimes it is important to let children initiate their own play freely (Whitebread et al., 2005). But we also need to be mindful that children's play can become quite repetitive, without sensitive intervention and support from adults. If children have a narrow range of interests and vocabulary when they come into a setting, then they will need practitioners to introduce them to new experiences and words. Even in a very wealthy country like England, many children are growing up in poverty. Those children need early years provision which offers them great riches. They also need us to drive social change to eliminate child poverty.

Child development

Practices like 'Sustained Shared Thinking' (Siraj-Blatchford et al., 2002; Siraj-Blatchford, 2009) require us to understand child development. We might visualise child development as a series of waves, overlapping each other, rather than seeing it like a stepladder, with one stage very clearly separate to the next.

To switch to a different metaphor: with child development, we know the overall direction of travel. But, at any one moment, we cannot say definitely what a child's typical development might look like. Just because some children achieve a certain set of developments at the age of 3, doesn't mean that all children will.

Imagine you are travelling out of a big city into the countryside. The overall change you will see is a shift from built-up streets, housing and shops to more open country with more sky and fewer buildings. However, at any moment, what you see may not exactly indicate where you are. You may look out the window and see lots of grass, trees and space, and be next to a large urban park. You may see shops and dense housing and be passing through a country town.

When we think of children's learning, we need to understand the big picture. As we consider children's emergent learning, we will carefully balance children's independent play with an intentional approach. Epstein (2007) usefully defines 'intentional teaching' as acting with specific outcomes or goals in mind for every area of children's learning. We will not serve the children's interests best if we look at a stepladder outline of early development and paste in 'next steps' onto a plan for the child, or group.

Sometimes, it is argued that children and child development have not changed. We should stick to practices which have served children perfectly well for decades. I would argue otherwise. Child development is an interactive process. It involves the child and their biology, and it also involves important people and the wider culture. For example, children now are 'digital natives'. They switch smoothly between the online world, and the real world. They watch a Spiderman cartoon on YouTube, fashion a cape from a bit of material and set about saving the world. The impact of ICT on child development may be cause for concern, or something to welcome. Either way it has changed childhood and child development. You could make the same argument about the loss of play out in the streets. As I write, I am looking out over a small street in East London lined with cars. Thirty years ago, it would have been teeming with children.

We have seen great changes to childhood. Children now spend much more time away from their families, in early years settings. They have many more social connections. This means that early education and care now provide a space for the experiences children would once have had in the home and on the street. Child development has changed. Early education and care has changed, too. These changes mean that play is, if anything, even more important in the early years than it used to be.

Play and curriculum

For play-based approaches to work, supporting children's communication is crucial. As children become better communicators, with a richer vocabulary, they are increasingly able to explore and discuss concepts. Sustained shared thinking rests on the foundations of play. Play is the most potent context for children to develop their communication and collaboration. Through engagement with literature, nursery rhymes and songs, children become increasingly competent, socially and culturally.

Play is also a powerful context for children to develop their metacognition and self-regulation. Again, this requires our sensitive intervention. Merely enabling children to choose from a range of paint brushes doesn't make them more independent learners. We need to support the opportunities in the environment with thoughtful interactions. We might say, 'I'm interested that you chose the biggest brush – what were you thinking then?' As children's choices become more intentional, they become more independent as learners.

Discussions about early years practice can quickly become confrontational. Should we focus on what children are learning? Or should we focus on developing their skills as learners, through the Characteristics of Effective Teaching and Learning? Should we focus on helping children develop as thinkers? Or should we focus on them learning the foundations they need for later school subjects like science and English? These are often false oppositions. We must hold both in mind at the same time. For example, sustained shared thinking requires the practitioner to consider:

- curriculum content: you need to think about *something*
- pedagogy: the skilful techniques we use to engage a child in an extended conversation on a shared topic

Similarly, as the Harvard Center on the Developing Child notes:

> Interventions that include an explicit focus on executive function skills do not need to be implemented separately from those focused on instruction in early literacy and math abilities. Indeed, the complex interactions that occur among executive functioning, social competence, and academic skills in preschool classrooms underscore the likely value of blending interventions designed to strengthen working memory, inhibition, and attention control with curricula focused on early literacy and math skill.
>
> (Center on the Developing Child, 2011, p. 9)

Achieving a balanced approach

I have argued above that we need a balanced approach to early education and care. As educators, we are using assessment all the time to identify the child's emergent learning. That way, we can plan to help children repeat, practise, enjoy and consolidate. That gives children secure foundations for their future learning. By thinking like this, we can avoid false polarities, like 'the child's right to play in the early years' versus 'preparing children for their future learning'. Play which is sensitively supported and guided by practitioners who are 'intentional teachers' will ensure that children are ready for the curriculum in Key Stage 1 and beyond. Similarly, thoughtful Key Stage 1 teachers will be mindful that we call the EYFS the 'foundation stage' for a reason. They will take care to ensure that children consolidate all that foundational learning, by applying the programmes of study flexibly.

Achieving this balance also means that we need to consider children's prior learning and experiences carefully. As I argued above, where a child doesn't yet have all the skills, concepts and vocabulary they need to start writing sentences, we will do them a disservice if we just make them write anyway. We will also do them a disservice if we merely wait for them to be 'ready' for writing. We need to consider all the prior skills and concepts the child needs, and then plan the activities which will promote this learning. Here are a few examples of what that might include:

- outdoor play with a focus on large muscle development (arms and shoulders)
- games which involve starting and stopping, going up and going back down
- activities to develop small muscle skills; for example: picking up bits of gravel and putting them in a pot (finger strength, coordination and pincer grip)

We must also be careful about mis-applying the insight that early learning is holistic. It's true that children in the early years are often learning in several domains at once. For example, as a child helps to prepare their own snack from a range of healthy ingredients, they may be learning in the areas of:

- personal, social and emotional development: making healthy choices
- physical development: using a knife to spread hummus on their cracker
- mathematical development: taking two crackers for their plate, and no more, so that there is enough food for everyone

However, we need to think carefully about what children already know, and what they need to know next. Otherwise, we can easily overwhelm them with too much to think about. When we add plastic numbers and letters to the water tray, we are confusing children, not helping their learning. We are expecting them to play with the water and somehow 'absorb' learning about letters and numbers as well. In most cases, where it appears that a child is learning well in a context like that, it is because they were already secure in the knowledge. They already knew how to recognise numbers, so they could do this whilst playing with numbers in the water. It gave them an opportunity to practise what they already know. However, for any child who does not know their numerals, this activity is merely confusing. They are likely to be too distracted to learn: are they supposed to be concentrating on the feel of the water, splashing, or learning number names?

This is why we cannot expect every child to 'learn maths through play'. We can certainly interact with children's play to prompt mathematical learning. As a child spreads their hummus, we can talk about 'covering' the cracker. We can draw the child's attention to the shape of the cracker (and maybe contrast square cream crackers with round water biscuits). This can help children with their early learning about shapes and areas.

However, we will also need to plan adult-guided activities up-front which focus children on key concepts, like shapes or numbers. We might work with a small group of children, using

Anno's Counting Book (Anno, 1986), to learn and practise saying numbers from 1 to 12 and match those with the number symbols. Children will need lots of repetition, in many different contexts, to become secure in their counting. This type of careful planning is good for all children, and especially good for children who haven't joined in with counting activities at home.

Every child needs a well-planned, high-quality early education which provides them with the knowledge, vocabulary and skills they need for a successful future in school and beyond. This is important to all children, and especially so for those children growing up in disadvantaged circumstances. As Iram Siraj and her colleagues point out:

> Although the importance of high quality ECEC [Early Childhood Education and Care] for fostering children's development and learning extends across the gradient of social disadvantage, it is particularly significant for children from highly disadvantaged backgrounds.
>
> (Siraj et al., 2016, p. 4)

Finally, it is important to reflect on the experiences of children with Special Educational Needs and Disabilities (SEND). The Education Policy Institute (EPI) (2020) reported that children with SEND are, on average, 10–15 months behind other children by the end of the EYFS. Nearly 20 years earlier, the REPEY (Researching Effective Pedagogy in the Early Years) team studied those children described as 'struggling learners' (Siraj-Blatchford et al., 2002) by practitioners. The researchers found that this group of children experienced a much narrower curriculum. They experienced more negative interactions with practitioners, and fewer interactions focused on learning. In the last 20 years, we have made huge strides to improve inclusive education in the early years. Yet the EPI findings suggest that we still have much to do. We need to consider our early years curriculum carefully, so that it includes all children. We need to give extra help when needed, so that all children can access that curriculum. This is where scaffolding, again, is such a powerful technique. To be more inclusive, we need to 'scaffold up' so that every child takes part in, and enjoys, the same early years curriculum. We need to call time on the type of 'differentiating down' which can leave children with SEND accessing an impoverished, watered-down curriculum.

Conclusion

Ever since the poet Wordsworth invented the concept of 'early childhood', we have been aware of what a special and sensitive time this is. Anyone who is regularly in contact with very young children will have a feel for their wonderful sense of alive-ness, joy and potential. As the nursery school pioneer Margaret McMillan wrote, 'to move, to run, to find things out by new movement, to feel one's life in every limb, that is the life of early childhood' (McMillan, 1930, p. 23). It is important that we do not over-programme early education and dampen that joy. It is important that we value every child and recognise their special talents and unique character.

However, that does not mean taking up a romanticised view. Every child's development will not flow as naturally as the caterpillar's development into a butterfly. High-flown rhetoric about childhood and vaguely invoking 'beliefs' is not enough.

As the Harvard Center on the Developing Child argues, 'brains are built, not born'. To support that building well, we need to understand the principles of construction, and we need effective plans which we carry out well.

We need to think through our approach to pedagogy, curriculum and assessment with care and precision.

That's exactly what the authors of the following chapters have done so eloquently. As Alison Peacock reminds us at the book's conclusion, this is a rich conversation which we need to carry on. There is much to celebrate in the early years. Yet there is still much we need to learn and do. The wide range of authors in this book offer practical and evidence-based ways to think about the curriculum in the early years. I hope you will join with them, in a spirit of challenge with partnership. That way, we can keep the conversation going about what's best for young children in the early years.

Throughout this book, 'parent' refers to parents, carers, adoptive and foster parents, and guardians.

2

A curriculum that promotes equality and challenges racism and sexism

Eunice Lumsden

Introduction

I began my career in higher education in 2002 and some of my earliest memories include visiting Early Childhood Education and Care (ECEC) settings that had sections labelled 'Multi-Cultural Area'. In my previous role as a social worker, valuing difference and diversity and addressing how they impact people's lives were embedded in practice. Consequently, I was rather taken aback that for some in ECEC inclusion was an 'add on'. They were unable to see that all children, regardless of the demographics of the setting, needed experiences that reflected the fact that England is a multi-cultural society.

Practice has evolved and the Statutory Framework for the Early Years Foundation Stage (EYFS) (DfE, 2021c, p. 5) states that every child deserves 'equality of opportunity and anti-discriminatory practice, ensuring that every child is included and supported'. In other words, differences should be 'seen as assets to be appreciated, rather than problems to be solved' (Thompson, 2021, p. 6). Early years practice must recognise and value 'differences' in gender, sexual identity, heritage, religion, family background, class, disability and country of origin.

This chapter will demonstrate why equality in our work is not optional; it is the right of every child and enshrined in law. The discussion will illustrate how different areas of inequality are connected and that a holistic approach in practice is important. The language of equality will be discussed, and you will be supported to examine and reflect on your own beliefs, including how unconscious bias can impact on your work with children and how you respond to others.

Exploring these areas, regardless of your background, gender, sexuality, disability, religion and culture, will be challenging. However, embracing anti-oppressive and anti-discriminatory practice is an essential, not a desirable, outcome in our work with children and families. Through addressing your values, beliefs and attitudes, you will begin to understand the role you play in providing a curriculum where inequality is addressed.

The legal and policy context

The importance of equality is firmly embedded in legislation and the policies that govern our work in the early years. The United Nations Convention on the Rights of the Child (UNICEF, 2019) is ratified by the United Kingdom and should underpin all our work in the early years. Article 2 is pertinent to the focus of this chapter:

> The Convention applies to every child without discrimination, whatever their ethnicity, gender, religion, language, abilities or any other status, whatever they think or say, whatever their family background.

> (UNICEF, 2019)

This right not to be discriminated against is also embedded in the Children Act (1989) and the Equality Act (2010). The Equality Act replaced and consolidated former legislation to simplify the law. It identifies all unlawful areas of discrimination and includes the legal duty for all institutions to ensure equality of opportunity and protection of rights for all. It is against the law to discriminate against someone because of:

- age
- disability
- gender reassignment
- marriage and civil partnership

- pregnancy and maternity
- race
- religion or belief
- sex
- sexual orientation

These are called protected characteristics. They can offer us a useful framework to reflect on our own values, beliefs and attitudes. The reflective questions at the end of this chapter will help you to consider how your setting ensures they are embedded.

We all live in a society that, despite legislation, is not equal, nor is the aspiration for an inclusive society held by all. Research by the Equality and Human Rights Commission (Abrams et al., 2018) found that at least 42% of people indicated they had faced prejudice. Some people also expressed negative responses to some of the protective factors, including sexual orientation, gender identity and specific ethnic groups. The pandemic that began in 2020 has also reinforced the inequalities in society and held a mirror up to the structural and health inequalities in the UK (Marmot, 2020a).

Recently, the debates on *intersectionality* (Bernard, 2022) have provided a theoretical framework for understanding the multiple and multifaceted oppression and discrimination faced by people. We are required to abide by the law and are held accountable for our actions. Therefore, understanding this interlayered area and the wider context that early years practice is nested in is vital for all that work in the sector. Legal requirements, policies and procedures should be explicit and known by all, as should the EYFS. Embedded within it is the importance of equal opportunity and principles of uniqueness, difference and inclusion, as well as the importance of partnership working with parents and carers.

However, it is not just about knowing – it is about actions. What is the ethos of your place of work and how do you continually focus on your development in this area? Those working with infants, children and families must be committed to learning, discussing, reflecting and developing their practice, as well as challenging others. It is this continual cycle that will enable settings to embed high-quality practice that meets the overarching principles of the EYFS.

The language of equality

Understanding the terms that are used in legislation, policy documents and practice to promote equality is an important starting point. One of the challenges is ensuring a shared understanding of the same terms. There also needs to be an understanding that practice in this area is about social justice. To promote social justice, you need to understand diversity and the challenges, inequalities, oppression and discrimination experienced by children and families.

For all of us who work with children and families, engaging in these debates will enhance our work and make us address our value base and reflect on the judgements we make and the language we use.

As you engage with the discussion that follows, hold in mind the quotation from the children that the *Nurturing Care Framework* (WHO, 2018, p. 2) uses to capture our work in early childhood: 'If we change the beginning of the story, we change the whole story'.

Social justice

This broad term and its principles are captured effectively by Tedam (2020), who states:

> Social justice is the fair, just and respectful treatment of all people, while recognising that unfairness, corruption and inequalities are the leading causes of war, conflict, inhumane treatment, suffering, pain, exploitation and many other ills that confront our world today.
>
> (Tedam, 2020, p. 60)

Embedded in this definition is the idea that social justice is broader than fairness for the individual. It is a *sociopolitical* term that embraces what is happening in society as well as at a political level. In short, social justice is about how the systems we operate in can perpetuate injustice. For those working in the EYFS, this is important as you will work with infants, children and families who have been discriminated against.

Anti-oppressive and anti-discriminatory practice

These two terms are closely aligned and often used together. For some, reading this chapter may be the first time you have explored the terms in greater detail. Anti-discriminatory practice is embedded in the EYFS and practitioner and professional standards. These terms are complex and need to be understood holistically, drawing on the sociological, economic and political contexts as well as the legal frameworks that govern our work.

Arguably, the language of oppression does not sit well with the language of the early years. However, to provide young children with the best start, we must understand the unique child and their story. In ECEC, we are ideally placed to work with children and their families. We can provide new ways to eliminate the barriers they may face now and in the future.

This can be done by embedding anti-oppressive practices which proactively address the oppression faced by individuals, groups and communities in our work. This involves understanding that some are oppressed, some are the oppressors, and that those who have been oppressed can become the oppressors. Also, being oppressed can lead people to fight for their rights and freedom (Tedam, 2020).

If we consider child poverty, the number of children in this category is increasing year on year, even though at least one of their parents is working (CPAG, 2021). The impact of child poverty is well documented, yet the research by Simpson, Lumsden, McDowall Clark and others (2015, 2017, 2018) highlights how the effects of poverty on child development are not always understood by practitioners. Understanding the causes and impact of poverty is important to meet the requirements of the EYFS. Staff need training that explores this. It will enable practitioners to address their views about families living in poverty and explore how practice can be enhanced. However, the challenges of this cannot be underestimated. Poor pay and working conditions permeate the sector (Bonetti, 2019), which means that members of the ECEC workforce are part of the 'in work' poverty statistics.

Through developing our knowledge, understanding and appreciation of the experiences of others, we begin to develop our empathy and skills in anti-discriminatory practice: practice that acknowledges our *power* in situations to make a difference. Understanding that in ECEC we all have the power to act in ways that can make a difference, is key to creating change. You can explore this further through the reflective questions at the end of this chapter.

When we exert power over someone, or someone uses it over us, we need to consider two things:

1. the occurrence itself
2. the feelings evoked in us

Our experiences, whether positive or negative, have an impact on our feelings. Those of us who choose to work with infants, children and their families have a responsibility to understand the *power* we have in our interactions with others. Through this understanding, we can begin to advocate more effectively and address specific areas of discrimination, including racism and sexism and unconscious bias.

Unconscious bias

It may be hard to comprehend that our actions towards others are influenced by factors that are not in our immediate consciousness. These factors are deep-rooted and have been formed from previous experiences and exposure, or lack of them, to certain groups in society. Even if we *think* we are being fair, unconscious bias may lead us to think about different groups in society in certain ways as well as influencing our decision-making and actions. It can influence the decisions we make about friends, the groups we join or avoid, how we think about certain issues and the things we buy – for example, buying boy dolls, men working in ECEC and the impact of the Travelling Community staying near an ECEC setting. For those we interact with, our actions can have wider implications. For instance, gender, sexual orientation, age, ethnicity and disability are some of the protected factors under the Equality Act (2010), yet at an interview for a job, our (unconscious) beliefs and prejudices may impact who is successful.

I appreciate the complexity of this area, but educators have an important role to play in creating enabling environments that are representative, inclusive and empowering for every child. Importantly, they need to understand that inclusion means that those being included need to feel they belong. If you think about the example at the start of this chapter – a 'multi-cultural' area: the message is one of exclusion, not inclusion. This shows that the environments we are in can leave messages in our unconscious that last a lifetime.

I want to share an example from my journey to reinforce this point. My special doll from childhood was something rarely seen in the 1960s as it was a 'Black Doll' and that is what I called her. I remember people asking me why she didn't have a name, but to me, she did. You can read many things into my actions as a child but, looking back as an adult, I think it reflected what I was experiencing. My mother was from Sri Lanka and my father was White British. I was often referred to by many names other than the name my parents gave me.

Can you think of examples when you have referred to others in a discriminatory way or challenged others who have? The language we use is powerful and can lead to discrimination.

To change this, we need to be open to learning, reflecting on our practice and personal and professional challenge. We also need to see the world through the experiences of others. This cannot happen unless we recognise that unconscious bias exists and, while we cannot change what has happened to us, we can explore where our views come from and undertake training. Through these processes, we can minimise their impact on our work.

Anti-racist practice

We live in a society where racism is prevalent. The murder in May 2020 of George Floyd in the USA by police officers arresting him led to a considerable public outcry. The 'Black Lives Matter' movement has led to a renewed focus on the role of the early years in addressing racism. The issues are not new in early years practice, but it is a multifaceted and challenging area. As Tedam (2015, p. 93) states, 'Early years practitioners will need to be aware of racism and its long-term effects on children's self-esteem and identity.' She highlights that if incidents of racism are not addressed, the message received by others is that 'the practitioners in early years provisions condone racist and discriminatory behaviours and attitudes'. Rather, the victims and perpetrators of racist behaviour need to know it is wrong.

Lane (2008) points out that we must not get into a 'blame' culture or feel guilty when mistakes are made; nor should practitioners think they are better than others if they understand issues and see racist actions that others cannot. The important point is that racism is a complex area where unconscious bias plays an important role in how we view the world. However, we must address it in our work and make it visible to others when we see it in action.

Understanding racism and the impact it has is an area of ongoing development for us all. Discussions and training need to be addressed sensitively and in non-threatening environments where people feel able to explore the issues, as well as seeing them through the eyes of others. This is not always easy to achieve. As the discussion in this chapter highlighted, you cannot fulfil your duties unless you open yourself up to the ongoing learning journey that is required. To be an anti-racist practitioner, you first need to understand the many different forms racism can take and that it is deeply embedded in the history of our society.

Jane Lane (2008, p. 32) argues that myths and misunderstandings about racism can be removed if the different types of racism are understood. She identifies these as:

- racial prejudice
- racial discrimination
- racial harassment
- racial hatred
- racial violence
- racial assumptions
- racial stereotyping
- cultural racism
- sectarianism and anti-religious racism
- xenoracism
- institutional racism
- structural racism
- state racism

The list shows that racism is not just about how we may act, or how it impacts the individual, but that it can be embedded throughout the workplace (institutional racism) and in the society in which we live (structural racism). You will also see how intersectionality as a framework can support your learning and understanding of different people's experiences. Understanding racism through these different lenses is an important step in the journey to create inclusive early years environments.

Anti-sexist practice

To understand why anti-sexist practice is important in the early years, practitioners need to understand:

1. what sexist behaviour is
2. the impact of sexual discrimination, and
3. how it can be addressed

Like other protective factors, discrimination because of your sex can be experienced personally as well as being embedded in the structures and organisations we interact with. While it can impact all, women are particularly affected because of the historical context of the relationship between men and women and gender assumptions. The terms 'patriarchy' and 'male privilege' are much used. These are complex areas concerned with understanding the dominance of men over women in all structures of society.

Anti-sexist practice is about addressing these gender assumptions and taking action to eradicate or minimise inequality because of your sex. In the UK, there is an ongoing focus addressing sexual discrimination, including action to proactively address the gender pay gap between men and women. This is gradually reducing (Office for National Statistics, 2021), though we have a long way to go. We now have women on active duty in the armed forces and more women in leadership roles, but equality of opportunity for all women is still an aspiration requiring considerable work.

The early years sector provides a mirror to the many challenges faced by women in the workplace. Despite the increasing requirements on the workforce to prepare children for school and their future as citizens, the early years is a low-pay, low-status occupation. The challenges of this were captured effectively by Cooke and Lawton (2008, p. 6), who highlighted the importance of early years services in 'delivering both economic prosperity and social justice' for young children, yet receiving no financial reward for the workforce to upskill themselves. Furthermore, debates still exist about whether pre-school provision is about early learning or providing 'childcare' while parents work. However, traditionally childcare is viewed as women's work and closely connected to motherhood. This has negatively impacted pay scales in the sector and how it is valued by others (Bonetti, 2019; Osgood, 2011).

Conclusion

This chapter has provided an overview of the areas that practitioners need to engage with to put into practice the EYFS requirement of 'equality of opportunity and anti-discriminatory practice, ensuring that every child is included and supported' (DfE, 2021c, p. 4). The key message is that to meet these requirements and those of the Equality Act (2010), practitioners must understand how inequality and discrimination manifest. We are all on a challenging learning journey in these areas. Not only do those working in the early years need the knowledge, but they also need empathy and insight into the lived experiences of others and the skills to promote anti-discriminatory practice for all.

In conclusion, I would like to draw on the words of Martin Luther King. In 1964 he stated, 'The time is always right to do what is right.' Yes, the meaning of his words is so true, but real change will only come when, one by one, we can say, 'I've noticed this…', 'I have challenged others to…', 'We need to…' and 'I am open to…' (Lumsden, 2021).

Reflective questions

1.   It is against the law to discriminate against someone because of:
     - age
     - disability
     - gender reassignment
     - marriage and civil partnership
     - pregnancy and maternity
     - race
     - religion or belief
     - sex
     - sexual orientation

How does your setting tackle prejudice and promote understanding between people from different groups? Are there areas of practice that you could improve?

2.   When was the last time you exerted power over someone? When was the last time someone used their power over you? How did it make you feel? How do you think it made them feel?

3

Communication and Language

Sandra Mathers

EYFS Statutory Educational Programme

The development of children's spoken language underpins all seven areas of learning and development. Children's back-and-forth interactions from an early age form the foundations for language and cognitive development. The number and quality of the conversations they have with adults and peers throughout the day in a language-rich environment are crucial. By commenting on what children are interested in or doing, and echoing back what they say with new vocabulary added, practitioners will build children's language effectively. Reading frequently to children, and engaging them actively in stories, non-fiction, rhymes and poems, and then providing them with extensive opportunities to use and embed new words in a range of contexts, will give children the opportunity to thrive. Through conversation, story-telling and role play, where children share their ideas with support and modelling from their teacher, and sensitive questioning that invites them to elaborate, children become comfortable in using a rich range of vocabulary and language structures.

Introduction

It is hard to overstate the importance of early language. Children need strong oral language skills to underpin their social communication, relationships, literacy and learning in all areas of development.

The aspects of oral language are outlined in Table 3.1. They include both receptive language (understanding) and expressive language (speaking). Understanding and speaking are related but can develop at different rates. For example, a child learning English as an additional language may have good understanding, but they may not yet be ready or able to communicate verbally in English. Most children follow the same pattern in their language development. But the different phases overlap greatly. This means that children reach milestones at very different times within the 'typical' range.

The role of the adult

As practitioners in the early years, we play a vital role in supporting young children's oral language development. There is a window of opportunity in the first five years, when children's language is more mouldable. The home environment has the strongest influence. Children's early education experiences are also very important. The quality of the language which children hear and engage with matters more than the quantity. For example, the range and sophistication of the words spoken to children predict their pre-school vocabulary growth and later literacy outcomes more strongly than the *number* of words they hear. Children need to hear many different words and to hear unusual as well as everyday words.

Conversations with a more experienced language partner are one of the best ways for children to develop their language and thinking. Conversations allow children to:

- hear new language in context
- practise using language within social interactions
- receive feedback on their communication and language from adults

Feedback is most powerful when it is responsive and adaptive – that is, when we adapt our own language, stepping up or stepping down as needed in response to the child.

To support young children's oral language development effectively, we need to consider:

1. planning
2. opportunities for communication and language within the daily routine
3. environment and resourcing
4. the language-supporting strategies we use in interactions with children
5. how to support language at home

We will consider each of these aspects in turn. Many of the practices described are appropriate for children with language delays as well as children within the typical range. This chapter does *not* provide detailed guidance on how to support children with specific speech, language and communication needs (SLCN). Noticing and taking prompt action if a child might have SLCN are vital. You can learn more about this through ICAN's short online course, which is free (https://ican.org.uk/i-cans-talking-point/cpd-short-course).

Table 3.1 Communication throughout the EYFS

Aspect of language development	Birth to 3 years old	3-, 4- and 5-year-olds
Vocabulary knowledge underpins children's understanding and use of language, and sets the foundation for later literacy and learning.	**From 6 months,** children begin to understand words. **Between 9 and 14 months** they typically produce their first words. Given the right conditions, vocabulary increases dramatically during the early years (an estimated 7-10 words per day) but the developmental range is great. **By 18 months,** word production can range from 10 to 200 words.	**Around the age of 3,** children will have more words to describe categories (*birds* or *fruit*), emotions (*happy, sad, angry*) and time and space. **Between the ages of 4 and 5** children will have more words for emotions (*upset, unsure, thrilled*). They will use words to explain position (*between, above, below*). They will use more adjectives (*rough, huge, funny*).
Social communication (pragmatics) involves learning how to use language in social contexts and mastering the 'rules' of conversation. This forms the foundation for building relationships, engaging in social interaction and later literacy and learning.	**At 4-7 months,** social communication begins with vocalisations (e.g. growls, squeaks). **From 7 months** babbling begins. **Between 7 and 15 months,** children begin to use gestures, eye-gaze and pointing. Through the **toddler years** up to the end of the EYFS, children continue to master the skills of social conversation, including initiation, turn-taking and using language in an increasingly wide range of contexts.	**Around the age of 3,** children's language becomes more adult-like. **By age 5,** children can typically express ideas and feelings using quite complex sentences, including connectives (*and, but, when, because*) and different tenses.
Grammar includes knowledge about the structure of words and the rules governing how words and phrases are combined into sentences.	**At 16-26 months** children begin to understand short sentences and create two-word sentences of their own (e.g. *Daddy shirt*). **Between age 2 and 3,** children typically begin to understand and produce more complex sentences (e.g. *Daddy putting shirt on*) including use of function words (*a, the, I, we*), word beginnings (*mis, un-*) and word endings (*-ing, -ed*). Errors such as' me runned' are common as children over-generalise the rules they are beginning to grasp.	**Between age 3 and 5,** children use these skills to increasingly talk about a wide range of topics (e.g. past events, causes and consequences, predictions and explanations). They are also important to underpin later reading comprehension and writing.
Higher-order language Narrative skills include the ability to link ideas together to retell events and tell stories coherently using all the important details (e.g. who, where, when). Children also need to develop the skills which bring narratives to life such as description and inference		

Plan to support communication and language

Every context, experience and interaction provide opportunities to support oral language. Careful planning helps us make the most of these opportunities. Think about:

- Planning for language **within all activities and contexts**. Include contexts which we may not be obviously language-focused. Identify key vocabulary and oral language goals for all planned activities. For example, during nappy changes, we might plan to focus on commentary. We might talk aloud to interpret babies' feelings and intentions (e.g. *I'm going to put your nappy on now. I know, you don't like that very much, we'll be done soon…*).
- Planning for language across the **week, term and year**. Make sure that **observations and assessments** inform language planning. Knowing where children are in their language development helps us to provide the right experiences for them. We need to plan experiences which are just above their current level. There is a range of tools which can support us. This includes simple free screeners like the TROLL (Dickinson et al., 2003) and comprehensive toolkits such as the Wellcomm (Hurd and McQueen, 2010), which have costs attached.

Choosing vocabulary for explicit teaching

The most important thing to remember about word learning is that it should form part of a broad approach to developing oral language. Word learning is best supported when we:

- plan interesting and meaningful experiences to talk about
- build on these experiences to support word learning *in context* and *through conversation*
- identify the **key words** which the children need
- explicitly teach and support the children to learn those key words
- reinforce the children's learning through engaging follow-up activities and in continuous provision

Beck et al. (2013) give practical and evidence-based guidance in their book *Bringing Words to Life*. They remind us that the words we introduce to children should be both **important and useful**. They set out three tiers for vocabulary:

- Tier 1: simple, everyday words which will be familiar to most children
- Tier 2: high-frequency words which are used in a range of different contexts
- Tier 3: words which are rare and specific to particular environments or activities (e.g. *stethoscope*)

We do not need to teach Tier 1 words because most children will hear and use them daily. Tier 3 words are too specific to be very useful for children. Tier 2 words form the best focus and will add richness to children's vocabularies. Where a word sits within the tiers will depend on children's age and abilities. For example, 'down' might be a Tier 2 word for a toddler but a Tier 1 word for a 3-year-old.

We need to remember to go beyond nouns when choosing target vocabulary. Children find verbs harder to learn than nouns, so these provide a good focus. Also include key grammatical items such as pronouns (*I, me, he, she*) and adjectives to support children with their descriptive language.

We need to plan for deep word learning. For example, choose words and concepts from the books you are using, or which relate to other planned activities and experiences. Children need to understand these words to engage fully in these activities. When we have introduced new words, we need to link them to a broader topic. We need to reinforce the meanings of new words in other activities. This will further support word learning.

Opportunities for communication and language within your daily routine

Think carefully about how to create time and space for communication. Research suggests that the 'ingredients' of a language-supporting day include the following.

Daily shared reading

In a language-rich setting, children of all ages share books with adults daily. Books are perhaps the single most powerful tool in our language-supporting toolkit. They contain richer language than everyday conversation. For example, they have around twice as many non-common words and more complex grammar than we use in everyday talk. They also offer great opportunities for interaction, communication and conversation in a context which is meaningful and engaging for children.

Shared reading can take place in any format (whole-group, small-group, pairs, one-to-one) but will be most powerful when it is *interactive*. This means that children will gain more from reading individually or in a small group than from whole-class reading. This is because they have more opportunity to be actively involved. We should not rule out whole-group reading, but we must think carefully about what children will gain from this.

Remember to read books more than once. Children love to re-read stories. Research shows that they learn words introduced in a new book much faster when that book is read three or four times in a short period (e.g. a week) than from a single reading.

Songs, rhymes and poems

Songs and rhymes provide a great opportunity to develop communication and language in a way that babies and children (and adults!) enjoy. *Development Matters* (DfE, 2021a) offers useful guidance. It suggests that we should sing songs with babies and toddlers often, play a wide range of music types, move with babies to music, use action rhymes, and encourage babies and children to join with and anticipate the words and actions in songs and rhymes. Older children should learn a wide repertoire of songs and rhymes and perhaps create their own. By Reception, the guidance reminds us to focus on the sound and structure of songs/rhymes. We should draw attention to rhyme, pausing for children to predict the next rhyming word and encouraging them to create their own rhymes or clap out the beats in words.

Small-group opportunities for talk

Once children become old enough to take part in short group activities, we should plan regular opportunities for structured conversations with adults. In a small-group context, children have more opportunity to engage in the back-and-forth conversational turns. These support language development most powerfully. Structured does not mean formal or adult-led. It means that we have a planned focus on oral language, and we are actively scaffolding children's communication, language and conversation. We should try to include children with mixed language levels in groups. That will enable children with lower language levels to benefit from the language of their peers. We also need to think about how we can scaffold children's conversations with each other. We might use techniques such as Talking Partners (Think, Pair, Share) for older children.

Meaningful and irresistible contexts

Rich and varied activities and experiences promote communication. They build on children's interests and existing knowledge to harness their enthusiasm to communicate. Make sure children have the experience and words they need to access new topics confidently.

Play, exploration and investigation offer particularly meaningful contexts for language learning. They build on children's interests and allow them to practise language, social and self-regulation skills with peers. While babies are playing with toys and resources, we can name objects and talk about what they (and we) are doing. This provides language in context. For toddlers and pre-schoolers, pretend, dramatic and role play offer rich early language and literacy experiences.

Informal and individual conversations

'Intentional teachers' (Epstein, 2007) make use of every opportunity for language and learning, both planned and unplanned. They create regular one-to-one opportunities to talk with children. This includes making the most of routines such as tidying up, mealtimes and getting ready to go outside. Routines provide rich opportunities for giving children the language they need to negotiate these routines, and for relaxed conversations in an informal context.

Connecting it all together

We need to think about how to link language and experiences across different activities and experiences. This will give children repeated opportunities to hear and rehearse new language. We can:

- provide activities which follow on from books, stories or songs
- choose books which relate to other experiences and activities in the class/room

Creating an environment which supports communication and language

Adult–child interactions are the 'engine-room' of language development. The physical environment and resources we provide are the fuel which lights the fire. We need to:

- think carefully about which areas are hotspots for communication and which are not
- consider whether our resources and activities are meaningful and irresistible for the children, thinking about *each* child's experiences and interests
- group resources together, in the way we naturally do in the early years. This enables children to learn the words related to these resources more quickly

For example, children will learn the words for different foods and kitchen tools more quickly and deeply when they hear and use them as part of home-corner role play. It will be harder for them if they come across these words out of context. Using concrete props, pictures and real experiences during activities and when reading books also supports language learning. This is particularly important for children with poor language or those learning English.

It is important to be intentional about the books we choose for our setting. Make sure that books reflect a wide range of types (fiction, non-fiction, rhymes), levels of challenge, topics and people. Choose books for the vocabulary and concepts they will introduce to children. Consider offering some wordless books, even for older children.

Interactions which support communication, conversation and thinking

We move on now to consider the evidence on adult–child interactions and the strategies we can use to nurture children's language skills. Sustained multiple-turn conversations (verbal and non-verbal) give children the richest 'package' of information to learn from. They give children the best opportunity to express their ideas, feelings and wishes. They allow children to use many different cues (social, linguistic, cognitive). This helps children to practise communication and language in a social context, while receiving immediate feedback from adults who adjust their language and responses to match the child's. Five evidence-based strategies for helping children engage in conversation are set out below.

Be a magnet for communication

The first step is to engage babies and children and motivate them to communicate with you. You can do this by:

- *Making children feel noticed and valued*. Children communicate most when they feel comfortable, confident, competent and listened-to. Encourage children to initiate communication by showing you are relaxed and have time to talk. When children do communicate, show interest using eye contact, body language and children's names. Know and enjoy your children as individuals and let this show. Give each baby and child individual attention and use specific praise and encouragement.
- *Putting children in charge*. Children are most confident and motivated to talk about things they have experienced, and which are meaningful to them. Talk about what babies, toddlers and children are doing, know about and are interested in. Let them lead in interactions and conversation.
- *Using non-verbal and verbal invitations*. Use eye contact, body language and facial expressions to engage children. Then, a mix of open comments and questions will get the conversation going. A comment (e.g. *I wonder what will happen next…*) can sometimes be more natural than a question, allowing children to respond in their own way.
- *Engaging with all children*. We need to ensure we interact and communicate with reluctant communicators, children with language delay and children in the early stages of learning English. These children may not 'ask' for our attention directly but will benefit greatly from interacting with us.

Support children to engage and reply

Help children communicate successfully by being an active listener and responsive language partner:

- *Give space and time* for children to think and respond. Try pausing for 7–10 seconds.
- *Listen and respond.* Tune in to what babies, toddlers and children are trying to communicate verbally and non-verbally. Let children know they have been understood and encourage more communication by:
  - confirming (e.g. nodding, repeating the child's words)
  - praising verbal and non-verbal communication
  - verbalising babies' gestures (*Oh, you want to give me the toy – thank you!*) and responding with interest.
- *Support turn-taking* using facial expressions and gestures to cue a baby or child to take their turn, verbally or non-verbally. Some children will need more help if they do not have experience of conversations at home.
- *Give extra support where needed.* For example, a child might find it hard to respond to the question *Do you want an apple or a banana?* We might repeat the question, pointing to the fruit to make the words more concrete. For an older child, instead of *How does he feel?* we might give a forced alternative like *Do you think he looks happy or sad?* Or we might interpret and verbalise what the child is trying to communicate (e.g. *Are you telling me that Teddy is tired?*) – but be sure not to jump in too soon. Support children with limited language using concrete gestures, props and pictures.

Converse with children

Classes or rooms need to be places for conversation. We should talk about a wide range of subjects with children and deepen topics over multiple turns. We should have genuine conversations about things that interest the children, and us. Pitching the conversation at the right level provides each child with 'just enough' challenge.

- *Low-challenge language and prompts* are grounded in the 'here-and-now'. Examples include: talking about what children are doing and experiencing, or what they can see on the pages of a book. We can use techniques like:
  - labelling (*That's your cup*)
  - commenting (*Mr Bear is going upstairs to bed*)
  - closed questions (*What is the mouse holding?*)
  - simple 'wh' questions (*What is the man doing?*)
  - completion prompts (*The bird is landing in the…*)
  - forced alternatives (e.g. *Do we put our shoes or our socks on first?*)
- *Mid-range language and prompts* extend language and thinking. We can:
  - use more open 'wh' prompts (*What's happening here?*)
  - encourage children to recall past experiences (*Which animals did we see on the farm?*)
  - encourage children to make links between a story and their life (*Have you ever felt scared like Ali?*)

- o   talk about preferences or opinions (*What's your favourite kind of fruit?*)
- o   make simple inferences or predictions, giving context to support their answer (*Mr Bear looks quite uncomfortable, I wonder if he'll be able to get to sleep…?*)

- *High-challenge language and prompts* extend children even further. We can:
  - o   think out loud (*I think I'm going to try turning the key this way and see if it works…*)
  - o   encourage children to infer (*How do you think he feels?*)
  - o   encourage children to speculate or predict (*What do you think will happen next?*)
  - o   encourage children to explain (*Why is Mr Bear carrying a torch?*)
  - o   ask open questions with no right answer (*Which one do you like the best? Why?*)
  - o   talk about abstract topics like feelings

Research shows that using language beyond the 'here-and-now' can support growth in language skills and later reading comprehension.

Support children to understand and build narratives

Children also need support to understand and create narratives. These might be fictional (e.g. stories) or personal (e.g. children talking about events in their own lives). Children need practice at:

- *Scene-setting* (who, where, when) – talking about the characters and where/when the event or story happened
- *Talking about events in order and linking ideas together.* Help children tell or retell events or stories, link ideas together (e.g. *After Sami threw the ball, what happened…?*) and summarise the 'story so far'. Support children to talk about their own experiences clearly (e.g. *And what did you choose when you went into the shop?*)
- *Ending a narrative* (e.g. *They all went home for tea…*)

Actively scaffold peer communication and conversation

Supporting peer communication and conversation will support children's social skills and relationships, as well as their language development. Hold and place babies where they can communicate with each other. Encourage children to talk with and listen to each other. Techniques such as descriptive commenting can help children to notice each other, drawing them into peer conversation. For older children, we need to plan for small-group discussions supported by an adult. We might consider talk-partner techniques during whole-group times.

Interactions which support children's words and sentences

Introduce and model new words and language

Adults play an important role in modelling new language for children. We need to use a rich and varied vocabulary which is appropriate to children's level. We need to support this by *planning* for the vocabulary we will use. We might:

- make new language meaningful by introducing it through concrete, engaging, playful experiences
- provide the words for objects, actions and feelings
- use commentary, description and narration to describe what children and adults do, experience and think (e.g. *You're standing up! I'm cutting the peel off the orange because we don't eat that part.*)
- speak slowly, clearly and match our language to the child
- model language just above children's current level

Word learning can be a slippery process. Children must be sure which word applies to which object, action, description – or even to which concept. We can support this by repeating the word and demonstrating gestures, actions, pictures or simple activities to ensure understanding. For example, to explain the verb *unlock* we might mime the actions, using pretend keys to unlock different objects.

Model and support word meanings

When learning new words, children need information about word meanings as well as the word labels. It can be easy for children with weak word learning strategies to misunderstand or have only superficial word knowledge. This information is best provided in context and by building on what children already know. For example, we might say '*Knitting* is a bit like sewing but you use wool and a really big needle. Your mum or dad might *knit* a jumper for you to wear in the winter.' Again, having physical objects available can help children's understanding.

Put new words and language to work

To build confidence and depth of understanding, children need to practise using new language in a range of concrete contexts:

- Prompt children to talk *about* words and the wider concepts they represent to build experience in using them in different contexts. For example, you might ask 'what do we use a *torch* for? What do we look like if we're *sad*?'
- Give children multiple opportunities to use and act out new words and concepts, to see how they work. For example, to reinforce the word *behind*, we might demonstrate it. We might ask the children to line up and take turns to stand behind each other. We might hide behind something in hide and seek or treasure hunting games. We might use small-world play to show which objects are '*behind*'.

Adapt, extend and deepen

We can extend and deepen children's word learning by expanding their own language. This can give children a more complete or more complex model which is just above their current level. We want our language to be not too difficult and not too easy – finding the 'just right' levels that allow for language growth. These are some examples based on the book *Good Night, Gorilla* (Rathman, 2012). We might:

- Expand on what children say to provide more information or ideas. For example, if the child says, '*that a lion*', we might say '*yes, that lion is* eating a juicy bone'.
- Add more grammatical information. For example, if the child says, '*climb out*', we might say '*yes*, he *is climb*ing out'.
- Expand with words to add richer meaning. For example, if the child says, '*mouse got banana*', we might say '*oh yes, the mouse is* pulling *that* heavy *banana*'.

Support language at home

Parents and the home environment are the most significant influence on children's language development. Let parents know how important their role is and how they can help children to develop their language. Support them in playing and talking with children at home, for example by sharing books and resources. We can discuss our themes or activities with parents and share ideas for talking about them with their children. We might ask parents to help us to understand their child's interests and experiences. What will they be keen to talk about? We might share our assessments and understandings about children's language development with parents. Then, we can ask them to help *us* in gaining an accurate picture of their child's language abilities and progress.

─Early Learning Goal─

Listening, Attention and Understanding

Children at the expected level of development will:

- Listen attentively and respond to what they hear with relevant questions, comments and actions when being read to and during whole-class discussions and small group interactions;
- Make comments about what they have heard and ask questions to clarify their understanding;
- Hold conversation when engaged in back-and-forth exchanges with their teacher and peers.

─Early Learning Goal─

Speaking

Children at the expected level of development will:

- Participate in small group, class and one-to-one discussions, offering their own ideas, using recently introduced vocabulary;
- Offer explanations for why things might happen, making use of recently introduced vocabulary from stories, non-fiction, rhymes and poems when appropriate;
- Express their ideas and feelings about their experiences using full sentences, including the use of past, present and future tenses and of conjunctions, with modelling and support from their teacher.

Conclusion

Early language ability is one of the strongest predictors of later development through school and in life. For example, children with poor vocabulary at age 5 are more than twice as likely to be unemployed at age 34 (APPG on Social Mobility, 2019). Children who struggle with oral language at school entry are unlikely to catch up without extra support. They are at risk of poorer outcomes throughout their lives. Language is essential for thinking, expressing our feelings, making friends and finding solutions to conflicts. For these reasons, it should be a priority in curriculum planning. You can use the insights and ideas in this chapter – and the reflective questions below – to take the first steps in creating a communication-supporting class or room.

Reflective questions

1. As a team, reflect on the ways in which you could **plan** more effectively for supporting communication and language across activities and contexts.
2. Make a map of your outdoor and indoor **environment**. Mark areas which are communication 'hot spots' and where communication and talk happen less often. What can you learn from this?
3. Consider **the 'ingredients' of a language-supporting day** set out in this chapter (shared reading, small group opportunities, etc.). Identify one aspect to focus on over the next term to improve language opportunities for your children.
4. Reflect on the **language-supporting interactions** set out in this chapter. Which are part of your regular practice and which might you need to work on? Choose one strategy to focus on for a week. Be intentional about *rehearsing* and *reflecting* on your use of this strategy during the week to refine your practice.
5. As a team, reflect on the ways in which you could work with parents more closely to support **children's language at home.**

Acknowledgements

The author would like to acknowledge Clare Williams, Janice Woodcock and Iram Siraj (URLEY), and Wendy Lee, Clare Williams and Julie Dockrell (Talking Time).

4

Personal, Social and Emotional Development

Julian Grenier and Fliss Dewsbery

EYFS Statutory Educational Programme

Children's personal, social and emotional development (PSED) is crucial for children to lead healthy and happy lives, and is fundamental to their cognitive development. Underpinning their personal development are the important attachments that shape their social world. Strong, warm and supportive relationships with adults enable children to learn how to understand their own feelings and those of others. Children should be supported to manage emotions, develop a positive sense of self, set themselves simple goals, have confidence in their own abilities, to persist and wait for what they want and direct attention as necessary. Through adult modelling and guidance, they will learn how to look after their bodies, including healthy eating, and manage personal needs independently. Through supported interaction with other children, they learn how to make good friendships, co-operate and resolve conflicts peaceably. These attributes will provide a secure platform from which children can achieve at school and in later life.

Introduction

Supporting children's personal, social and emotional development (PSED) has always been central to the early years. Many of the pioneers of early education and care in England, like Anna Freud, made this their priority. Over time, this led to a split between the care tradition and the early education tradition. Practitioners in the care tradition emphasised the importance of children feeling happy and well-cared for. Others, with a stronger focus on early education, judged that it was most important for children to get a head start with their learning.

Research challenges this polarisation. The biggest research project ever undertaken in England and Northern Ireland, the EPPE project, reported that:

> For most practitioners the declared priorities in the early years are on the development of positive dispositions to learning, self-confidence and independence. Staff and parents normally give priority to social development, but our evidence suggests that those settings which see cognitive and social development as complementary achieve the best profile in terms of child outcomes.

> (Siraj-Blatchford et al., 2002, p. 10)

Much of a child's development is a process of learning, shaped by culture and environment. Of course, there are definite, biological stages in a child's development. Newborn babies don't walk or talk. But, as Usha Goswami, professor of cognitive developmental neuroscience at the University of Cambridge, argues, 'children think and reason largely in the same way as adults. However, they lack experience, and they are still developing important metacognitive and executive function skills' (Goswami, 2015, p. 25).

When we turn our attention to PSED, we know that children do pass through important developmental stages. For example, young babies do not have 'object permanence'. They do not understand that when things, or people, are out of sight, they continue to exist elsewhere. Once a baby has this concept, coming into nursery or to a childminder setting can become more difficult. The baby becomes consciously aware of the presence, or absence, of a parent. As the parent leaves, the baby feels the loss, and this can make the goodbye very distressing. This is just one example of supporting a child's emotional development by remaining calm and supportive. It is unhelpful to deny the child's emotional state ('there's no need to cry') or to become cross or rejecting. These responses can confuse children. They can be left wondering if there is something wrong with their emotions, or if adult support is conditional on not showing upset or anger.

Part of the adult role is about 'being': being there for the child, being compassionate and accepting. We need to show that we understand how difficult it can be to lose the presence of someone you love very much.

But another important part of our role is about teaching children strategies to manage their emotions. This is especially relevant for children aged 2 and over. For example, some settings use 'Zones of Regulation' with children. Sometimes, children feel overwhelmed by their feelings, like sadness or anger. We can sensitively use the zones to help children to reflect on how they are feeling. By naming the feeling, the child may feel a little less overwhelmed. In this way, we are gradually and sensitively handing some control to children. In contrast, a 'time out' approach means that we have all the control. It does not help the child to process their emotions. As children get older, it is increasingly important to help them to talk about and elaborate on their feelings. We might talk with a child about why they are feeling angry, and what happens to us when we are angry. We might share a picture book, like *I Really Want to Shout!* (Philip and Gaggiotti, 2020). How can we express anger in a socially acceptable way? What can we do to calm ourselves down?

Over time, this cycle of recognising the emotion, and actively finding a way to feel calmer, can become second nature to the child. This strengthens an aspect of the child's executive function: their ability to inhibit impulsive behaviour.

This is not only important whilst children are in the EYFS: it is also vital for their future. As the leading researchers Cybele Raver, Clancy Blair and Michael Willoughby argue:

> … children's executive functioning plays a key role in supporting early learning and positive behavioral outcomes in school … Put simply, children who can remember information, who can regulate their attention, and who can maintain inhibitory control are in better position to take advantage of opportunities for learning than children who struggle with problems of memory, inattention, and impulsivity.
>
> (Raver et al., 2013, p. 292)

Attachment and the key person role

The EYFS requires that each child in a group setting should have a 'key person'. Sometimes, we view this requirement through an organisational lens. Key people take on the responsibility for updating the child's records, for example.

The thinking behind the key person approach (Goldschmied and Jackson, 1993) is not primarily organisational. It builds on decades of research about children's needs for attachment and warm, responsive care. In a busy group setting, the adults and children will be engaged in lots of activity. Within that busy-ness, it is important that the child knows there is a special person in the team of adults who knows them intimately. That person will have worked closely with the parents during the settling-in phase, getting to know the child. When a key person is settling in a baby, they will get to know the baby's routines in the day, and how they show happiness, frustration and tiredness. By learning from the parent or parents, the key person will get to know how to soothe the baby and help them through difficult times.

Key people also play an important role in ongoing liaison with the parent. As practitioners, we have general experience of many children and their development. Drawing on this experience, we can really help parents who are struggling with:

- toddler tantrums
- fussy eating
- a 3-year-old who wants to be like a little grown-up one minute, and like a little baby on their lap a moment later

We need to remember that parents are the experts on their own children. We have a lot to learn about the uniqueness of the child and their family. Working together, in a mutually respectful and cooperative partnership, we can act in the child's best interests.

Research suggests that this way of working with children can be emotionally demanding on the adults. That can sometimes lead to adults becoming a bit withdrawn and detached from a child who feels rather 'difficult'. Working with young children can be exhausting and can push staff to the end of their tether. In this next section, Fliss Dewsbery considers how leaders can help staff to manage this.

Supervision and Work Discussion by Fliss Dewsbery

Supervision is a statutory requirement in the Early Years Foundation Stage (EYFS) (DfE, 2021c), which applies to everyone who works in the sector. In her 2011 review of the EYFS, Clare Tickell recommended that it should be 'clear what supervision means in practice, including some good practice examples, and that settings should agree their own procedures for supervision. Childminders should also have access to the challenge and professional support that supervision can provide' (Tickell, 2011, p. 47).

One of the most influential versions of supervision is 'Work Discussion', developed by Peter Elfer. Elfer (2018, p. 4) describes the aim of Work Discussion as being to enable 'practitioners to be more attuned to the child holistically, in the context of that child's family culture and wider culture, in order to support their practice and strengthen outcomes for children'.

Michael Rustin describes the purpose of a Work Discussion group as providing an 'understanding [of] what is going on, and the emotions and anxieties that are in play in a situation, but also of actively trying to help a participant observer to cope better with a situation and, through this, to enable practice to become more thoughtful' (Rustin, 2008, p. 269).

A Work Discussion group offers practitioners a space to wonder about and reflect on children's experiences and anxieties. It also offers a space to discuss a wide variety of work-related issues. It facilitates group reflection and containment on such issues.

The psychoanalyst Wilfred Bion developed the theory of containment, which Douglas (2007) has defined in an accessible way. She describes containment as occurring 'when one person receives and understands the emotional communication of another without being overwhelmed by it, processes it and then communicates understanding and recognition back to the other person. This process can restore the capacity to think in the other person' (Douglas, 2007, p. 33).

Peter Elfer argues that supervision must not be understood as a 'tick-box approach'. It is not a system for setting and monitoring staff targets, for example. Instead, he proposes that 'supervision should be part of a setting's culture, recognising that there are many dilemmas in early years work. Thoughtful reflection, including attention to emotion, may not produce simple solutions but it is an integral part of a respectful, whole-setting approach to the complexities of the work' (Elfer, 2015).

However, others have argued for a broader understanding of supervision. We can understand supervision as offering an individual or a group a reflective and containing space to discuss a variety of different work-related issues. John (2012) suggests that supervision should:

- offer a developmental or formative aspect to supervision, providing an opportunity to discuss skills and understanding
- provide a management/organisational aspect to discuss aims, principles, policies and standards
- be supportive or restorative, offering an opportunity to discuss how the work is affecting supervisees

Supervision means different things to different people. Scaife and Inskipp (2001) suggest that supervision varies depending on professional context, but that there are some common features. They define supervision broadly as 'what happens when people who work in the helping professions make a formal arrangement to think with another or others about their work with a view to providing the best possible service to clients and enhancing their own personal and professional development' (Scaife and Inskipp, 2001, p. 4).

Supervision has been of particular importance since 2020. The COVID-19 pandemic has had a negative effect on children and the early years workforce. Many early years practitioners have reported facing difficult circumstances in their work with young children who they felt were undergoing social or emotional difficulties or mental health problems (Nelinger et al., 2021). Supervision could become a mechanism to explore some of these difficulties.

The EYFS states that:

3.22. Providers must put appropriate arrangements in place for the supervision of staff who have contact with children and families. Effective supervision provides support, coaching and training for the practitioner and promotes the interests of children. Supervision should foster a culture of mutual support, teamwork and continuous improvement, which encourages the confidential discussion of sensitive issues.

3.23. Supervision should provide opportunities for staff to:

- discuss any issues – particularly concerning children's development or well-being, including child protection concerns
- identify solutions to address issues as they arise
- receive coaching to improve their personal effectiveness

From co-regulation to self-regulation

Young babies do not yet have the capacity to manage their emotions. As soon as a baby is hungry, or cold, or wet, they are likely to become distressed. In an early years setting, the baby depends on their key person to understand the different ways they communicate their feelings. We can learn many important things about babies from their parents:

- how the baby shows tiredness, distress and unhappiness
- what different gestures mean – for example, some babies start to scratch their heads when they feel tired, signalling it's a good time to settle them for a nap
- what their emotional flow across the day is generally like: When are they most likely to feel happy and confident? When are they likely to get tired and need extra support?

It is also important to spend time carefully observing how babies respond to different situations, so we learn for ourselves, first-hand.

As a key person, we learn to understand when a baby's cry means they are tired. As we soothe them and get them ready for sleep, we are 'regulating' their emotions. We make sense of their crying, and then act on our understanding.

Gradually, the baby begins to adopt this thinking for themselves. They begin to understand the feeling of hunger, and gesture to their bottle or the snack area. The baby is moving on from needing us to regulate their emotions, to a new phase of 'co-regulation'. This means that the baby can self-regulate a bit, and still needs us to regulate their feelings a bit too. Gradually, children take this on more and more. Older children in the EYFS find ways to self-regulate, including:

- talking to themselves: 'if I just wait, soon it will be my turn' – rather than getting frustrated and pushing another child out of the way
- using language: telling us that they are feeling tired, or cross, or upset
- self-comfort: as they begin to feel sad, or angry, they might do something soothing like sit in a quiet area and look at a book, or seek out their key person

By supporting children with their emotional self-regulation, we help them to install a set of brakes and an accelerator pedal. We enable them to manage their emotional pace and flow through the day.

At the same time, children are developing their cognitive self-regulation. In the EYFS, children become increasingly aware of focusing their attention and efforts, to achieve a goal.

Case Study

A nursery team set up an obstacle course in the garden for the trikes. They plan the course so that the children will need to concentrate hard to go round the cones and over the slope, which is made with blocks and planks of wood.

At first, the children find it difficult. Many of them go too fast around the cones, sending them flying. Some of the children approach the slope at their normal speed on the trike and find that they run out of steam halfway up and roll backwards.

With encouragement from the practitioners, the children become more aware of the strategies they need to succeed. They realise that they need to slow down for the cones, and then speed up as much as they can in the run-up to the slope. The children are learning to monitor the strategies they use, and work out which strategies work, and which are ineffective.

The case study above shows how a challenging physical development curriculum can support children's growing self-regulation. Cognitive self-regulation is a bit like a powerful search engine: it gives us focus and helps us to prioritise all the information and stimuli around us.

Early Learning Goal

Self-regulation

Children at the expected level of development will:

- Show an understanding of their own feelings and those of others, and begin to regulate their behaviour accordingly;
- Set and work towards simple goals, being able to wait for what they want and control their immediate impulses when appropriate;
- Give focused attention to what the teacher says, responding appropriately even when engaged in activity, and show an ability to follow instructions involving several ideas or actions.

Children learning to manage themselves

Linked to children's growing capacity to self-regulate is their capacity to manage themselves throughout the day.

Practitioners play a key role in helping children to become confident. First, there is the crucial importance of helping children to settle into their early years setting or class. It can be tempting to rush this process.

It is important to have a clear approach to settling-in, which allows the process to be gradual and humane. Children will benefit greatly from the support of their parents in the early days, as they get to know us and the setting. It is useful to think ahead about the possible downsides and consider how we might manage them positively:

- Are you worried that some parents might stop their children from exploring freely and be a bit interfering? Consider the types of guidelines you might draw up and share, and what you might say if that happens.
- Do you sometimes feel that parents find the separation harder than children? You might decide to offer some practical advice to parents. A kindly meant suggestion can help: 'once you've said goodbye, I will show you out. We don't prolong this in a painful way.' Parental distress is real, and we should be sympathetic whilst also putting the child's wellbeing first.

At all phases in the EYFS, children's confidence develops from feeling safe and secure. This is especially important for babies and toddlers. Children need to know that their key person is a reliable 'safe base', an adult they can return to when they need a little extra care or sympathy. It is equally important for the adult to transmit a positive sense of 'you can do this' to the child. This helps children to develop resilience in the face of difficulties.

It is tempting to think that constant positivity and praise will help children to develop their confidence. In fact, research suggests the opposite. The important work on 'growth mindset' by Carol Dweck (2007) shows how constant praise can lead children to focus on pleasing the adult. Children become so accustomed to praise that they choose easier things to do, knowing that they will succeed and gain praise. It is more important to help children to develop their confidence in tackling difficult tasks. The best way to promote this is through feedback. Focus on the child's efforts: highlight what has gone well, and sensitively point out where they might have tried something differently.

We might think about rules in a similar way. It is important to have secure routines and rules: children don't do well in chaotic settings. But an excessive focus on rules can lead to what researchers call 'situational compliance'. This means that children follow the rules when the adult is there because they want praise. But when they think there are no adults around, children with 'situational compliance' might behave poorly. They are not developing self-control and self-discipline.

We must help children to understand the reasons behind rules. Simple rules help everyone to feel safe and secure. This approach helps children to learn 'committed compliance'. Whether an adult is around or not, they know it is wrong to hurt another person. Children's developing understanding of rules is outlined in Table 4.1. Children develop at different rates. It is also important to note that changes in circumstances, like transition into a new group or class, the arrival of a new sibling, or moving house, can lead to children seeming to regress in their PSED for periods of time.

Table 4.1 Helping children to learn about rules throughout the EYFS

	Birth to 3 years old	3- and 4-year-olds	4- and 5-year-olds: Reception
Attitudes and dispositions	Begin to show 'effortful control'. For example, waiting for a turn and resisting the strong impulse to grab what they want or push their way to the front.	In addition: Find solutions to conflicts and rivalries. For example, accepting that not everyone can be Spider-Man in the game, and suggesting other ideas.	In addition: Identify and moderate their own feelings, socially and emotionally.
		Increasingly follow rules, understanding why they are important.	
Concepts and skills	Waiting	In addition:	In addition:
	Sharing	Listen to someone else and agree a compromise.	Reflect on their feelings and the feelings of others, in different scenarios.
			Respect class rules.
Vocabulary	Wait	In addition:	In addition:
	Turn	Agree	Respect
	Next	Disagree	Strategy
		Suggestion	Reflection
		Rules	Scenario
		Calm down	

Finally, one of the changes to the EYFS in 2021 was moving personal care, toileting and eating into PSED. This brings together all the different aspects of how children manage themselves through the day. As we explained above, the EYFS integrates care with cognitive development. We can approach nappy-changing like we're at a supermarket checkout. A single practitioner can process one baby after another, which makes the process rather dehumanising. On the other hand, we might organise the day so that each baby has their nappy changed by their key person. This can make the experience emotionally warm, full of little communications and loving moments. We might have a special song, or toy for the baby to hold. This way, the nappy-changing routine also boosts the baby's sense of self, belonging and early communication.

Instead of planning 'toilet-training' at a fixed age, we might use a process of ongoing assessment to explore, with the child's parent, when it's best to start. We will watch out for the child's awareness or discomfort when their nappy is wet, or soiled. We will talk to the child about this. We might show them how other children are using the potty or share a book about using the toilet. We need to give children just enough help at each stage. As we gradually and sensitively withdraw our help over time, children can become independent in managing their personal needs.

Early Learning Goal

Managing Self

Children at the expected level of development will:

- Be confident to try new activities and show independence, resilience and perseverance in the face of challenge;
- Explain the reasons for rules, know right from wrong and try to behave accordingly;
- Manage their own basic hygiene and personal needs, including dressing, going to the toilet, and understanding the importance of healthy food choices.

Building relationships

Making friends, tolerating disagreements and relating confidently with a wider circle of people are important. They are also difficult developments for many children as they move through the EYFS. Research suggests that 'physical aggression by humans appears to reach its peak between 2 and 3 years of age. In the following years most children learn alternatives to physical aggression' (Tremblay, 2002, p. iv17).

The implications of the research for our practice are clear. We need to have a carefully planned approach to help children learn alternatives to aggressive behaviour. Approaches that focus on conflict resolution and helping children to understand, as well as follow, rules are powerful.

Children in the EYFS need adults' support and scaffolding to manage the ups and downs of friendships. We can model polite and cooperative behaviour as adults working in teams, and in our relationships with parents. We can usefully spend time talking through difficulties with children. It is also important to avoid 'jumping in' too quickly to resolve any difficulties between children (Whitebread et al., 2005). This can prevent children from learning the skills they need to overcome a conflict or a problem in a friendship.

All children will find these developments hard at some time. Some children will have very significant difficulties. Some young children in the EYFS will have already suffered adverse childhood experiences (ACEs), including:

- abuse and neglect
- living in a household where there is domestic violence, drug or alcohol misuse, mental ill health, criminality or separation
- living in care

(Marmot, 2020b, p. 45)

ACEs disproportionately affect children growing up in poverty. We cannot solve these problems on our own in the early years. We need to work collaboratively with other services. We might develop a professional relationship with our local Sure Start Children's Centre, Family Hub, or Early Help team. Specialist services also support children who have suffered a damaging experience, like a bereavement. Longer term, we need to make the political choices which will reduce the rate of child poverty in England. This is currently well above the average rate for economically developed countries (Marmot, 2020b, p. 44).

─Early Learning Goal─

Building Relationships

Children at the expected level of development will:

- Work and play cooperatively and take turns with others;
- Form positive attachments to adults and friendships with peers;
- Show sensitivity to their own and to others' needs.

Conclusion

Supporting children's personal, social and emotional development is at the heart of the EYFS. At every phase, high-quality care is vital, so that children have a positive environment for this important learning.

This is essential, difficult and skilled work which places great demands on us. Supervision, or Work Discussion, helps us to develop a positive environment for children's emotional growth.

It is crucial to remember that this area of the EYFS is about learning, as well as care. As adults, we play a key role in helping children to make sense of their emotions. By helping children talk about and elaborate on their feelings, we help them develop vital skills in self-regulation. By helping children manage the inevitable difficulties and responsibilities of life in a group, we are offering them a life-long benefit. The same could be said about managing the ups and downs of friendship. The complexity and the importance of this work are often under-appreciated. But, perhaps above all else, this is what makes the early years so special.

Reflective questions

1. How might you explain the importance of settling-in to a parent who is under pressure not to take time off work?
2. Why is it important to help children understand rules, rather than just follow them?

5

Physical development

Lala Manners

EYFS Statutory Educational Programme

Physical Development

Physical activity is vital in children's all-round development, enabling them to pursue happy, healthy and active lives. Gross and fine motor experiences develop incrementally throughout early childhood. They start with sensory explorations and the development of the child's strength, co-ordination and positional awareness. They develop through tummy time, crawling and play movement with both objects and adults. By creating games and providing opportunities for indoor and outdoor play, adults can support children to develop their core strength, stability, balance, spatial awareness, co-ordination and agility. Gross motor skills provide the foundation for developing healthy bodies and social and emotional well-being. Fine motor control and precision help with hand-eye co-ordination, which is later linked to early literacy. Repeated and varied opportunities to explore and play with small-world activities, puzzles, arts and crafts and the practice of using small tools, with feedback and support from adults, allow children to develop proficiency, control and confidence.

Introduction

Young children's physical health, development and wellbeing have always been central to early years education and care. From the 18th century philosopher Jean-Jacques Rousseau, to the Victorian reformer Robert Owen, children's physicality is recognised as being essential to their growth and development. This is echoed in the work of Froebel, Steiner and Montessori.

It is now our turn to prioritise physical development in our practice. It needs to be a strong thread through all planning and provision.

This is perhaps more difficult than it once was. We have screen time to contend with. We have an obesity crisis to address. We have the grave health effects of a pandemic. In all, we are working at a time when children's health is under ongoing strain.

Physical development is a discrete area of learning in the EYFS. However, as the Statutory Framework for the Early Years Foundation Stage says, 'all areas of learning and development are important and inter-connected' (DfE, 2021c, p. 7). In everything a child does, every moment of every day, something physical is going on. This may be external and visible (jumping, running) or internal and invisible (heartbeats, digestion).

Maybe surprisingly, children use a lot of effort being quiet, still and alert. Staying in one position while looking and listening is a huge challenge for the growing body. It is more difficult to achieve than big, energetic movements.

Learning through everyday movements

Let's have a think about *crawling on hands and knees*:

- Physically: it is challenging. The body must be balanced before moving forwards. Hands need to be flat and in the correct supporting position. The eyes and head must be aligned for direction. Overall strength is needed to push forwards and stop. Breathing must be steady. Coordination is needed to move fluently and change speed and direction.
- Emotionally: the baby experiences frustration and disappointment, triumph and accepting or refusing support.
- Communication: crawlers make their plans clear by sound and gesture. They tell us what they are aiming for as they crawl towards something they want.
- Mathematical thinking: the baby works with gradients, levers, shape, weight, length, speed, angle, direction, estimation, cause and effect and sequencing.

We can deduce from this that physical development involves endlessly varied learning opportunities. Of course, children will grow and develop regardless, but if they are to *thrive,* we need to play a proactive role. Our daily planning must include a wide range of opportunities that supports their movement.

What is physical development?

Physical development concerns the overall and progressive changes in the body and the journey towards maturity. This includes all senses, systems and reflexes. Evidence for change is mainly qualitative: it will include observations, recordings, conversations and case studies. It is often gathered over a long period of time.

Physical development influences growth because physical activity has a positive effect on bone growth and joint stability.

Children's physical development may be negatively affected by:

- overuse of sitting devices: car seats, baby-walkers, bouncy chairs
- unsafe or inappropriate environments
- inherent medical conditions
- lack of opportunities to move safely and freely
- negative adult attitudes to physical activity

Physical growth is closely related to physical development and concerns the progressive increase in the size of the child, or parts of the child. It relates to changes in physical aspects of the body, including shape, size, form and structure. Evidence for growth is primarily quantitative: it can be measured on graphs and scales.

Growth positively affects physical development. As children grow taller and their bones lengthen, they can reach, kick, throw further and climb higher.

Conversely, if children carry excess weight, their ability to move fluently may be adversely affected.

Several factors may compromise a child's growth:

- poverty
- housing
- poor sleep
- nutrition
- illness
- medication
- inadequate care
- lack of stimulation
- biological or genetic factors

The framework makes clear that *physical activity* is intrinsic to supporting physical development. Physical activity here refers to gross motor skills and fine motor skills. This encourages us to think about providing well for these two areas of development.

The individuality of physical development

Every child's physical development journey is unique. Although biologically programmed, we can play a critical role in providing movement opportunities that help their physical development unfold in a smooth and fluent way.

Children come from different backgrounds, cultures and communities. Being aware of the cultural capital linked to their physical development is important. For some, a significant aspect of daily life will include physical skills: tending livestock, planting, servicing machinery, cooking, sewing, cleaning, washing and dancing. These require significant strength, balance, coordination and agility. These children bring a wealth of previous physical experience with them.

For many children, their environment cannot adequately support their physical development. The reasons may include cramped housing, main roads and unsafe outside spaces. Time and appropriate support may be limited, as well as access to local amenities.

Here are two approaches to help smooth out the inequality between those children whose day involves a wealth of movement and those for whom it is difficult to be active:

1. *Thread* opportunities for children to move freely throughout every day:
    - At arriving and leaving times, create a daily challenge: put a line of masking tape on the floor and think of ways to move along it.
    - At circle and story time, allow children to change position: squat, kneel, sit with legs straight or crossed, lie on back or tummy with knees bent.
    - During transitions, use different ways of moving: walking on knees with hands on head, sliding on hands and knees, taking wide steps between stickers placed on the floor.
2. *Embed* a culture of physical activity and movement in the environment:
    - Afford time in planning meetings to determine how physical development may be supported both inside and outdoors.
    - Value and understand the different ways in which children may develop physically and respect their individual approach to progression and practice.
    - Encourage children to reflect on their movement skills.

The development of the physical

There are two key principles to remember:

1. Motor and muscular development is *cephalocaudal*. This means that it works from top to bottom, head to toe. Control of the head is achieved before musculature to gain control of the shoulders. Once babies can hold up their head, the spinal muscles then develop

to enable sitting aided then unaided. The legs gain strength once crawling begins and, with continual practice, they become strong enough for standing and walking. As the muscles around the ankles and feet mature, running and jumping may be added to their movement repertoire.

2. Motor and muscular control is *proximodistal*. This means that it emerges and extends from the centre to the extremities, inside to outside. For example, muscles need to be strong and stable around the shoulder girdle to support the smaller muscles in the elbows, wrists, hands and fingers to gain strength for later handwriting. Other challenging tasks, like using zips, buttons and handling cutlery, are equally informed by this developmental sequence.

Keeping these principles in mind helps us understand why children sometimes struggle with activities or avoid them. They may be motivated, but if the requisite strength, balance and co-ordination are not in place they may need to go back a few steps. For example, if handwriting is difficult, provide a range of activities that strengthen the shoulder, wrist and fingers. Hanging from hands, swinging activities, washing cars, carrying and digging and big painting with brooms all help with this.

What do we know about movement and learning?

From birth onwards, 'Movement is essential to the wiring and firing of the brain, creating the connections needed for the foundations of all future learning. The more we repeat movements – the stronger these connections become, enabling us to gain automatic physical mastery of our bodies so that we can use them without thinking' (Early Years Alliance, 2018, p. 11).

Multisensory experiences have a central role to play in supporting a child's development. Offering a wide range of activities to stimulate the senses requires specific planning. It is not just the five main senses we need to look at, but also the three lesser-known ones. These are *proprioception*, the *vestibular* sense and *interoception*.

Proprioception

What is it? It tells us where we are in space, how our bodies relate to the environment around us, where they begin and end. Proprioceptive sensors lie under the skin and continually send information to the brain about where we are and what we are doing. Birds have these sensors at their wing tips to help them fly in formation. A well-developed proprioceptive sense enables children to do things quite unconsciously. They can take something out of their pocket, tie up their hair, sit in a group and, as the framework says, 'negotiate space and obstacles safely'.

How to support: Encourage whole-body movements such as carrying, digging, pushing–pulling, stretching, jumping, running, climbing, kicking and throwing.

Impact: Proprioception supports children with their handwriting. It helps form proportional letters, directionality and spacing between words. When playing, children will be able to judge the amount of force needed for a particular task.

The vestibular sense

What is it? The vestibular mechanism is situated in the inner ear and is the oldest of our sensory systems. It is critical in the development of balance and helps us understand our relationship to gravity. It helps determine when we are moving or still, upside down or upright. When moving, the vestibular system works with the neck, head and eye muscles to stabilise vision and ensure we know where we are going and don't fall over. It is also connected to hearing and the processing of language.

How to support: The vestibular system takes around seven years to mature and needs a wide range of varied movement opportunities. Lots of 'dizzy play', swinging movements, turning, being upside down, spinning, tilting, leaning, rolling and toppling help develop this sense. Outside spaces provide the best environments to do these, but small indoor spaces can also work.

Impact: A well-functioning vestibular sense supports all learning that includes an element of left and right. It also helps keep children calm and alert. It will support children to move over uneven surfaces, use escalators and be confident in open spaces.

As their balance develops through experiencing daily movement opportunities, their ability to be still, concentrate and listen will increase. Their emotional security is also supported through the relationship between the vestibular system and the limbic system in the brain that generates emotionally based behaviour.

Interoception

What is it? This is when the internal organs of the body send messages to the brain via the skin and blood. It lets us know when we are hungry, thirsty, tired or need to evacuate bowel or bladder. Children need to interpret these signals, act accordingly and trust themselves. Interoception starts early and is linked to emotional security. It's all about developing the capacity to listen to the body, regulate responses and describe physical and emotional states.

How to support: Varied sensory and movement play refines this sense, particularly repetitive and rhythmic movements: pushing and pulling, sweeping, digging. Temperature activities such as exploring hot and cold are also effective.

Impact: The interoceptive sense helps children tune into emotional cues and respond appropriately. It enables them to decide if they are tired because they are hungry, if they need to rest, if they scared or excited by a new challenge.

Children experiencing and learning about their own physicality

Physical skills matter greatly to children. Movement provides a supportive environment in which language and communication may be practised and friendships created. Knowledge about themselves and the world is gained as they collaborate over ideas and resources.

Getting better at something is important to children: moving faster, climbing higher, throwing further. We can help children work out what went right, what went wrong, and why. They can explore the reasons why a skill may be difficult to achieve and understand the steps involved in becoming more proficient.

Moving for its own sake also plays a critical role in supporting physical development. Simply experiencing *the feeling of me* is important for children as they roll on the grass, plait their hair, sway to songs and enjoy the feel of rain or sunshine on their bodies. We should recognise and value these movement moments, however random or trivial they may seem.

We should also be aware that progression in physical development is not always smooth, and that regressions and plateaus are an equally valuable part of the process.

Children of a similar age do not acquire skills at the same time. Walking may happen any time between 10 and 20 months. Often, they revert to earlier skills like crawling if it seems a better or faster option. There may be periods when little progress is visible, and movements seem less mature and fluent.

Progress may also appear in other areas of development – for instance, different friendship groups emerging, or extended use of movement vocabulary in writing or verbally. Allowing time for children to watch and listen, get used to space and noise, feel and explore the properties of different resources and learn the social behaviours expected during physical activities, is essential.

─Case Study─

The Running Project

The children in my Reception class became interested in running. I'm not sure why! We looked at animals that run like lions and tigers and thought about why. We then thought about those that don't run much, like cows and sheep.

We moved on to thinking about human running and the reasons why people run. We looked at types of running: park runs, running for the bus, sprinting, marathons, cross-country, parkour. We discussed speeds and distances, watching videos on YouTube.

Next, we explored our own running. Would we run better barefoot, in trainers or wellies? We realised slippers were useless! How fast could we go? What helped or hindered us? What did we need to do to improve our running?

We examined how we felt when we ran. Were we puffed-out, tired, happy?

All these involved long discussions.

Finally, we made a collage of the areas we had explored and did a presentation in assembly. We invited parents to come in and talk about running.

Planning for progress in physical development

Planning for physical development should be simple, manageable and sustainable. Inside and outdoor environments should provide a range of physical opportunities that children may enjoy independently or in a group. Resources should be accessible and include a mix of large, moveable loose parts for building and construction and smaller materials to cater for a range of manipulative activities.

Aspects of children's physical development and movement are outlined in Table 5.1. Children vary considerably in their health, confidence and fitness. As a result, children will achieve these skills at different times. It is important to develop an inclusive culture so that all children enjoy movement and develop their skills throughout the EYFS.

Physical activity and health

We know that being physically active has these benefits:

- strengthens bones
- stabilises joints
- generates muscle mass
- encourages strength and endurance
- builds healthy tissues and tendons
- increases lung capacity
- boosts circulation
- establishes core strength and control

Being active outdoors

The Finnish framework for physical activity in early childhood, 'Joy, Play and Doing Together', states that 'Children are most physically active during guided play that involves physical activity and has rules, and during free spontaneous play. Among children aged 3–4, free spontaneous play accounts for about 20% of the time, and they play more freely outdoors than indoors' (Ministry of Education and Culture, Finland, 2016, p. 29).

As Jan White reminds us, 'the outdoors offers a perfect companion to provision indoors, working in harmony and providing a complementary environment that enhances and extends what we are able to offer children inside' (White, 2013, p. 3).

We should make sure that children can have access to move about in a space without obstruction. The outdoor provision should include a variety of surfaces to move on: large vertical and horizontal surfaces; places and materials for digging and filling; lots of things to lift, carry, transport and move around; wheeled vehicles; and quiet spaces to recuperate and revive.

Table 5.1 Physical development and movement throughout the EYFS

	Birth to 3 years old	3- and 4-year-olds	4- and 5-year-olds
Attitudes and dispositions	Explore movement and sensory experiences with primary caregiver or independently – inside and outdoors. Support and include those differently abled.	In addition: Plan for more complex movement play. Negotiate and collaborate with others. Enjoy more challenging play outdoors. Begin to reflect on activities and how to refine them.	In addition: Increase independence in self-care. Create more interesting opportunities to be active outside. Persevere to keep practising and improving skills. Be resilient and determined. Explore wider possibilities of using skills in different contexts.
Concepts and skills	**Skills:** Rolling, crawling, sitting, standing Climbing, walking, jumping, running Stretching, swinging Pedalling, scootering, grasping Holding, prodding Squeezing, wiping, brushing	**Skills** In addition: throwing, catching, kicking, aiming, passing, batting, hopping, galloping, cycling, swimming, constructing, writing, drawing, painting, cutting/scissors Processing instructions Combinations/sequences	**Skills** In addition: skipping, galloping, turning Balancing, sewing, modelling **Concepts** Precision, accuracy Rhythm, sharing Imitating, copying Following, leading, demonstrating, practising
Vocabulary	Position: On, off, under, above, below, near, far, over, beside, in, out Directions: Around, backwards, forwards, sideways, through	In addition: enjoy, happy, frustrated, sad, cross, bored, tired, exhausted, free, relaxed, energetic, calm, pleased, disappointed	In addition: dither, meander, rapid, adjacent, topple, wilt, dangle, slump

Being happy

A 10-year study conducted by the movement play specialists Jabadao suggests there is a strong link between young children's wellbeing and their movement play. Their evidence indicates that children's enjoyment, relaxation, vitality, openness, self-confidence and self-knowledge are all increased through their participation in movement play (Jabadao, 2009).

If children are physically confident and competent, daily routines become manageable and enjoyable: taking coats off, washing hands, sitting in a circle, cutting up snacks, and moving between rooms and activities. Growing independence in self-care is important for supporting their agency and self-image.

We should do all we can to make sure that children's movement experience is happy and fun. If memories are positive, children are more likely to engage with future movement opportunities and physical activity.

Inclusive practice

The physical development component of the framework should be effective in supporting inclusion. Careful planning may account for children who have language difficulties, identified additional needs or are overweight. The spaces in which children move inside and outside should be safe places where each child is welcome and supported.

When cooperating physically, children learn that different bodies move differently and that some children are more confident in their movements and physicality. They will learn when other children may benefit from being helped and, more importantly, become sensitive to when help is and is not wanted.

Children learn to wait their turn, so that everyone can participate. They learn about sharing spaces and resources when moving together. They use language in a relevant and meaningful context.

Negative behaviour or language related to race and gender may be addressed through careful observation and planning for physical activity and movement play – for example, how to deal with the 'zoning' of gender specific spaces and resources; children from similar backgrounds always playing together; the 'labelling' of less confident or competent individuals; and children creating and enforcing random 'rules'.

It is the responsibility of practitioners to ensure that all children have equal access to all physical activities.

Gross motor skills

These are also known as generic, fundamental or functional. They are the basic movements associated with human activity.

Essentially, gross motor skills are whole-body movements. They provide the strength, coordination, balance and agility needed for all other skills. They are the critical building blocks.

Practising rolling, crawling, climbing, running, jumping, kicking and throwing provide effective preparation for later, more complex physical skills. The importance of continuous and varied experience of these skills cannot be overstated. Even when they are fluent and used effectively, children will benefit from repeating and refining them.

How to practise these skills

Inside (shoes off if possible):

- Rolling: ask the children to curl up into a ball by hugging their knees tightly – now rock backwards and forwards, slowly then getting faster. Ask them to lie on their front with long arms and legs – now flip onto their back without losing the shape – now flip back onto front again – try going left and right very fast
- Crawling: try going at different speeds, forwards and backwards, around and under tables and chairs
- Jumping: invite the children to hold the back of their chair with both hands – jump with feet together on tiptoes, with flat feet, with feet out and in, forward and back
- Running: put tables together in a line to create one big one – invite children to place one hand on the table and face forwards – now ask them to run around the table, keeping their hand on the table at all times – change direction
- Ball skills: use rolled up socks or crumpled paper bags to throw, kick, catch, pass and aim
- Obstacle courses: invite the children to construct a course themselves using the available resources like cushions, tables, chairs, carpet, walls, floor, steps

Outside:

- Provide a range of large loose parts, including car tyres and crates for children to lift, carry and construct
- Suggest ways in which the available resources may be used to challenge jumping (across/onto/down), running (in a circle/back and forth), climbing, balancing and swinging
- Encourage group activities that include digging and pushing resources around the space – sweeping up afterwards

Gross Motor Skills

Children at the expected level of development will:

- Negotiate space and obstacles safely, with consideration for themselves and others;
- Demonstrate strength, balance and coordination when playing;
- Move energetically, such as running, jumping, dancing, hopping, skipping and climbing.

Fine motor skills

These are sometimes called manipulative skills as usually they apply to the hands only. However, we should include the mouth, feet and eyes. These body parts play a significant role in fine motor skill development.

Reaching the goals for fine motor skills depends mainly on prior gross motor skill development. Children need to be able to sit still in the right position. They need to keep their head in alignment with the body and maintain eye focus. The shoulder girdle must be strong enough to carry the weight of the arm and stabilise the elbow joint. It must also be flexible enough to allow for the wrist to rotate. Significant experience of gross motor skills will support the balance, strength and coordination needed for fluent handwriting.

Hands are extraordinarily complex and one of the final body parts to mature. The range of skills that hands perform can become increasingly complex and develop over a lifetime: music, sewing, cooking, calligraphy, knitting, hairdressing, card games, board games, modelling, painting.

Children need repeated and varied opportunities to use all the muscles in their hands. This will support them to achieve the 'tripod grip' for handwriting. Some children may already have highly developed fine motor skills owing to their cultural background, such as through their use of chopsticks in the family home.

To strengthen the hand muscles:

- Try playing with sponges in water, playdough, rolling pins, twisting tops off bottles, prodding, squeezing, rolling and pinching appropriate materials
- Peel small pieces of fruit, add a pinch of salt or spice to a recipe, find small objects hidden in a bowl of dried rice, feed the fish
- Thread material through a lattice or put pasta and breads on a string
- Create intricate patterns with small buttons, beads and paper straws
- Peel off stickers and place on a sheet of paper
- Enjoy sand play with small utensils like teaspoons and egg cups

- Play 'dancing and talking' fingers – draw faces on fingertips and hold conversations between hands
- Practise finger drumming

Towards the dynamic tripod grip

- Children may start with the *palmer grasp* when the whole hand is used to hold a crayon
- The *digital pronate grasp* usually comes next when the pencil is held between two fingers and thumb
- Between 3 and 4 years, children will start to use the *static tripod grasp* when the thumb is separated from the fingers and movement comes from the wrist not the fingers
- Finally, the *dynamic tripod grasp* is achieved, and letters may be joined together with ease

Throughout this often-lengthy process, provide continual opportunities to practise the pincer grip:

- Enhance sorting activities by picking up small items with tweezers or clothes pegs
- Evenly place pegs around a circle of card
- Drop a range of small objects into a bottle – try marbles and paper clips

───────────── ▰Early Learning Goal▰ ─────────────────────────

Fine Motor Skills

Children at the expected level of development will:

- Hold a pencil effectively in preparation for fluent writing - using the tripod grip in almost all cases;
- Use a range of small tools, including scissors, paint brushes and cutlery;
- Begin to show accuracy and care when drawing.

───

Thinking beyond the goals

Health and self-care have been repositioned in PSED, yet gross motor and fine motor skills impact greatly on the development of self-care. Manipulative skills help with cleaning teeth, holding cutlery and getting dressed. Gaining physical competence and confidence supports children's safety in the wider environment and encourages healthy behaviours around food and drink.

The current goals for physical development are narrow in focus and not very ambitious. To extend their reach, consider the following:

- Invite children to create their own movement sequences, using music to provide a steady beat
- Practise challenging combinations of movements: they can spin or jump and balance on one leg
- Introduce interesting materials to move with: chiffon scarves or coloured ribbons
- Encourage the exploration of different ball skills: batting, passing and aiming

Conclusion

The physical development component of the framework informs, supports and underpins all the other areas. At every moment of children's lives, something physical is happening, especially when they are pretending to sleep or stand guard and be very still.

Every child's movement journey is different. It unfolds in its own way, following a personal timetable. Early movement experiences that are enjoyable and meaningful will provide a wealth of long-term health benefits.

Being a competent and confident mover impacts on children's ability to create and maintain friendships and to try new experiences. Moving together provides a supportive environment in which new vocabulary and language skills may be practised and refined.

Providing opportunities for children to move throughout the day and ensuring the value of physical development is reflected in planning, will effectively support overall learning and development.

Reflective questions

1. What practical measures do you take to ensure all children are active throughout the day?
2. How do you ensure physical development is properly valued by parents and staff?

6

Literacy

Sinéad Harmey

EYFS Statutory Educational Programme

It is crucial for children to develop a life-long love of reading. Reading consists of two dimensions: language comprehension and word reading. Language comprehension (necessary for both reading and writing) starts from birth. It only develops when adults talk with children about the world around them and the books (stories and non-fiction) they read with them, and enjoy rhymes, poems and songs together. Skilled word reading, taught later, involves both the speedy working out of the pronunciation of unfamiliar printed words (decoding) and the speedy recognition of familiar printed words. Writing involves transcription (spelling and handwriting) and composition (articulating ideas and structuring them in speech, before writing).

Introduction

Mohammed-Jawad bursts into his classroom and runs up to hang his coat on his peg – proudly pointing to his name, he declares 'that's my one'.

Seeing children recognise their name for the first time is one of the joys of being an early years teacher. It used to be thought that children move from a 'pre-reading' to a 'reading' stage. Another perspective, an emergent literacy one, is that the journey to becoming a reader and a writer is more fine-grained and that children emerge into literacy from birth. Children are in the process of becoming literate: aware that print contains meaning and that speech matches print. We see this in lots of subtle ways in early years classrooms. What do we mean by literacy? The Statutory Framework for the Early Years Foundation Stage (EYFS) (DfE, 2021c) describes literacy as reading and writing:

- reading consisting of two dimensions: language comprehension and word reading
- writing involving transcription and composition

This framework helps us think of the components involved in skilled reading and writing. But it can be difficult to match that definition with literacy learners in early years settings. As an early years teacher and researcher, I find it more helpful to define literacy as a process that involves learning that symbols in print make meaning:

- I can read these symbols and listen to someone else's message
- I can write these symbols and this carries meaning (even if the symbols do not quite look conventional yet)

As Mohammed-Jawad joyfully demonstrated, these symbols arranged in this way mean something – his name.

This chapter builds on the idea that literacy is a meaning-making activity, and that oral language is the foundation of literacy. First, I consider how oral language feeds into literacy. Then, I consider how to support emergent readers by fostering a love of books and building foundational reading skills. Finally, I examine emergent writing and how to support emergent writing.

Literacy builds on oral language

Written text is thoughts and language in print. Understanding language or language comprehension is essential for reading and writing. It starts from birth and the development of language 'underpins all seven areas of learning and development' (DfE, 2021a, p. 21). Chapter 3 in this book focuses on language and communication. In this section, I want to focus on:

- how literacy and oral language are interconnected
- how we can support children's literacy development through the development of oral language

Research supports the idea that strong oral language skills are linked to later reading ability (Law et al., 2017). Some of the aspects of oral language that support literacy include the development of:

- narrative skills
- vocabulary
- print knowledge
- phonological awareness

I focus next on narrative skills and vocabulary; print knowledge and phonological awareness will be developed later in the chapter.

Narrative skills

Narrative skills are the ability to tell a story, describe or retell events, or provide instructions. There are many places in the early years curriculum where we can support the development of oral narrative skills. Stories span cultures and form the backbone of poems, rhymes, story books, drama and play. Most stories follow a 'story grammar' – a setting, event, characters, with (typically) a beginning, middle and end. Children's narrative skills develop by providing opportunities to listen to and engage in stories, poems and rhymes. Providing opportunities to retell stories with a light touch emphasis on the 'grammar' of the story supports children to develop narrative skills. Planning to support children to expand their own stories will also support narrative skills.

Narrative skills can develop further via opportunities to tell stories through:

- engaging in sustaining conversations with peers and adults
- using props and puppets
- pretend play

Narrative skills, however, go further than fiction and storytelling. The day-to-day routines of the setting provide opportunities for children to sequence and retell events. Later in children's education, the ability to describe and sequence events will be part of subjects like science, geography and music.

Vocabulary

Knowing and using a wide variety of words is another essential component of literacy development and underlies language comprehension. The rate at which young children accumulate vocabulary is astounding. Children who have a limited vocabulary, however, are unlikely to just 'pick up' words. They need sustained and directed teaching to develop a vocabulary of basic and more complex high utility words. By high-utility words, I mean words that will be used often across subjects. It is useful to think about vocabulary not just as words but also as types of words. Beck et al. (2013) provide a useful framework for this and describe three tiers of words that children need to learn:

- Tier 1: basic everyday words used often (book, bear, door)
- Tier 2: more complex high utility words used across subjects (turn, next, over)
- Tier 3: content-specific words used infrequently (photosynthesis)

In planning the curriculum for early years, it helps to think about how to embed teaching of different types of words across subjects, particularly Tier 2 words. We can do this intentionally through modelling, expanding on what children say, labelling, repeating and rephrasing. It is important to provide repeated opportunities to use and hear words through sharing stories and poems and in small-world play. This supports the development of a rich and varied vocabulary.

Intentionally planning to develop narrative and vocabulary skills fits well with shared reading in the early years. For example, in planning to read *We're Going on a Bear Hunt* (Rosen, 2000), there are opportunities to:

- support children to retell the story in sequence
- encourage a retelling of the story in their play
- directly teach Tier 1 words (e.g. bear, stick)
- directly teach Tier 2 words (e.g. under, over)

Ultimately, the Early Learning Goals for Language Comprehension (below) will be supported by a sustained and intentional focus on narrative and vocabulary skills. Regular sharing of books across a wide variety of topics and genres will expose children to a varied 'diet' of words.

───────**Early Learning Goal**────────────────────────────────

Comprehension

Children at the expected level of development will:

- Demonstrate understanding of what has been read to them by retelling stories and narratives, using their own words and recently introduced vocabulary;
- Anticipate - where appropriate - key events in stories;
- Use and understand recently introduced vocabulary during discussions about stories, non-fiction, rhymes and poems, and during role-play.

───

Emergent reading

The Early Learning Goals for Reading (DfE, 2021c) are the end goals of the EYFS. In this section, I consider what a supportive literacy curriculum needs to include to support children to reach this goal, and beyond. I am framing literacy as a meaning-making process that starts at birth. This process can be supported from birth by:

- fostering a love of books
- providing meaningful opportunities to engage with print
- learning how print works
- developing phonic knowledge

Fostering a love of books

As adult readers, motivation to read guides what and how we read:

- Can you remember the last book that you could not put down?
- What was it about that book that captured your attention?
- Can you remember how this felt compared to the last text you 'had to read'?

At these moments, you were impacted by two factors: motivation and engagement. Your ability to maintain attention and your unwillingness to put this book down was because you were motivated to read. You had a goal – to get to the end of the book! You were engaged or involved in the reading process (Wigfield and Guthrie, 2000). You maintained your attention because you engaged in the story and made connections with it. Apart from the personal enjoyment that reading brings, it is well established that reading motivation and engagement are linked to later academic achievement. This makes sense when we consider how the amount children read will increase opportunities to develop reading skills and exposure to words and knowledge. It is useful to think about motivation and engagement when considering how to foster children's love of books. Children who are motivated to read will pick up books that they are interested in and seek out favourite stories to be read to them. Children who are engaged enjoy listening to stories. They pay attention to stories and share ideas. They talk about books that they are reading and that are being read to them.

We can help children to develop a love of books by paying attention to how motivated they are to read and how engaged they are in book-reading activities.

The social reading environment plays an important part in promoting and fostering a love of books. Think back to where you read that last book you read for pleasure. As adults, we usually seek somewhere comfortable to read books and the same goes for children.

- Where can children read in your setting?
- Is it comfortable and inviting?
- Are the books in good condition and can children easily see and access a range of titles?

We can help children to develop a love of books by reading aloud a variety of children's literature. This helps inform children's motivation to read independently. Reading aloud provides opportunities to learn about stories and engage with print. It also promotes informal book talk through:

- a culture of recommending books to each other through display areas
- involving parents and carers to encourage a culture of reading within and beyond the setting

Learning how print works

Reading starts the moment we look at print. But, accessing print requires some key conceptual understanding about how print works, or concepts about print, as *Development Matters* explains (DfE, 2021a, p. 79). First, children need to understand that print has meaning and has different purposes. Fostering a love of books and creating multiple opportunities to engage in meaningful writing activities support this. There are also more 'technical' things to learn about how print works. Written English follows certain rules, that we need to understand to access print. We write in English from top to bottom and start at the top left of a page. Then writing moves left to right, before going to the next line and starting at the left again. To read a book, we start at the front and turn the pages to the left until we reach the back of the book. Letters make up words and words make up sentences. To read a word, we need to start at the first letter and move left to right. It is all quite complicated really! It is important to teach children in Reception:

- the 'meta-language' we expect them to understand and use (letter, first letter, sound, book, page, title, sentence)
- the literacy behaviours they need to control to read (where to start and which way to go)

This teaching supports emergent reading and should be part of the literacy curriculum.

We can support conceptual awareness about print through print referencing during shared reading (see Justice and Ezell, 2004). Consider this extract from Naomi's classroom – she is reading *Open Very Carefully – A Book With a Bite* by Nick Bromley (2014):

Naomi:	OK everyone, sitting comfortably? Today I'm going to read this book – it's called '*Open Very Carefully – A Book With a Bite*'!
Alex:	A crocodile!!
Naomi:	That's right, Alex – you saw a crocodile on the cover of the book! Let's open this book very carefully so (turns the page) and here on the first page I see a beautiful lake…
Amy:	With a mother duck and baby ducks
John:	Ducklings
Naomi:	Yes – I can see them too – mother duck and three yellow baby ducklings and a little grey duckling with a red hat. Let's see what's happening. Where should I start reading?
Jamie:	Up the top
Naomi:	Yes, right up here on the top left-hand side – I'm going to start here (points to the first word) and then go this way (gestures left to right under the first line of text). Once upon a time, there was a mother duck with three pretty ducklings and one… Wait a minute… what's that…?

In this exchange, Naomi is building engagement with the story by talking about the pictures. She is helping the children to learn new vocabulary by expanding on what the children are contributing and by print referencing.

- Talking about pictures allows children to build a 'mental model' of the story that they are about to hear and supports comprehension
- Print referencing draws children's attention to how print works

Print referencing is an effective strategy to develop conceptual awareness about print. It provides a kind of meta-language for children to use: the cover of the book, the first page, where I should start reading. Building in print referencing, like Naomi does, demonstrates the kind of things children need to be able to do in order to use letter-sound knowledge. We expect children to know where to and how to look at print whilst we are teaching them more complex phonic skills. Deliberately teaching conceptual awareness about print as part of the literacy curriculum in the early years lays the foundations for this.

To read letters and words, children need to match speech sounds (phonemes) to symbols (graphemes). This demands phonological awareness – the ability to perceive and manipulate sounds in words (Cain, 2010). Supporting the development of phonological awareness is an essential component of any literacy curriculum. Difficulties in phonological awareness are linked to later difficulties in reading. To support phonological awareness, engage children in activities like:

- recognising words that sound the same
- saying words that sound the same
- identifying and segmenting syllables
- playing with individual sounds through songs, word games and rhymes

Phonics instruction supports children's understanding of the link between what they hear and what they see. Evidence suggests that the teaching of phonics should be 'explicit and systematic' (EEF, 2018b) for children in Reception. There is less evidence about the impact of phonics instruction with younger children (aged 3–4). Children need to learn how to decode words, analyse word parts and recognise words. There is strong evidence that 'once children know a few consonant and vowel sounds they can start to blend those letters into simple words' (Foorman et al., 2016, p. 14) and indeed read simple sentences by the end of Reception.

―――――(Early Learning Goal)―――――――――――――――――――――――――――――

Word Reading

Children at the expected level of development will:

- Say a sound for each letter in the alphabet and at least 10 digraphs;
- Read words consistent with their phonic knowledge by sound-blending;
- Read aloud simple sentences and books that are consistent with their phonic knowledge, including some common exception words.

Emergent writing

Writing starts when a child picks up a tool and makes marks that express some sort of mean-ingful message. The message, however, might not be obvious to the reader. Writing is a very complex process. It requires bringing together a huge amount of knowledge and skills, both cognitive and physical. It is a physical act requiring fine motor control and self-regulation. It involves knowledge about letter-sound relationships and spelling patterns. It involves composition – so it could be thought of as the bringing together of ideas and shaping those ideas in written form. In this section of the chapter, I consider how we can support children with:

- the physical act of writing (transcription)
- the act of composition (writing a message)

I also consider how writing can support reading and language more generally.

The physical act of writing

The fine motor control required to write letters develops first through the coordination of larger muscle groups. This happens in the early years areas of physical development and expressive art and design, and as children play. As early years educators, we have all seen the intense look of concentration as children grip writing tools in an effort to reproduce symbols. Rowe and Wilson (2015) studied children's writing from age 1 to 3. They found that children's early mark-making may seem random, but that children follow developmental trajectories:

- moving from using their forearms to make big purposeful marks
- repeating patterns like lines and circles
- producing semi-conventional letters

We can support these early interactions with print by providing lots of opportunities to make marks using a variety of media and tools. Tools like sticks, large paintbrushes and sponges, together with media like chalk and paints, provide opportunities to grasp and use tools to make marks. Cutting with scissors helps develop hand strength. *Development Matters* describes how sensory play with sand, flour and mud can support the development of gross motor con-trol. Writing is part of children's play – for example, shopping lists, sending notes and letters at the post office and writing menus. Providing a clipboard, whiteboards, notebooks and paper all encourage the child's motivation to write. This provision will put them on the path to being able to write and form some letters correctly by Reception.

Over time, children can develop emergent writing skills by using a variety of media like felt tip markers, pencils, chalk, charcoal and smaller paintbrushes. As children move towards producing more conventional letters, it is supportive to think again about the meta-language that is necessary to support writing letters – words like up, down, round and back. Thinking back to conceptual awareness about print, it is important to help children to write accurately and develop concep-tual awareness about print. As we teach children to write in Reception, we might focus their attention on:

- where to start
- which way to go
- how to group letters into words
- leaving spaces between words

The act of composition

The prime purpose of writing is to make meaning. Providing the opportunities to practise the act of transcription will help children to understand that writing is a meaning-making process. As I sit here writing this chapter, I am thinking about a message I want to convey. I am thinking about how to organise that message into recognisable symbols so that you, the reader, can understand my message. In today's society, however, it is worth thinking about text as being multi-modal. We express meaning in text. But we can also use pictures and symbols, using either traditional tools (pens and pencils) or digital means (photos and apps). Indeed, using pictures in tandem with writing is supportive for emergent writers as it helps children to organise their ideas.

There are many opportunities for teachers to model how ideas can become print by modelling and scribing for the child. We can annotate children's paintings and mark-making messages (for example, by asking children to provide simple phrases for their work and writing them for them). Shared writing can become a part of daily routines by writing on flipcharts and asking children to add letters or punctuation they know and can write. As children begin to attempt to write on their own, their first attempts may be phonically plausible but incorrect (for example: cr for car or byk for bike). This is absolutely fine. Children who use invented spelling are 'flexing their muscles'. They are using their growing phonological awareness skills and linking sounds to letters. Ouellette and Sénéchal (2017) found that invented spelling in kindergarten (Reception) is linked to later success in spelling and early reading.

All of the opportunities described in the last two sections bring children to a point where they will have the physical ability to write recognisable letters and words and write simple phrases.

—Early Learning Goal—

Writing

Children at the expected level of development will:

- Write recognisable letters, most of which are correctly formed;
- Spell words by identifying sounds in them and representing the sounds with a letter or letters;
- Write simple phrases and sentences that can be read by others.

Speaking, reading and writing: Interconnected and not separate

I have written about oral language, reading and writing separately in this chapter. You might think that I am suggesting that we should teach these three aspects of literacy separately. Not quite. There is evidence that there is a need for discrete and intentional teaching of certain elements of literacy – for example, phonics and vocabulary teaching. But there are distinct benefits to considering how the elements support each other. How might this look in practice? Take, for example, the following extract as Lizzie, Mohammed-Jawad's teacher, works with him to caption a painting.

Lizzie sits beside Mohammed-Jawad as he finishes painting. On the page is a big yellow sun and some green stripes at the bottom.

Lizzie: Tell me about your painting, Mohammed-Jawad.
Mohammed-Jawad: It's sun and park.
Lizzie: Oh nice – and is that the grass there at the bottom of the picture?
Mohammed-Jawad: Yes, it's sun and grass.

Lizzie takes a strip of card and says, 'where shall I start?' and Mohammed-Jawad points to the left. She writes the sentence as she says it – It's sun and grass.

Lizzie: Now we'll put your name here. You know the first letter, so you start for me.

Mohammed-Jawad takes the pen and writes the M for his name.

This exchange exemplifies how language becomes text. It illustrates the interconnected nature of literacy. Mohammed-Jawad provided the meaning – it became written text which can be read – and opportunity to learn about print works. Inviting children to add letters to text allows them to start making these connections. The literacy curriculum should offer opportunities for children to make these connections across reading, writing and speaking. Books authored by children bring the connection between speaking and writing even closer. We can share these pieces by reading them aloud to the other children and put these books in the library for children to read independently. This demonstrates to children that literacy is about making meaning and that they can be authors. In my work with struggling writers, the first place I often start with is small caption books that include the child's name.

Conclusion

The developmental trajectory in becoming literate is rapid in the early years setting. Looking at the Early Learning Goals, we can forget that children need a solid foundation of language. They also need to integrate a range of physical and cognitive skills. The road to reading and writing simple sentences and understanding texts is built on these foundations. Reading and writing require motivation, engagement and self-regulation. Above all, as the first

Table 6.1   Literacy throughout the EYFS

	Birth to 3 years old	3- and 4-year-olds	4- and 5-year-olds: Reception
Attitudes and dispositions	Enjoy stories/songs/rhymes. Enjoy sharing books. Seek out favourite stories. Pay attention to songs/rhymes/stories. Enjoy drawing/making marks. Confidently share ideas about reading/writing.	In addition: Engage in storytelling and sequence events. Confidently converse and express what they need. Engage in more extended conversations. Plan writing and persist to try and form some shapes while writing.	In addition: Engage in extended stories/learn new vocabulary. Reflect on likes and dislikes (e.g. stories). Seek out opportunities to write messages. Engage in more extended writing episodes.
Concepts and skills	Say some words/songs/rhymes. Repeat words and phrases in songs/rhymes/stories. Ask questions about books. Share ideas about books. Talk about writing/drawing. Add meaning to marks by talking about writing. Hold a book and turn pages. Notice some features of print.	In addition: Understand some concepts about print. Sequence stories/narratives. Recognise words with the same initial sound or that rhyme. Clap syllables. Write some letters and some or all of their name. Use some print to represent meaning. Use a variety of language structures.	In addition: Recognise, name and write some letters. Blend sounds in some short words. Read/write their name and read some exception words. Read simple phrases. Form letters correctly and revise. Reread what they have written. Match sounds to letters. Write short sentences using a capital letter and a full stop.
Vocabulary	Book, name	Front/back of book, page, first, next, last, turn, start/end	Letters, words, phoneme, grapheme, digraph, left/right, full stop, capital/lower case

sentence of the EYFS Statutory Educational Programme says, literacy is about enjoyment (DfE, 2021c). Motivation and engagement in reading and writing provide children with positive dispositions towards literacy. They need this to persist with becoming more expert readers and writers. In Table 6.1, I outline how early learning might look in the EYFS across different phases. In the vocabulary section, I refer to the meta-language which might be helpful at each phase, assuming that reading and writing themselves are vehicles for developing vocabulary across the wider curricular areas.

Reflective questions

1. The development of narrative skills and vocabulary is essential in supporting children's language comprehension. How can we integrate this into shared reading opportunities?
2. Are the social reading environments of the classroom inviting?
3. Are children motivated to use the social reading environments independently?
4. The Early Learning Goals separate reading and writing into components. Are there components that receive more/less emphasis in your curricular provision? What areas need more emphasis?
5. What opportunities are there to link together reading, writing and speaking?

7

Mathematics

Fliss James

┌─EYFS Statutory Educational Programme─┐

Mathematics

Developing a strong grounding in number is essential so that all children develop the necessary building blocks to excel mathematically. Children should be able to count confidently, develop a deep understanding of the numbers to 10, the relationships between them and the patterns within those numbers. By providing frequent and varied opportunities to build and apply this understanding – such as using manipulatives, including small pebbles and tens frames for organising counting – children will develop a secure base of knowledge and vocabulary from which a mastery of mathematics is built. In addition, it is important that the curriculum includes rich opportunities for children to develop their spatial reasoning skills across all areas of mathematics, including shape, space and measures. It is important that children develop a positive attitude and interest in mathematics, look for patterns and relationships, spot connections, 'have a go', talk to adults and peers about what they notice and not be afraid to make mistakes.

Introduction

Early mathematics is astoundingly important for children's development. Positive early experiences and achievement in mathematics lay the foundations for future learning and success. Fascinatingly, babies are born mathematical, and research shows that very young children have an instinctive sense of quantity, pattern and spatial relationships. From an early age, children develop their ideas about maths through play, exploration and routines. They have a natural desire and curiosity to learn and find out about their world. Many of the things children wonder about are bursting with mathematical ideas!

Maths anxiety

It is common for adults to express negative feelings and a lack of confidence about maths. Unfortunately, poor school experiences are often the cause.

Early years practitioners need to be mindful of expressing negative feelings about maths. Myths about maths abound: there is no evidence of a 'maths brain' or that particular people are 'wired up for maths' or are 'maths people'. It is important that we shift this false narrative. It is time to empower all adults and children to be able to engage with the wonder and creativity of maths.

Early maths is incredibly important, and all young children have a right to thrive in challenging and enjoyable maths teaching.

Maths is all around us

The world we live in is highly mathematical. Do you ever stop and look at the patterns and shapes that surround us? There are many examples in the natural world, from the spirals in seashells to the arrangement of sunflower seeds.

Our daily lives are filled with maths; from the moment we wake, we encounter mathematical ideas. Getting up on time, making breakfast and navigating our way to work all involve mathematical thinking. It is important to develop an understanding of the mathematics that is embedded in everyday life.

The importance of mathematising

Children engage with mathematical ideas in their play from a very young age:

> In their free play, children naturally engage in mathematics. Observations of preschoolers show that when they play, they engage in mathematical thinking at least once in almost half of each minute that they are playing.

> (Clements and Sarama, 2017)

Yet, despite this natural mathematical play, we know that young children need *our input* to make sense of these ideas. Children's interests, actions and experiences are rich, but they are not enough in themselves. They are a starting point. Children need adults to help them build on mathematical knowledge and make connections.

So how can we do this?

The term 'mathematising' has arisen in the literature to make abstract mathematical ideas 'real' for children. When adults mathematise experiences for children, they help them to 'see' the maths. Through engaging children in back-and-forth conversations, adults can encourage children to recognise and talk about maths in everyday situations. Use of open-ended questions can prompt children to make connections, reason, reflect and apply their knowledge. It is vital to understand that without the sensitive, responsive, intentional action of adults, these mathematical ideas do not develop into concepts that children truly understand.

Effective mathematics teaching in the early years

The Education Endowment Foundation's (EEF) guidance report *Improving Mathematics in the Early Years and Key Stage 1* identifies three important aspects:

- adults' own understanding of mathematics
- children's mathematical development and how they learn
- effective mathematical pedagogy

(EEF, 2020a)

Firstly, sensitive, supportive relationships are vital. Adults need to know children well. It is essential to foster a culture that supports and celebrates children's curiosity, problem-solving and reasoning skills.

Adults need to understand how children typically develop mathematical concepts and skills. It is also vital that adults are aware of how the following factors influence development:

- higher level thinking skills: executive functions, self-regulation and metacognition
- language skills
- motor skills
- previous experiences, interests, enjoyment and attitudes

(EEF, 2020a)

It is key that adults plan experiences that challenge young children's mathematical knowledge. This is neatly described in the New Zealand Education Review Office report *Early Mathematics: A Guide for Improving Teaching and Learning*:

> Without a balance of deliberate teaching and spontaneous learning, a 'hands off' approach does not benefit children's learning. When teachers do not deliberately or intentionally extend children's interests and build on their learning over time, children are disadvantaged.

(New Zealand Education Review Office/Te Tari Arotake Mātauranga, 2016, p. 24)

Practitioners need to have a strong understanding of maths so that they can identify the maths the child is engaging with, tune in and extend it. To quote the Erikson Early Math Collaborative:

> This knowledge will also help you recognize the kinds of structured activities that do the best job of making these ideas real for young children, which means you will be able to make them fun without losing the important concepts under the 'glitter and glue'.
>
> (The Early Math Collaborative, Erikson Institute, 2014, p. 6)

Understanding how children learn mathematical ideas will help you to work out what a child does and does not understand. You will be equipped to know what they need to learn about next.

Teachable moments

Teachable moments involve spotting and capitalising on opportunities to promote mathematical learning in everyday play and routines. As Clements and Sarama (2018, p. 3) state, 'teachable moments, handled well, can be wondrous and satisfying'.

Relying on teachable moments, however, is not enough.

We must seek out and take advantage of meaningful, spontaneous situations. Many adults do not spend enough time observing children to tune into such opportunities. Additionally, many adults do not have the necessary mathematical concepts, skills and vocabulary at their fingertips.

Teachable moments are important but need to be part of a 'hybrid approach'. We need to dedicate time for children to learn mathematics and integrate it throughout the day:

> Math can be integrated with children's ongoing play and activities, but this integration usually requires a curriculum and a knowledgeable adult who creates a supportive environment and provides challenges, suggestions, tasks, and language. Combining free play with intentional teaching, and promoting play with mathematical objects and mathematical ideas is pedagogically powerful.
>
> (Clements and Sarama, 2017)

How does children's understanding of number and counting develop?

Subitising

Developing a strong sense of number and counting in the early years is essential. An important aspect of number sense is *subitising*. Adults working with young children need to fully understand this. It is described in the non-statutory guidance and in the Early Learning Goals.

Subitise comes from the Latin 'to arrive suddenly' (Gilmore et al., 2018). *Subitising* is the ability to quickly recognise and say the number of things in a group without counting. For example, if there are 5 cherries on a plate, subitising is when the child knows there are 5 without counting them one by one. Research shows that subitising is one of the main skills that very young children should develop. Attuned and knowledgeable interactions are essential to develop subitising (Clements and Sarama, 2014; Frye et al., 2013).

There are two kinds of subitising:

- *Perceptual subitising:* when you 'just see' how many items there are in a very small collection, you are using *perceptual subitising*
- *Conceptual subitising:* this involves seeing the parts and putting together the whole. For example, when looking at a domino, you might see two groups of 4 as one 8

Subitising supports counting and lays the foundations for arithmetic. It helps children develop important ideas such as understanding 'how many' and how numbers are composed.

When children subitise, it is important that we acknowledge this. Equally, we need to be aware of when we might inadvertently discourage subitising – for example, if a child shows an amount using their fingers, saying '3', and the adult responds by asking the child to 'count them to check'.

Everyday experiences and routines offer purposeful opportunities to develop subitising. This case study describes how snack time can be a meaningful and engaging context:

Case Study

A team of practitioners wanted to promote subitising in their setting. They intentionally focused on using number words up to 5 in their interactions with the children during snack: 'We have 4 apples to share for snack today' rather than 'We have apples today'. The impact of mathematising this experience started to have an impact quite quickly. The children started to notice and talk about quantity (as well as using their fingers): 'I have 2 crackers', 'I took 3 pieces of banana!', 'We need 4 cups.'

The practitioners encouraged the children to see the amount, not just the objects. This enabled children to start to build up a concept of number and connect number words with specific amounts.

Number words and numerals

Another aspect of number sense involves understanding that numbers – both the words and the numeral – are used in different ways. Numerals are visual symbols: they are abstract. Words for small numbers are among the first words that children learn, and numerals come a little later. The full meaning of number words and numerals is acquired over a longer period.

Cardinal numbers

These are used to represent quantity: 2 means two things. We want children to develop an understanding that we use numbers (both words and numerals) to name specific amounts. Many young children will recognise the numeral 2 though not understand that it represents two things. Knowing that the word two and the numeral 2 cannot be used with any other quantity is an important development.

Ordinal numbers

These are used as labels for putting things in order. They refer to a position in a sequence. For example: first, second, third.

Nominal numbers

These do not give us information about quantity, but function purely as labels – for example, door numbers or telephone numbers. These numerals are not about 'how many'.

Referential numbers

These are used as a reference point. When we talk about time or temperature, we are using number words and numerals to refer to something that we have a shared agreement of. For example, 'Let's meet at 5 o'clock.'

Counting

Children love to count; it is a big part of their day-to-day life. It is the first recognisably mathematical activity that children engage in and something that adults tend to place a lot of emphasis on. Counting is often a social experience for very young children. Adults encourage children to use rhymes, stories and songs to promote their counting. Yet, the point of counting – that is to find out how many – is often *not* established in these experiences. Counting is deceptively complex! It is, therefore, essential that adults have a detailed understanding of *how* children learn to count.

We can explore this by looking at the *counting principles*. Gelman and Gallistel (1986) identified five principles that underpin young children's counting:

1. The *one-to-one principle*: one number word from the counting sequence is named for each object

2. The *stable-order principle*: number words must be said in the same order every time
3. The *cardinal principle*: the final number word tells you how many objects have been counted; it signals the end of the count
4. The *abstraction principle*: any collection of 'things' may be counted
5. The *order-irrelevance principle* – the order in which the objects in a set are counted does not change the total; the total is always the same.

Cardinality

A significant stage in the development of children's counting is when they understand the connection between counting objects in a collection and the total number of objects in that collection. The Early Math Collaborative (2014, p. 185) describes the principle of cardinality as the 'cornerstone of competent counting'. At first, children may not realise how many objects there are in a collection even after counting them. Children must learn that the last number word tells them how many things have been counted. It is a complex process, involving more than stating the last number word. To be able to count a collection of objects, children need to know the count sequence as well as pointing to or moving the objects. They need to know the last number word provides them with the total in the collection.

For us to understand if a child has grasped the principle of cardinality, we must have a sound understanding of what it means. Often, when children are asked to count how many children are in a group, practitioners focus on:

*   the correct sequence (stable order principle)
*   one number word for one item (one-to-one correspondence)

It is less common for adults to draw the children's attention to the last counting word and ask, 'how many?' Yet, it is *this* part of the process that is essential. We can emphasise the importance of this by explaining why we are counting: 'We are counting the children because we want to know how many are here today.'

We need to offer both planned and spontaneous opportunities for children to count. When we ask children to count, there must be a genuine reason to do so. Unless the context is purposeful, it can be confusing for children. Moreover, it can make them reluctant to count. The whole point of counting is to find out how many – so it is important to ensure that children know why they need to do so.

Operations

By the end of the EYFS, we aim for children to be able to count confidently, have a deep understanding of the numbers to 10, the relationships between them and the patterns within those numbers.

Young children have a sense of quantity from a very early age. They explore concepts of more, less and same; they add and take away things throughout their play and day-to-day routines. Number operations involve understanding how to use numbers to describe relationships and solve problems, including:

- how sets or collections can be changed by joining and separating
- comparing and ordering
- the relationships between numbers – that larger numbers contain smaller numbers

It is important that adults intentionally plan meaningful and purposeful opportunities for children to learn about joining, separating, comparing, and parts and wholes of sets. To support children to add and subtract with automaticity, they need a clear understanding of the parts of numbers and how they relate to other numbers. Children need to grasp the idea that the quantity of five, for example, is not just a collection of ones but can be understood as a group of two and a group of three. A focus on conceptual subitising can help children to build a strong visual sense of quantity and a deep understanding of part/whole relationships. Engaging children in sustained back-and-forth conversations in which children are encouraged to talk about their strategies to solve number problems, can be especially powerful.

In the Reception year, there should be a focus on the composition of number to 10:

- Focus on the composition of 2, 3, 4 and 5 before moving onto larger numbers.
- Provide a range of visual models of numbers: for example, six as double three on a dice, or the fingers on one hand and one more, or as four and two with ten frame images.
- Model conceptual subitising: 'Well, there are three here and three here, so there must be six.'
- Emphasise the parts within the whole: 'There were 8 eggs in the incubator. Two have hatched and 6 haven't yet hatched.'
- Plan games which involve partitioning and recombining sets. For example, throw 5.

Early Learning Goal

Number

Children at the expected level of development will:

- Have a deep understanding of number to 10, including the composition of each number;
- Subitise (recognise quantities without counting) up to 5;
- Automatically recall (without reference to rhymes, counting or other aids) number bonds up to 5 (including subtraction facts) and some number bonds up to 10, including double facts.

─Early Learning Goal─

Numerical Patterns

Children at the expected level of development will:

- Verbally count beyond 20, recognising the pattern of the counting system;
- Compare quantities up to 10 in different contexts, recognising when one quantity is greater than, less than or the same as the other quantity;
- Explore and represent patterns within numbers up to 10, including evens and odds, double facts and how quantities can be distributed equally.

Subitising, counting and number operations are not the only aspects we should focus on in the early years. It is equally important to ensure children are given rich opportunities to learn other mathematical topics, including shape, spatial reasoning, pattern and measures.

There is no longer an Early Learning Goal for shape, space and measures. Yet, as the EYFS Statutory Educational Programme states, it is essential that children experience a curriculum which offers rich and challenging opportunities to develop mathematical knowledge in these key areas:

> In addition, it is important that the curriculum includes rich opportunities for children to develop their spatial reasoning skills across all areas of mathematics including shape, space and measures. It is important that children develop positive attitudes and interests in mathematics, look for patterns and relationships, spot connections, 'have a go', talk to adults and peers about what they notice and not be afraid to make mistakes.
>
> (DfE, 2021c, p. 10)

It is critical to note that the Early Learning Goals are *not* the curriculum for the Reception year. They are 17 checkpoints to help us summarise what a child knows and can do, and where they might need more help. We need to ensure that children experience a rich early years curriculum, not a focus on the end goals.

Spatial reasoning

Spatial reasoning is very important for mathematical development and our everyday lives. The Early Childhood Maths Group explains what spatial reasoning involves:

> Spatial reasoning involves our interpretation of how things, including ourselves, relate to each other and our spatial environment and includes interpreting images and creating representations.
>
> (Gifford et al., 2022, p. 5)

It is essential to give young children time, space and freedom to explore the world physically. When you observe a baby, you will see how they try to reach for and grasp things dangled in front of them. This is part of learning how to locate objects in space.

As children's physical skills develop, so do their spatial abilities. Crawling, cruising and walking are ways young children develop an awareness of space. As they figure out how to move from one area to another, they negotiate obstacles. As children get older, they need opportunities to run, roll, jump, crawl and hide. They need to experience different heights so that they can begin to learn about different perspectives (Gifford et al., 2022, p. 24).

The role of the adult is vital for learning spatial language. Research shows that using gestures helps children learn spatial words. When adults use precise language and explanations in back-and-forth conversations, it enables children to develop a deep knowledge and understanding of mathematical concepts.

Case Study

Fatima spends part of every day in the block area. Over the last half term, her constructions have become increasingly complex and detailed. Fatima's key person has noticed her interest in the blocks and dedicates time to sensitively engage in her play. She knows that using precise language is important to extending Fatima's mathematical understanding. As Fatima constructs, her key person pays attention to what she is focused on.

Fatima comments:

'I got a square!'

Her key person responds by describing what she is doing to mathematise her play and expand her language:

Key person: Yes, it is a square, you used four blocks to make a big square.
F: It's going to be a castle!

They engage in a back-and-forth conversation about how to build the castle. Fatima's key person intentionally uses specific language and models her thinking out loud. At tidy-up time, she helps Fatima to replace the blocks, drawing her attention to the shadows on the shelves.

Key person: We need to turn this block sideways so it can fit. This block is curved, can you see the matching shadow?

The next day, to extend her thinking, she suggests that Fatima makes a plan before she starts creating her construction.

Pattern

Children experience patterns in their daily lives, particularly through routines. Patterns help them to predict what is going to happen next. Developing an awareness of pattern helps young children to notice and understand mathematical relationships.

The Early Math Collaborative (2014, p. 83) defines pattern as: 'any predictable sequence found in physical and geometric situations as well as numbers'.

Often, when we consider pattern, we think about regular repeating patterns that are visual, such as stripes on clothing. Generally, these are the first patterns children notice.

What makes a pattern a pattern?

Patterns require a rule. A regular repeating pattern contains an element that repeats continuously. This is called the unit of repeat.

If children are given many and varied opportunities to find out about patterns, they will come to learn that patterns involve a rule. When children understand the rule in a particular pattern, they can start to predict and then make generalisations.

How can we support young children's understanding of pattern?

Children need lots of opportunities to see how patterns exist in the world around them as well as in maths. An engaging way to support this understanding is to go on a pattern walk. Exploring the local environment to spot patterns is a great way to mathematise the patterns around us.

Children need to learn that patterns involve a rule. Though children need opportunities to copy and extend patterns, it is important to note that being able to copy a pattern does *not* mean that the child understands the rule. Children need experiences that help them to learn the rule. One way to do this is to break the rule of the pattern, with the adult supporting the children to understand it.

Pattern can often be focused on simple, regular repeating patterns. These repetitive patterns are important for children to understand the building blocks of numerical patterns. Yet, we need to expose children to many and varied patterns. Patterns can be visual, auditory, temporal and involve movement. Visual patterns are much easier compared to movement patterns such as dances or auditory patterns such as drumbeats or claps.

Children's developing understanding of pattern, and how adults can support this, is outlined in Table 7.1. Every child experiences pattern in their daily life, at home and in their setting. The key is to ensure that adults intentionally draw children's attention to patterns that exist in the world, in their own play and in maths itself.

Table 7.1 Pattern throughout the EYFS

	Birth to 3 years old	3- and 4-year-olds	4- and 5-year-olds: Reception
Attitudes and dispositions	Enjoy exploring the world, through open-ended resources indoors and plenty of time outdoors. This requires a well-organised, rich, sensory environment. Children need access to materials, freely combined with sensitive adult interactions.	Plan and think ahead about playing and exploration. Reflect on choices: 'I notice you have created a pattern that repeats with the sticks and leaves.' Keep trying when things are difficult: when the rule of a pattern is broken, persevere to correct it.	Reflect on what they are learning and how this links to what they have learnt before. Adults might ask questions like: 'What were you thinking when you chose to add the shiny gems into your pattern?' 'What did you learn from the book about the patterns in shells/leaves/flower?'
Concepts and skills	Notice patterns and arrange things in patterns.	Talk about patterns using everyday language. Create and extend regular repeating patterns. Identify where the rule of repeating pattern is broken and correct it. Describe a pattern of events.	Continue, copy and create repeating patterns. Add in additional elements to regular repeating patterns to make them more complex.
Vocabulary	Same Different Say the words for items in treasure baskets and heuristic play	Pattern Notice Copy Stripy Spotty Design First Then After	Continue Repeat Recognise Rule Extend Sequence Mistake Correct Discuss Explain

Conclusion

Children need rich, stimulating playful experiences that connect purposefully to their interests and everyday lives. They need sensitive, responsive adults who will support their thinking and learning both spontaneously and in carefully planned intentional ways. All children can be powerful maths learners. The input they receive and the experiences they have influence their mathematical thinking and learning. We know that specific types of input are crucial for children's early mathematical development: hearing and using mathematical language in sustained back-and-forth conversations, physical play, use of manipulatives, and seeing and using gestures (including using fingers for representing quantities and counting) are experiences that support the development of mathematical ideas.

The evidence is clear: adults play a critical role in building young children's brains. Children learn more in the first five years of their life than at any other time. What happens early, matters for a lifetime. We have a big responsibility to enable children to feel confident and to enjoy maths! The dispositions and attitudes we instil and the opportunities we provide will have a lasting impact on children's future development and life chances.

As Clements and Sarama state:

> Early math learning, from birth, is critical for all future learning … and living. Early math promotes math, but also social, emotional, literacy and general brain development.

(Clements and Sarama, 2021, p. 15)

Reflective questions

1. Can you think of a time when you helped a child to 'mathematise'; to notice and reflect on the maths in their play or in an everyday routine?
2. Can you make a list of genuine, purposeful reasons for children to count?

8

Understanding the world

Julian Grenier, June O'Sullivan, Liz Pemberton and Aaron Bradbury

EYFS Statutory Educational Programme

Understanding the world involves guiding children to make sense of their physical world and their community. The frequency and range of children's personal experiences increase their knowledge and sense of the world around them – from visiting parks, libraries and museums to meeting important members of society such as police officers, nurses and firefighters. In addition, listening to a broad selection of stories, non-fiction, rhymes and poems will foster their understanding of our culturally, socially, technologically and ecologically diverse world. As well as building important knowledge, this extends their familiarity with words that support understanding across domains. Enriching and widening children's vocabulary will support later reading comprehension.

Introduction

From their earliest days, children are exploring and learning about the world. Babies and young children engage in non-stop looking, touching, climbing, smelling and tasting everything around them. A baby playing with a Treasure Basket will put things in their mouth and feel them with their hands and fingers. The baby will return to some favoured objects and set aside others. A toddler in nursery looks back at their key person. The child is checking it is okay before skipping across the room to grab hold of something that looks exciting. The child's confident exploration depends on the sympathy and reliable support of their special adult. From a very young age, children can distinguish between living and inanimate objects. So many children love animals, being outdoors, touching and smelling the earth or sand, enjoying trees and other plants. These deep feelings towards the living world play an important part in helping children to feel happy, healthy and calm.

Children are like swimmers in an ocean of smells, foods, drinks, languages and people from their earliest days. Children in the early years:

- constantly explore and learn about their family culture and the cultures all around them
- become increasingly aware of the wider world of shops, parks, libraries and places of worship; they spend time with people from families other than their own and notice how people are different
- need confident and sympathetic support to explore the physical world and they need adults to reassure them that something different is still okay
- need to be able to talk about the differences they notice between different people's hair texture, skin colour and languages
- need confident, positive attitudes towards diversity to thrive
- are growing up in 21st century England: a dynamic and diverse society
- are growing up during the climate change emergency; they need to learn how they can become part of the solution to this crisis, and not part of the problem

We can already see why this area of learning is so important to children in the early years. This early learning will build strong foundations for subjects that come later in schooling. However, it is important to note that children in Reception do not learn history, science or geography as subjects. It does not make sense to design a primary school geography curriculum that begins in Reception. But it does make sense to consider how early learning in understanding the world will give children the foundational concepts and vocabulary to help them learn geography when they are older.

The revised Statutory Framework for the Early Years Foundation Stage (EYFS) (DfE, 2021c) and *Development Matters* (DfE, 2021a) put a greater emphasis on the foundations of science, history and geography. They also place more emphasis on teaching and learning about equality. These changes can help children to form positive attitudes about diversity, preparing them for life in an increasingly interconnected world.

Strong foundations to support later learning in science

Children are inquisitive – young children are often described as being 'into everything'. They have a strong disposition to explore and learn about their world. As young children mix different substances together, they may feel, notice and talk about the changes. That will be true whether they are mixing mud, leaves and water together in the mud kitchen, or flour, yeast, salt, oil and honey to make bread. We can understand activities like these as early experiences of learning chemistry. As children push toy boats under the water, they are experiencing forces (pushes and pulls). These will be part of their later learning about physics. Children planting cress seeds on cotton wool or searching for woodlice under logs are learning about living things – biology.

How can we maximise children's early scientific learning? We need to think about the importance of a richly resourced, stimulating environment. In my experience, this is a strength in many early years settings and in schools. If you are working with children aged 3 to 5 years old, you might use the ECERS-E environmental rating scales (Sylva et al., 2003) to check quality and set priorities for improvement.

Adult interaction is crucial. We need to think about how we help children to develop their early scientific skills in observation, and their early understanding of key concepts. This is a much trickier area. Some early years staff may not feel confident about their own scientific knowledge. They may not know the correct terms to use. The New Zealand government's Te Ihuwaka/Education Evaluation Centre argues that we need to 'take a deliberate, scientific lens to the learning opportunities available. This will support children with the opportunities to develop the knowledge, skills, dispositions, and working theories that serve as the foundation for ongoing learning in science, and for developing scientific literacy' (New Zealand Education Evaluation Centre/Te Ihuwaka, 2021, p. 7).

The child as a 'natural scientist'

It is appropriate that children from birth to 3 years old should enjoy open-ended exploration of the world and different materials. This will build on their natural curiosity. We can also widen children's interests and experiences by introducing new materials and experiences. We can supplement this by visiting places which some children may not have been to before, like a forest or a beach.

However, it is important to step beyond a simplistic view of the child as a 'natural scientist'. As children grow older in the phase, it is important to think ahead about what we want them to learn. We need to consider the key vocabulary that will be part of this learning. Children might love an interesting and memorable early scientific experience, like seeing Diet Coke exploding out of a bottle when they pop a couple of Mentos in. But a memorable experience is not necessarily rich in memorable learning. The idea that children develop early scientific and mathematical concepts solely through hands-on exploration of materials has been widely challenged. We cannot expect children to stumble across key scientific concepts and vocabulary through self-directed investigation and play.

Professor Robin Millar (2004, p. 7) argues that scientific education is 'not the discovery or construction of ideas that are new and unknown. Rather it is making what others already know your own.' The implication of this argument is that an early years scientific experiment would illustrate an early concept. It would provide a context for using new vocabulary to describe and explain what we see. However, the science behind the Diet Coke and Mentos experiment is quite complex: it is not an example of a chemical reaction, like baking soda reacting with vinegar.

On the other hand, when it is snowy the children are likely to talk excitedly about skidding and falling over. We could build on this by introducing words like 'slippery', 'smooth' and 'rough'. We could set up an experiment where we slide a block of wood down a smooth surface, and down a rough surface. This sort of activity and investigation communicates key concepts and models the key vocabulary in a natural way, so that children enjoy learning it. Millar (2004, p. 7) comments that practical activities 'should be seen, and judged, as acts of communication and not as opportunities for enquiry'.

Play

Children cannot learn scientific concepts simply through playing freely with materials. However, a recent analysis of the research by the Play in Education, Development and Learning (PEDAL) Centre at the University of Cambridge finds that guided play can be highly effective (Skene et al., 2022). Guided play consists of playful activities which are steered gently by an adult who also makes sure that the children can explore the intended learning goal in their own way. This means that the adult needs to have a clear intention behind the activity and needs to understand the scientific concept or concepts they plan for children to learn. An inspiring example of this approach is Professor Marilyn Fleer's 'Conceptual Playworld' (Fleer, 2021) in which practitioners create an imaginary scenario with the children. The adult leads and models the play, which motivates the children to find solutions to problems and learn scientific ideas along the way. For example, through a 'playworld' based on the book *Charlotte's Web* (White, 2014), children explored the imaginary world of Zuckerman's Farm and found out how to solve the insect problem in the apple orchard. This type of play is rich in potential learning, because the adults and children play together in an imaginative, language-rich way, exploring concepts which would otherwise be difficult to teach to young children.

The dangers of being 'activity focused'

Part of the joy of working in the early years is that so many spontaneous opportunities arise in well-resourced, play-based environments. When an unplanned situation arises, like finding a mouldy piece of apple behind the Lego box during tidying up:

- We must take advantage of that opportunity
- We need to be clear about key scientific concepts, skills and vocabulary

That is why early years teams need effective programmes of professional development in science. Otherwise, we are in danger of being too 'activity-focused' rather than focused on the vocabulary and concepts we want children to learn. When that goes wrong, children have lots of fun and engaging experiences, but there is an insufficient emphasis on learning.

Case Study

When I was teaching in Reception, I planned to teach children about floating and sinking. But I did not think ahead about what I intended for the children to learn, and how the activity might communicate that. After a week of investigating different objects in the water tray with the children, I put up a large display outside the classroom saying, 'We have been investigating floating and sinking'. Next to a picture of one of the children was a speech bubble saying, 'heavy things sink'.

When the primary science advisor visited, she asked me if this was really a useful idea to share. Is it true that heavy things sink? Would I be boycotting ferries in the future?

Although I was able to laugh along with the advisory teacher, there was a serious point to her comment. I have always remembered it. We must never teach children wrong things because we do not know the science ourselves, or because we have not thought ahead enough. I have made this mistake countless times myself, as a nursery and Reception teacher.

On reflection, I wish I had done things better. I could have introduced and regularly used the word 'push' with the children, as they pushed boats and other objects under the water. In Reception, the children could recap that experience to remember the feeling of 'pushing down'. The children could then talk about what they feel when they push a boat under the water. They might comment that it feels hard to do this. They will notice that when they let go, the water pushes the boat back up. They will also notice that they need to push quite hard on the boat to get it to sink. This would be the moment to introduce the term 'upthrust' to describe how the water pushes the boat up. In this example, the practical experience helps to communicate a small number of carefully chosen scientific ideas. When children use the vocabulary naturally, we know they have remembered the word and the concept. That will be a secure little block of learning to support their later scientific education.

In addition to first-hand experience, books can be an excellent way of helping children to learn early scientific concepts. Just as children (and some teachers!) might think that heavier things sink, it is also common for children to imagine that heavier objects will fall faster to the ground than light objects. In their excellent study, Venkadasalam and Ganea (2018) show how this common misconception can be challenged with high-quality picture books (fiction and informational). Children who enjoyed the books also learnt that weight does not affect the speed of an object's fall.

This discussion of how children learn early scientific concepts might seem daunting. Does every early years practitioner need to be a science specialist? I would turn that around in two ways. First of all, we often plan far too much learning in understanding the world. If we are choosier and more parsimonious, we might find things more manageable. Secondly, in my experience many adults enjoy having a chance to refresh their scientific understanding through focused and engaging practical investigations.

Early science should be fun: it should also give children strong foundations for their later science learning in Key Stage 1.

Introducing scientific vocabulary

The New Zealand government review on Science in the Early Years comments:

> When teachers introduce scientific concepts, using the correct terminology for those concepts, they promote children's scientific thinking and knowledge. This helps children share their thinking and explore ideas. It helps move their thinking from 'everyday' concepts to 'scientific' concepts. Using scientific terms is likely to help children understand that they are 'doing science'.

> (New Zealand Education Evaluation Centre/Te Ihuwaka, 2021, p. 8)

How might this look in practice? Table 8.1 shows one way we might think about early learning about science in the different phases of the EYFS. I think it is also important not to downplay the importance of pleasure and the sheer enjoyment children show. Joy and enthusiasm are at the heart of learning in the early years. The examples of vocabulary are just some of the words to use in regular, natural conversation with the children.

Learning about sustainability by June O'Sullivan

Although the term sustainability is much used these days, it is not a new idea.

Three pillars underpin sustainability: economic, social and environmental. It describes how we can protect the Earth's resources around the world in a way that treats all communities fairly. We can no longer ignore the environmental exploitation of poorer countries and global poverty. The Statutory Educational Programme for Understanding the World reflects this theme. It specifies that children should learn about 'our culturally, socially, technologically and ecologically diverse world'.

The 17 Sustainable Development Goals

In 2016, the United Nations launched 17 Sustainable Development Goals (United Nations, 2016) (see Table 8.2). These are designed as a blueprint for countries to create a more sustainable future. The fourth goal states that all children must receive an equitable quality education. The deadline for delivering the goals is 2030, with an annual global monitoring of progress.

	Birth to 3 years old	3- and 4-year-olds	4- and 5-year-olds: Reception
Attitudes and dispositions	Enjoy exploring the world, through open-ended resources indoors and plenty of time outdoors. This requires a beautifully-organised indoor environment where children can access materials freely, together with sensitive adult support and enthusiasm.	In addition: Plan and think ahead about playing and exploration. Reflect on choices: e.g. adults might say, 'I'm interested that you chose the fine brushes to paint the daffodil.' Keep trying when things are difficult, e.g. using equipment that requires greater dexterity like using pipettes to suck up and squirt out water in the water tray.	In addition: Reflect on what they are learning and how this links to what they have learnt before. Adults might ask questions like: what were you thinking when you chose to roll over the big log to find woodlice? What did you learn from the book about butterflies?
Concepts and skills	Holding, tipping, filling, emptying, mixing	In addition: Close observation, sometimes with magnifying equipment. Caring for plants and animals. Fitting three or more cogs together so that when you turn one, they all turn.	In addition: Exploring objects safely using all their senses – smell, touch, hearing, sight and taste. Creating close observational drawings and paintings. Describing some common plants and animals.
Vocabulary	Wet Dry Stamp Splash Puddle	In addition: Fill Empty Float Sink Bark Seed Magnify Investigate Wind-up Cogs Mouldy Push Pull Attract Repel Melt	In addition: Push down Push up Upthrust Close observation Vibration Transparent Shadow The names of the seasons The names of some common plants and animals in the local environment

Table 8.2 The 17 Sustainable Development Goals

1 No poverty	2 Zero hunger	3 Good health and wellbeing	4 Quality education	5 Gender equality	6 Clean water and sanitation
7 Affordable and clean energy	8 Decent work and economic growth	9 Industry, innovation and infrastructure	10 Reduced inequalities	11 Sustainable cities and communities	12 Responsible consumption and production
13 Climate action	14 Life below water	15 Life on land	16 Peace, justice and strong institutions	17 Partnerships for the goals	

(United Nations, 2016)

In 2021, the UNESCO World Conference on Education for Sustainable Development reaffirmed the fourth goal. Children of all ages must learn about our endangered planet and act for sustainability. The United Nations Convention on the Rights of the Child (2019) says we should be preparing each child to become a global citizen. This includes our youngest citizens.

Early childhood is a period when the foundations of thinking, being, knowing and acting are developing. Relationships with others and the environment are becoming established. Children are influenced by the environment, culture and people around them. However, they can also become agents of change once they begin to understand the consequences of their behaviour.

Sustainability is central to early education

Sustainability is not a distinct subject or part of an environmental topic. It is central to the child's whole experience. It needs, therefore, to be part of a broad and inclusive quality education. Learning about sustainability will enhance children's learning across the whole early years curriculum. It will also promote critical thinking, problem-solving, discussion and project work.

Teaching sustainability means taking account of the three pillars: economic, social and environmental. How we teach sustainability is consistent with how we teach everything else in the early years. We can build on children's interests and their sense of enquiry, both in settings and beyond. Practitioners, children, families and the wider communities can work together for a more liveable world.

Case Study

The Healthy School Streets scheme is an example of the 17th Sustainable Development Goal, working in partnership. A Healthy School Street is closed off to traffic at school drop-off and pick-up times. Achieving this begins with persuading your local council to start a consultation period. That means reaching out to the wider community: local councillors, residents and business owners.

Reducing pollution from cars enables children to play outdoors with less risk of damage to their young lungs. Car-free streets encourage families to walk, cycle and scoot to nursery.

The Greater London Authority reported in 2021 that 'children growing up in polluted areas in London showed significantly smaller lung volume, with a loss of approximately five per cent in lung capacity – equivalent to two large eggs – compared to their peers in the rest of England' (Greater London Authority, 2021).

This social action for a more sustainable world can also support children's early learning and development. Walking, scooting and cycling help children to develop their fitness, strength and stamina.

(Continued)

Children also get into the habit of walking and cycling around their local area, which is a more sustainable way of travel and living. In London Early Years Foundation (LEYF) nurseries, a pilot bike-lending project meant that children had access to bikes regardless of family income. Children quickly grow out of bikes, and a lending scheme significantly reduces the need to buy bikes (which are often disposed of when outgrown). LEYF and Bikeworks, who supplied the bikes, are both social enterprises – the scheme is a powerful example of how community, not-for-profit organisations can work together for the common good.

How to start teaching young children about sustainability

An accessible way to start this journey is with basic everyday activities. We can explore water conservation by turning the taps off and collect rainwater for watering the plants. We can think about not wasting energy by switching the lights off and lowering the thermostat. Over time, children will start to apply this learning at home.

Being around nature can make us feel happier. Again, simple everyday activities connect us with nature. We can introduce plants and build gardening into our daily activities. We can learn how to compost; develop a wildlife sanctuary; and build a bird box and bug hotels. These are all ways of discovering the interconnectedness of people and nature. The children soon appreciate that we are not the only ones living on the planet.

We can take this learning beyond our settings. Children can get involved with a local community garden. They can take responsibility for growing vegetables on a local allotment. They can simply go for a litter walk. This can encourage us to think about what we buy, where we buy it, how it is packaged and delivered. Do we choose items that can be recycled? Are we prepared to collect rubbish?

In LEYF nurseries, chefs do not just produce tasty and nutritious meals and snacks. They also involve children in cooking and eating activities, to broaden their culinary horizons and embed healthy life-long habits. Learning about correct portion sizes, and making food appealing to young children, leads to less food being scraped into the bin. This is another example of how we can reduce our consumption of resources in early years settings from an organisational point of view and help children to learn the attitudes and habits they need to create a more sustainable future.

We can introduce children to social justice through simple community activities. One way of doing this is to invite someone in from a local charity to talk about the work they do. The setting could also make a donation to the local food bank – this must be approached delicately as some families may use food banks themselves.

The chef can be included in our sustainability conversation. Children might consider how to waste less food and which ingredients are the most sustainable. These are examples of early learning about economic and environmental issues.

Early education and care is a natural place to introduce the theme of sustainability. It requires teachers and practitioners to have a vision of a world in which our children will thrive for generations to come.

We do not have all the answers to sustaining our planet. We will have greater success if we teach our children about their planet from the earliest age.

—Early Learning Goal—

The Natural World

Children at the expected level of development will:

- Explore the natural world around them, making observations and drawing pictures of animals and plants;
- Know some similarities and differences between the natural world around them and contrasting environments, drawing on their experiences and what has been read in class;
- Understand some important processes and changes in the natural world around them, including the seasons and changing states of matter.

Strong foundations to support later learning in history

Children are always curious about aspects of the past which they can relate to. For example, I remember putting up a display which showed all the children's teachers and early years educators as babies and young children. This prompted a great deal of discussion and amusement. Similarly, families often share photos and videos with their children, as a way of helping them understand the family's past, culture and some precious moments.

How can we help children learn some of the important knowledge and vocabulary that will help them to learn history in Key Stage 1? Children up to 3 years old in the EYFS do not need us to plan this learning for them. It will be enough that we spend time talking with them about anything important which comes up spontaneously. The birth of a new baby in the family is a natural time for a conversation with a child about how they, too, were once a small baby.

For older children in the phase, we can introduce the concept of past and present in ways which will make sense to them. Children in nursery do not need detailed knowledge about the past, or particular periods of history. Sensibly introducing them to a small amount of new knowledge will be sufficient to stimulate their curiosity and also enable future learning.

Simple timelines

For children aged 3 and 4, simple timelines can show a series of events in order. Those timelines might be about the order of the routines of the day, illustrated by photographs or symbols.

For example, you might put the following routines in order: coming in, registering yourself, brushing your teeth, deciding where you want to play first, and so on. You might also create timelines about children's growth from babies, to toddlers, to being 3 or 4. You might have a set of photos showing the school or setting from its earliest days. Children's early understanding of the past will be simple and imprecise. They might know there was an important woman from the past called Mary Seacole who nursed injured soldiers, and still expect to see her in real life. They might be fascinated about dinosaurs and know they lived a long time ago. They will not have a full understanding of what this means, and nor would we expect them to. How many adults know that the T-Rex is closer in time to the iPhone than it is to the Stegosaurus?

We do not know with any precision how children get a more detailed understanding of history. It is likely that it happens gradually, through repeated discussion of information. Children's early, imprecise ideas give them footholds for their later learning about the past.

Children can meaningfully explore the past through books, stories, poems and rhymes. This is most likely to be appropriate in the Reception year. We need to think carefully about diversity when we make these choices. It is important to include examples which focus on different parts of the world and different traditions. We also need to ensure we feature the stories of important women: it is all too easy only to share books about 'great men' in history. Children will often relate to some of the themes in simple books about the past, like compassion or bravery. Again, it is important that they relate to a range of figures from the past whilst exploring these themes. They should not be learning only about brave men and caring women, all of them white and European.

A focal point like Black History Month might be a positive way of raising awareness amongst staff, families and children. But is a month-long focus really adequate? Planning for diversity from the beginning, as a consistent feature in all our practice, is likely to have the most impact.

Helping children relate to the past: Trips, photos and books

Children are fascinated by visits to old buildings and sites. Trips to see castles, other ruins, old churches or houses with thatched roofs will prompt much observation and discussion. Young children do not need a detailed understanding of historical periods or other information at this stage. They might focus their observation and discussion on what aged bricks, stones and glass look like, for example. As part of a museum trip, it might be possible to make connections between the exhibits and some children's family history.

Case Study

When I took a Reception class on a visit to the Young V&A museum, I prepared for this by asking the children to bring in any photos of their grandparents when they were small, playing with toys. We ended up with a small handful of black and white photos. They showed East End children after the war, playing with dolls outdoors, building with wooden bricks, and holding little toy cars made by Dinky and Matchbox. This helped the children to connect the history they saw in the museum with the family context they knew.

As with science, picture books can be a powerful way to introduce children to some early historical concepts. Examples include kings, queens and palaces. Children can explore these through books about different periods and places: African, Indian and European kingdoms and palaces, for example. Again, children could link some of this learning by going to see a palace or a statue of a king or queen. We can also introduce children to some early concepts of chronology by drawing attention to the different terms we use. We might use the word 'ancient' about the pharaohs and pyramids. On a trip to see the King Edward VII memorial in Birmingham, we might use the word 'old'.

Early Learning Goal

Past and Present

Children at the expected level of development will:

- Talk about the lives of the people around them and their roles in society;
- Know some similarities and differences between things in the past and now, drawing on their experiences and what has been read in class;
- Understand the past through settings, characters and events encountered in books read in class and storytelling.

Strong foundations to support later learning in geography

Children's earliest learning in geography is practical and closely linked to their everyday lives. As Gopnik et al. (1999) explain, even very small babies have a sense of space and movement. They can track moving objects as they go out of view behind a screen. They will reach for an object where they know it has been hidden. Babies and toddlers remember how to find their way round places they know well, like their home and their early years setting. We have a sense of space and place from our earliest days, and it establishes the first building blocks of our understanding of geography.

As Adam Phillips noted in a talk for the *London Review of Books*, there is a big 'difference between taking a three-year-old child for a walk, and going for a walk with a three-year-old. You can take a three-year-old to the park, to the shops. But if you go for a walk with a three-year-old, you'll sort of go round in circles' (Phillips, 2019).

Young children are often fascinated by almost everything they see. This contradicts the casual notion we sometimes hold about them having short attention spans. They might want to stop and linger, looking into shop windows, touching tree trunks and talking about the cats and dogs they see around. It is generally us, the adults, who want to rush along. Unhurried walks around the local neighbourhood and small trips to shops, parks and libraries are important. They help the youngest children to develop their sense of place.

As they approach their third birthday, some children like to tell us about their sense of place through narratives as they draw or paint. They might say 'this is mummy in my home' or rapidly draw a bold line across the paper, saying 'I'm running in the park'. Chris Athey (1991, p. 188) observed children making their own maps to represent familiar places like the nursery garden. These types of drawings show objects in fixed locations relative to other objects, like the nursery slide being next to the sandpit.

Alison Clark (2010) further explores children's sense of space. Her work shows how we can consult children from around the age of 3 about proposed changes or redevelopments of buildings and outdoor play spaces. Technology now makes it even easier than it was in 2010 to ask children to take photographs or make films about the spaces they learn and play in. This way, they can put across their views about how they would like those spaces to be. The emotions we associate with places are an important part of geography.

Children's connections to different environments

Many 3- and 4-year-olds can tell us about their local environment. Benjamin, aged 3, was walking to Forest School when he stopped and told his teacher 'this is dangerous'. He was remembering what she had said the week before about not crossing the road near the bend. He pointed to the zebra crossing as a safe place to cross.

Children who have been abroad on holiday can often tell us what they liked. They can talk about how the place, language and food were different to what they are familiar with. Holiday photos shared online, and postcards, can stimulate these sorts of discussions. Many children have family living in different parts of the world. Through their first-hand experience of visiting relatives, or through video calls and photos, they can talk about similarities and differences. For children without experience of the world beyond England, videos and books can create spaces for conversations and ideas which would otherwise be closed off to them.

All of this reminds us that the foundations of geographical thinking lie in the early years. Geography is about our own sense of place in our diverse, interconnected world, our curiosity and our emotions. As President Barack Obama memorably argued, 'the study of geography is about more than just memorising places on a map. It's about understanding the complexity of our world, appreciating the diversity of cultures that exist across continents. And in the end, it's about using all that knowledge to help bridge divides and bring people together' (Obama, 2012).

In Reception, children build on their earlier sense of space and place through a more precise vocabulary of position. It is important for children to learn to describe the position of objects, and their own position in space, with specific vocabulary. Some examples of this are: close, near and far, left and right, behind and in front, on top and underneath. The contexts of this learning will build on the interest and experience that children already have, which is noted above. I think it is important to avoid unmotivating, assessment-driven activities. I would not ask children to 'put teddy under the chair ... put teddy to the left of the chair' and so on. It is much better to engage naturally and enthusiastically with young children who are figuring out how to show the location of the 'treasure' on a map they are drawing. We might also talk with the children about their positions at different stages of a dance routine, too.

Building mental maps of places

Young children hold mental maps of familiar places. They will often show those places in drawings and by making early versions of maps. Building on these experiences, we can introduce older children in the EYFS to simple maps and teach them how to use them. I remember visiting a school where a Reception teacher had created a set of installations around the outdoors area. These were all based on the story of Goldilocks. Small groups of children found Goldilocks's house. Then they went onto the house of the three bears. Finally, they went to the woods and saw a cut-out of Goldilocks running away. The children needed some help at the beginning to work out how to follow the map, but soon got the hang of it.

Research suggests that children 'start to acquire geographical knowledge about their own country by 5 years of age' (Barrett et al., 2006, p. 72). At this early stage, children may be able to show some different countries if asked to draw a map of the world. They will not have an accurate sense of shape, size or position. For that reason, it is unlikely that young children will understand formal maps. Descriptions of the geographical features of different countries, like climate, mountains, coastlines and cities, will not be meaningful either.

Instead, what is most likely to make sense to children in the Reception year is talking about the different places they know. Children can talk about what different places look like, what they do there and what happens whilst they are there (Barrett et al., 2006, p. 61).

Examples of similar and contrasting places in other countries will help children to widen their early sense of geographical place. But young children are unlikely to integrate that knowledge into a bigger frame of reference. So, if children are familiar with their local market, they will understand it as a place where people come to buy and sell a range of goods. They will be able to talk about how the activity in a market in, say, Bangladesh looks similar and how it looks different.

More affluent families travel more, and this means that some children will know more places than others. Equally, children with families abroad may know more about Asia or Africa, for example, than Europe. This means it is important to prioritise visiting different local areas as part of the curriculum, to widen children's horizons. It is also important to consider the knowledge children already have about the world. We should reflect on whether it is wise to refer only to Europe in the Reception year and leave the rest of the world until later.

A space becomes a place

The foundations of geography are personal: they depend on children's experiences. A space becomes a place because of the emotions we attach to it and the knowledge we have about it.

Young children can talk readily about familiar places: my home, my nursery or my street, for example. They may be able to talk about shopping areas and places of worship, too. Children will additionally have many experiences of linking places to people. They may talk about seeing relatives, shopping trips with family members, or where they go to worship. In my experience, there are also children who have not been to many places. In London, they may never have ridden on a red bus, been on the Tube, or seen the River Thames. Even a small trip out, like a ride on the bus to a local market, can be a source of days of conversation, play, drawing and model-making. Children need these foundational experiences to make connections between people, activities and places. Otherwise, they will find learning geography in Key Stage 1 very difficult.

Similarly, learning about weather is founded on direct experience. It is important for children (in appropriate clothes) to feel the rain falling on them or the wind blowing in their faces. If it snows, children can feel the compression of fresh snow under their feet as they leave snow prints behind them. There is a rich tradition of outdoor learning in the early years, including approaches like Forest School. These first-hand experiences provide children with much to talk about, using early geographical vocabulary. Adults can support this by using simple terms like sunny, windy, rainy and snowy. Vocabulary that may be less familiar includes words like hail, stormy, gale, downpour or blustery.

Learning about diversity

Children learn more from birth to 5 years old than at any other time in their lives. That includes the values and attitudes they need for life in modern England. We can set the scene for children to develop positive attitudes about diversity and difference. That means challenging stereotypes about what boys and girls, or men and women, can do. Research suggests that from 3 months of age, babies notice the physical differences that define ethnic groups (Kelly et al., 2005). That's why it is important to encourage children's curiosity as they notice and talk about differences. We can celebrate racial and cultural diversity through our attitudes and our selection of books and play resources. It is important to tackle prejudice, like racism and sexism, directly. This isn't just behaviour that is 'not nice'. It can cause long-lasting distress and damage.

Research also suggests that parents appreciate guidance from practitioners about challenging stereotypes (Fawcett Society, 2020). So, it is important that we explain how we tackle comments like 'we don't want any boys here' or 'that's for girls'. We also need to explain how we tackle racist comments about children's skin colour, hair, or clothing whilst encouraging children to be curious and talk about the differences they notice.

None of this introductory section should imply that we 'teach diversity' to young children as a separately planned item. Instead, this work is all about regular discussions, challenging assumptions and getting the right books and resources. When we are teaching about figures from the past, it means we achieve a balance of men and women, white people and people of colour. It means we include examples of women being brave, and men being sensitive and caring. Lots of small steps every day will have much more impact than a one-off week. It is also important to note that the sections below do not imply that practitioners are at fault. All of us – adults and children – have attitudes and values which come from our family, from our experience and from wider society. The aim of these sections is to raise everyone's awareness and encourage discussion and debate. This will help us work together for a fairer future for every child.

Gender equality

Many of the toys young children play with and the media they see on television and online are very gendered. Shops may have different shelves for boys and girls. As a result, some children in early years settings may have rigid ideas about gender. The following tips are adapted from the suggestions of the Fawcett Society (2020, p. 108) to help combat gender stereotyping:

1. Encourage children to engage with a range of activities by offering play options that actively challenge gender stereotypes and demonstrating that activities and spaces are inclusive to all. If the home corner is available for everyone to use but only the girls use it, practitioners can challenge this by actively engaging all children in that space. Similarly, all children can be invited and given space to play football.
2. Be supportive of children when they take part in activities that run counter to gender stereotypes. All children should be encouraged to engage in risk-taking play and caring activities. Keep a watchful eye for other children's reactions to their peers who challenge gender stereotypes, and ensure that any bullying related to non-conformity with them is addressed.
3. Practitioners should offer children a wide range of worldviews – include stories with diverse lead characters based on gender, ethnicity and other characteristics, so that they don't just see the 'default male'. Try counting the number of male and female characters in the books and materials used in the setting – if characters, and lead characters, aren't equally present, can you find books where they are? Are female and male characters shown equally in different roles, or are, for example, male firefighters or builders, and female teachers or mothers, much more common?
4. Where possible, practitioners should try to use non-gendered language when talking to children, e.g. 'Those children are good at video games'. If using gendered language is necessary, be clear that we are referring to specific people, not boys and girls in general: 'Those boys are good at football', not 'boys are good at football'.
5. Have conversations about gender with children and challenge any stereotypes they try out. When children are younger, practitioners can ask them to explain why they think a particular thing is 'for girls' or 'for boys'. Use examples to challenge any stereotypes they repeat.
6. Similarly, practitioners can have conversations with colleagues about gender stereotypes. We should be willing and ready to challenge colleagues who repeat gender stereotypes.

This can be as overt as telling a colleague you disagree when they tell children something is a 'boy' or 'girl' activity, or as subtle as suggesting a less stereotypical book if they often select a traditional fairy tale to read to the children.

7.   Explore whether anything in the environment or practice of the setting encourages unnecessary segregation – that is, separating children by sex when it is not relevant. This might include queuing up, sports or games, or where children keep their coats and bags.

8.   Ensure that all children are given equal space and time in our settings. Research suggests that girls are given less attention – think about who we call on to answer and who gets our attention during carpet and group times. Look regularly around the setting to see whether staff are talking and playing more with girls than with boys.

Practitioners must reflect on our own practice and unconscious biases. We are all immersed in stereotypes, and these tips represent a starting point for practitioners to think about how they impact on our work – and what we can do to challenge them.

Disability equality

Nearly 25 years ago, I was on the edges of one of the most inspiring projects I have seen in the early years. In Haringey, London, disabled children with the most complex conditions had been cared for in a hospital-based nursery for many years. The council planned to move the children to Rowland Hill Nursery School in 1997. During the early stages of the project, there was huge anxiety; even claims that some children might die without hospital-based care. I was privileged to see the children move out of the hospital and flourish, with meticulously planned care and education at Rowland Hill. I also saw how all the children benefitted, learning to communicate with peers using sign language and visual symbols, for example, and being able to talk matter-of-factly to their parents about disability.

That changed my opinions, and feelings, forever. I previously worked in an excellent special school as an early years teacher. Since 1997, I have been strongly committed to ensuring that disabled children in mainstream settings receive the best possible standard of early education and care, and that all children learn positive attitudes about disabled people.

All of the curriculum, all of the time, must enable children to:

•   Play with resources which show disabled people in an ordinary, everyday way
•   Enjoy books which include disabled people in regular activities and events

As adults, it is important that we challenge negative attitudes or language associated with disabled people. For example, calling someone 'dumb' means equating not speaking with being unintelligent or deficient. Yet there are many ways people can communicate. Blanket terms like 'the deaf' or 'the blind' can de-individualise people. Referring to disabled people as 'inspirational' can also be unwelcome. What if a person simply wants to feel that they are living an ordinary life, supported by equipment or technology?

Racial equality by Liz Pemberton

Case Study

Kemi is a confident and self-assured child. Her smile is huge and her imagination is expansive! She has beautiful, tightly coiled Afro hair separated into two sections with multi-coloured bobbles, and she is holding an imaginary microphone.

One hand is grasping her 'mic', the other hand is waving in the air. Her eyes are tightly closed as she bellows out her high notes with enthusiasm and passion, oblivious to anybody else around her.

Max is an energetic child who often plays alone but has always had an affinity with Kemi. He is racialised as white and has the hood of his coat on his head with his arms outstretched inside of the main body of his coat, pretending to be an aeroplane.

Both are 4 years old and they are in the garden at their nursery.

Something catches Max's eye as he whizzes around Kemi. His attention focuses on her outstretched hand waving. He pauses and then asks loudly: 'Kemi, why are the insides of your hands pink and the other side is brown?'

Kemi stops suddenly, looking momentarily confused by Max's question, and she inspects her outstretched hand by bringing it closer to her face.

Before she can form the words to respond, Ethan, the nursery practitioner who has overheard, interjects: 'Max, that isn't a very nice thing to say; say sorry!'

This case study tells us about how we can send out dangerous messages on the subject matter of 'race' in the early years.

As an educator, there are many ways in which Ethan could have responded to this incident. It may (or may not) surprise you that there *is* a right and a wrong way to do this if we are to think about this as a perfect opportunity to lean into a conversation with children about race. Debbie Epstein says that 'the anti-racist educator needs to have an ear for the opportunities provided by children's own comments and questions' (Epstein, 1993, p. 324), and Max's question is a perfect example of such an occurrence.

Birth to 5 Matters, the early years guidance document, explicitly states that 'talking about race is a first step in countering racism' (Early Years Coalition, 2021, p. 22) and this is sage advice. We must do this as Epstein tells us, by having an ear for the opportunities to do so. How do we do this if racial literacy is so poor within the sector and there is a seeming reluctance to want to engage in dialogue about the impact of racism for children during their earliest years?

For many parents of racially minoritised children, the sad reality is that 'the talk' – a colloquial term coined in the US which is almost seen as a rite of passage for Black parents to pre-warn their children about the inevitable day when their racialised identity is perceived as a negative thing or as a threat – is always looming. But this may not necessarily be the case for white parents of white children when it comes to them having the conversation about the injustice of racism in the same way one would talk to their child about the concept of not being violent by having 'kind hands', or introducing the idea of consent to children with regard to touch as an introduction to the wider subject matter of sexual abuse.

Max's passing inquisitive comment about the colour of the palms of Kemi's hands illustrates how children, in the words of *Development Matters*, 'notice differences between people' (DfE, 2021a, p. 103). To respond to it in the way that Ethan did has a negative ripple effect, and as educators we must be aware of this. Undoubtedly his response was what he believed to be appropriate, and we would like to think that those of us who are responsible for the care and education of children would never intentionally respond to their needs inappropriately, but within this exists a challenge, the challenge to accept correction.

When matters pertaining to race in the early years are mishandled by practitioners in a nursery environment, it is not uncommon for intention to be used as a pacifier. By this, I mean the excuse of one not meaning any harm by it. This is supposed to excuse the impact of what could indeed be very harmful to the child who is on the receiving end. We must be aware of this. If we start to prioritise one's intention over the impact of a statement that may harm a racially minoritised child, it feeds into a dangerous cycle of upholding a system that effectively says, 'if I didn't mean it, then it doesn't matter'. We wouldn't apply that same theory if a child unintendedly bumped into another child, knocking them to the floor. If that child subsequently hit their head, they would still have suffered an injury and we wouldn't dismiss that child's pain because the other child didn't mean it. There would be a process of learning and accountability, an apology and a reminder to the child about their spatial awareness as they were running.

Ethan's dismissal of Max's statement would not only attach a feeling of shame to Kemi's understanding about the colour of her skin, but it may convey a deeper and even more harmful message to Max, the white child. That message is that conversations about race are 'not very nice'. What if this happens repeatedly throughout Max and Kemi's nursery and school experience? What is the cumulative impact for both children when it comes to their understanding about race and racism? Neither child's skin colour is going to change, and given that we live in a racist society, this is a very dangerous situation.

Table 8.3   The 4 Es for anti-racist practice

Step 1 EMBRACE all children's racial, cultural and religious backgrounds, especially when they are different from your own.

Step 2 EMBED a culture of belonging and value amongst practitioners and children.

Step 3 ENSURE that your practice is culturally sensitive and places the child as the expert of their cultural, racial and religious identity.

Step 4 EXTEND learning opportunities for the child by showing interest, expanding conversations and using diverse resources.

In 2020, I created the '4 Es of anti-racist practice' (Table 8.3). If we extend this learning opportunity for Max and Kemi by 'showing interest, expanding conversations and using diverse resources', there will be a very different outcome and impact for all of the children. An informed response from the educator would have left Kemi feeling affirmed and proud of the colour of her skin and Max educated about the reasons why skin colours come in a range of shades.

If you were a white child who was raised to think that talking about skin colour was unkind or impolite, you can perhaps see why now, as an adult responsible for the care of children, you find it so uncomfortable to talk about race.

So, where do we go from here?

We can draw on *Development Matters*, which suggests we should 'model positive attitudes about the differences between people including differences in race and religion' (DfE, 2021a, p. 103), to support Step 4 (extend) from my framework. But before we start to think about the array of multi-cultural posters that we have on our nursery walls or in our classrooms, and all those skin-coloured paints that we use, we should reflect on that deep inner work that we must do on ourselves first. That way, we can develop our ability to respond to those uncomfortable feelings that arise when the topic of race is brought into the arena by the children that we are caring for and educating.

Flex your anti-racist muscle

I want to begin by posing some reflective questions for you to ask yourself and answer honestly. These are not responses that you are required to share with anybody, but they will start a process of unlearning and start the preparation for what I like to call an anti-racist workout. See these questions as the pre-stretch and me as your personal trainer getting you ready to flex your anti-racist muscle:

1.   What are you bringing to your practice from your own lived experiences about race?
2.   In your practice, how do you encourage a balance of child-initiated and practitioner-led provocations that can lead to exploring things around race, ethnicity and culture?
3.   Are you confident with the language that you should be using when it comes to explorations of the concept of race, ethnicity and culture?

When you start to unpack the answers to these questions in your own mind and start to connect them to your everyday interactions with all children, you will start to be able to consider your own positionality as an early years educator. Perhaps you are a white teacher, and your concept of your own racialised identity is something that you have never considered. That in and of itself is something to look at more deeply because it would suggest that because you have deracialised yourself as a person and as an educator, you have also deracialised the children that you care for. Adopting an 'I don't see colour' approach is part of the problem.

Development Matters suggests that we should 'encourage children to talk about the differences they notice between people, whilst also drawing their attention to similarities between different families and communities' (DfE, 2021a, p. 107). That cannot only apply when we are talking about the differences in the colour of the children's coats, or their eyes, as we saw with the example of Max and Kemi. Children see the colour of their skin, even if we would like not to because it makes us feel uncomfortable.

The best response that Ethan could have given would have been to:

1. Assess Kemi's reaction, detect whether there are any feelings of confusion, upset or dismissal and also give her the opportunity to respond before he took the lead. It may have been the case that Kemi's response is 'it's because I'm Black and Black people have lots of shades!' She might have said 'I don't know': it isn't anything she would have ever considered before, given that this is her normal. Either way, we must give children the opportunity to be the expert on their own racial identity. You cannot assume that their own families have not equipped them with racial literacy and a strong sense of self pertaining to their own racial identity. You will only find out if you provide space and opportunity for this to happen.
2. If Kemi has no response or a response that indicates that she is embarrassed or upset, process this response and understand that this is indicative of a society that constantly 'others' Blackness as something to not take pride in. Widen the spectrum of the conversation so that it is inclusive of everybody in the playground. What you want to reinforce to both children is that, in fact, there are differences with everybody, including skin tone and colour, even amongst the white children (if the setting is predominantly white).
3. *Building Futures: Believing in Children* (DfE, 2009) focuses on provision for Black children in the EYFS. It notes that 'the learning environment should be a place where children feel confident, so that they are willing to try things out. Seeing themselves and things familiar to them will help them feel confident and secure' (DfE, 2009, p. 25). In my webinar, *Inclusion in Role Play for the Under 5's*, I stress the need to ensure that the home corners, hairdressers and shops in your space should feature a range of hair products and diverse food. You can use empty containers and packets from the supermarket, and different eating utensils such as chopsticks, as permanent features in these spaces. Be sure to explain to the children why these objects are in the respective areas in the setting. It is important that the children are introduced to the various items. So, use additional supporting resources such as books that can help introduce these things to the children in a culturally sensitive way.

The topic of 'race' is a huge one but it isn't one that should be approached with trepidation or reluctance in the early years. If we continue to perceive this as a 'no go' area for young children, then we do more harm than good in the long run. Let us be as excited about learning and engaging as we expect our children to be because it is only then that we can truly help our children contribute to the momentum of change that we want to see in the world.

LGTBQ+ equality by Aaron Bradbury

As early years professionals, we can make real change by educating children about the acceptance of LGBTQ+ people (those who identify as lesbian, gay, bisexual, transgender, queer, or any other minority sexuality or gender identity). In his ecological systems theory, Bronfenbrenner (1977) explored oppressive practices including poverty, racism and sexism. We could include homophobia, transphobia and other forms of LGBTQ+ phobia here, and how we support ever-changing family structures in the 21st century.

Encouraging the way forward

We should encourage all early years settings to engage with a diversity of families, not just those in our immediate communities. The Statutory Framework for the Early Years Foundation Stage (DfE, 2021c) is explicit about the importance of equality of opportunity and anti-discriminatory practices, 'ensuring that every child is included and supported'.

We may have heard it said that we are inadvertently talking about sex if we promote LGBTQ+ inclusion in the early years. This is false. When discussing gender and sexuality, we are exploring and celebrating identities, love and family, as well as the way people are positioned within our society, and the love and respect we need to develop for one another. We do this in an age-appropriate way. For example, with children under the age of 5 we might discuss different family arrangements, but we do not have involved conversations about sexual choice (Price and Tayler, 2015).

What should we be doing in the early years to promote LGBTQ+ representation?

We can make a start by reflecting on the following questions:

- Do we support members of the team who are open about being LGBTQ+ at work?
- Do we support the families of children whose parents identify as LGBTQ+?
- Does our curriculum represent a diversity of family structures and give voice to each unique child who we know has LGBTQ+ parents?
- Are we reading and keeping up to date with research and discussions about LGBTQ+ work in early childhood?
- Have we created a supportive and inclusive environment for all children, one that affirms all LGBTQ+ identities, in recognition of the children's current and future selves?

As early years professionals, building meaningful partnerships with all parents and carers is crucial. Exploring relationships and each other's attitudes and practices to these is part of a progressive curriculum. It is important that all families, including those that identify as LGBTQ+, are treated differently and uniquely. We don't treat all heterosexual families the same, do we?

We can put this into practice by asking parents or carers questions such as:

- What name(s) does your child call you?
- How would you like us to refer to you when we speak to your child?
- How would you like us to describe your family to others?
- How would you like us to respond to questions about your family?

Creating a welcoming environment

It is important to create an environment that is welcoming and nurturing for members of the LGBTQ+ community. Here are some of the ways we can do this:

1. Intake forms: change the space for the name of the 'father' or 'mother'. Use 'parent' or 'guardian' instead.
2. Make diverse images more visible, in a child-centred way. This will help children to explore their different cultures and family structures.
3. Have posters representing a range of families on display in the entrance and around the setting.
4. Think about your use of pronouns. Pronouns are a part of everyday speech and we often assume the pronouns people use for themselves. Have you made the effort to ask colleagues and families what pronouns you should use for them?
5. Have you had professional development that addresses these topics? They can be hard to approach without expert input.

Let's not forget that our work is all about educating, caring for and providing children with a nurturing environment in which they can thrive. The notion of a *loving pedagogy* is emphasised by Grimmer (2021). This includes engaging with the representation of LGBTQ+ people.

Crucially, we must examine our personal values and beliefs, and the power they have. Who decides on what is right and wrong? Are we stifling children's development because our own values get in the way?

By becoming more open to, accepting of and loving to everyone in our society, we can begin to share the beauty of the world. We can celebrate diversity in its widest sense.

─────**Early Learning Goal**───

People, Culture and Communities

Children at the expected level of development will:

- Describe their immediate environment using knowledge from observation, discussion, stories, non-fiction texts and maps;
- Know some similarities and differences between different religious and cultural communities in this country, drawing on their experiences and what has been read in class;
- Explain some similarities and differences between life in this country and life in other countries, drawing on knowledge from stories, non-fiction texts and - when appropriate - maps.

───

Conclusion

The area of learning called 'Understanding the World' has a lot packed into it. It includes the foundations of science, history and geography. It also includes the crucial early learning about diversity children need for life in the 21st century.

Sometimes, the structure of the EYFS is misunderstood. Practitioners think that children should learn the prime areas first, with the specific areas coming afterwards. A more helpful image is weaving. We weave the prime and specific areas together, creating a unified curriculum. Much of the learning children do as part of Understanding the World builds on their earliest interests and feelings of curiosity. As children explore their world, they want to tell us what they notice. Over time, this helps them to build their vocabulary. As they see new places, they are broadening their horizons. They build a store of cultural knowledge: what happens in a theatre, what you see in a museum, how public transport works, how you get a freezing sensation when the tide rolls over your bare feet. Wider experiences and broader vocabularies help children to feel more confident to talk about what they know, beyond the 'here-and-now' of their everyday lives. This will also help children when they are older and learning to read. When you see the word 'castle' in print for the first time, you can focus on sounding it out. You do not also need to puzzle over what it means.

Events in the news are always telling us how important scientific literacy is. We see how important it is for everyone to treasure and care for our local environment and for the whole world's ecology. We see how urgent equality issues are. For all these reasons, understanding the world is a crucial part of the early years curriculum, and relevant to children at every age.

Reflective questions

1. Professional development is central to effective practice. Understanding the world has been neglected in the early years for many years. How will you take your learning forward about the foundations of science, history and geography? If you lead a team, how will you do this for everyone?
2. Understanding our culturally diverse world is key to children living in 21st century England. How will you go beyond a general acceptance of different children and embrace a more positive set of attitudes to promote diversity and challenge prejudice?

Note

An extract from this chapter first appeared in the Chartered College for Teaching's Early Childhood Hub.

9

Expressive arts and design

Anni McTavish

EYFS Statutory Educational Programme

The development of children's artistic and cultural awareness supports their imagination and creativity. It is important that children have regular opportunities to engage with the arts, enabling them to explore and play with a wide range of media and materials. The quality and variety of what children see, hear and participate in is crucial for developing their understanding, self-expression, vocabulary and ability to communicate through the arts. The frequency, repetition and depth of their experiences are fundamental to their progress in interpreting and appreciating what they hear, respond to and observe.

Introduction

Seven-month-old Ines is exploring the handle of a dumpling spoon. Grasping the smooth bamboo, she lifts and mouths the sieve-shaped end. She seems fascinated by both the shape and texture of the spoon. With her close adult nearby, Ines is finding out about the materials in her world. She is developing her confidence, her curiosity and her physical abilities to explore the things around her.

Young children need relaxed time to investigate the properties of materials as well as creating and making. They need the chance to experiment with sounds and listen to a diverse range of music. They need an enticing selection of media to explore mark-making, drawing and painting on different scales. Along with songs and rhymes, they need to hear a variety of stories and be encouraged to tell their own. They need to be introduced to different cultures, artefacts and artists, and be invited to explore their own.

Developing your curriculum

To develop your curriculum, it can be helpful to think first about the art activities that children already enjoy. For younger children, this might be the sensory pleasure of exploring runny glue or paint. For older children, or those with more experience, this might be about having an idea and developing it.

It is also important to respond to what children and families bring. These things may include:

- warm conversations
- songs
- rhymes
- role play

All these help to develop communication and language.

Movement and dance, and mark-making on different scales, support both fine and gross motor skills. Materials such as pinecones, shells and pebbles will provide opportunities for sorting and counting. Building and designing with wooden blocks and boxes will help to build strength.

A broad and balanced curriculum

A broad and balanced arts curriculum values both spontaneous and guided learning. There also needs to be an overview or 'bigger picture' of what you want children to experience and learn. Your long-term plan might include links to the seasons, outings and special celebrations. It is important to expand on these so that they are not stand-alone events.

Case Study

During the autumn, a team of childminders take their children to gather leaves, conkers and grasses. They use the materials as a basis to explore colour and colour-mixing. The children mix their own colours and paint with large brushes on a variety of surfaces, including paper and cardboard. As their skills develop, the children begin to use a wider range of tools. They use shaving brushes to explore 'stippling', a technique of dabbing paint onto paper, and fine brushes and small sponges for detail and texture. The adults model printing and stamping techniques. They encourage the children to experiment, utilising the natural materials on black and white card.

To explore mixing and blending further, the team introduce a new medium - 'brusho'. This is a highly pigmented, water-based ink. Inspired by the rich autumn colours, the children create a large, floor-based artwork. They start by drawing with crayons, then add washes of diluted brusho colours. The brusho 'lifts off' the wax crayon, creating a vibrant, layered effect. The stories *Leaf Man* (Ehlert, 2014) and *Pumpkin Soup* (Cooper, 1999) expand on the autumn theme.

You will also need to consider how to address and highlight sustainability with the children. Free, found, natural and recycled materials have less impact on the environment and often are more likely to promote creativity. You can make links to environmental artists, such as Thirza Schaap, who creates beautiful constructions using rubbish like toothbrushes and lighters. You need to consider the detrimental effects of some of the materials you use. Many practitioners, for instance, have banned glitter due to the harm microplastics cause to freshwater habitats.

The following framework, suggested by Eglington (2003), is helpful in the development of a holistic art and design curriculum. It comprises three elements:

1. Practical: this is exploring, making and doing.
2. Aesthetic development: this is connecting with beauty. It might be through nature or sensory explorations of different media and materials. This may also include exploring the world around, like visiting a beautiful building.
3. Encounters with real art: this is seeing, hearing, exploring artists' work. It may be looking at images, hearing music, examining artefacts, taking part in a dance or visiting a gallery.

The idea is that these elements ebb and flow, helped along by sensitive adult interactions. It is possible that all three aspects will be present in an art and design experience, but more likely that one or two will motivate and enrich the others. In the practice example above, the children's aesthetic experience of gathering leaves, conkers and grasses inspires the *practical* making and doing. This framework offers plenty of scope to develop children's artistic and cultural awareness, emphasised in the Statutory Framework for the Early Years Foundation Stage (EYFS) (DfE, 2021c).

The quality and variety of activities are also highlighted in the framework. This means that children will need to take part in plenty of enjoyable ways of exploring and representing their ideas, thoughts and feelings. The focus on depth and repetition recognises the importance of children revisiting activities to deepen their understanding and to continue their creative investigations. These possibilities will help children to develop as imaginative and adaptable thinkers, well-prepared for a changing, developing world.

Early music, early art and early drama

Early music

Before they are born, infants can hear sounds and begin to distinguish their mother's voice. Early musical activities such as vocalising, moving and responding to sounds form important foundations for later language, literacy and mathematics. The infant's fascination with the human voice suggests that it is the ideal instrument for developing young children's musicality. The flexibility of the voice allows for a range of sensitive musical responses. From a soft lullaby to a jaunty finger-rhyme, musical exchanges can help to model conversational turn-taking, and be an important tool in building warm, loving relationships.

Burke (2018) suggests four areas of musical learning and development:

- hearing and listening
- vocalising and singing
- moving and dancing
- exploring and playing

These are detailed with excellent examples in *Musical Development Matters* (Burke, 2018) and in *Development Matters* (DfE, 2021a).

The ability to distinguish sounds and recite and learn rhymes will help to boost children's phonological awareness. This is an essential skill for later reading (EEF, 2018b, p. 12). Children should have a diet rich in songs – a core list of songs and rhymes at hand will mean you keep track. Children can start with simple rhymes and gradually progress to more complicated ones. Learning will be extended if your rhymes link to a similar list of quality core books – for example, the rhyme 'Ten in the Bed' with the picture book by Penny Dale (Dale, 1990) and 'I Know a Teddy Bear' links with *Brown Bear, Brown Bear, What Do You See?* (Carle, 1997).

Regular occasions for relaxed musical play can lead to creative music-making. This includes listening and engaging with music from a range of different genres and cultures. Children can create their own movement and dance using instruments and adaptable materials such as lengths of fabric, ribbons or scarves. A key element for the success of this is an adult who facilitates and joins in with children's play, offering a choice of adult-guided activities and introducing musical vocabulary.

As well as being fun and challenging, a 'singing-grid' is a creative way of making choices and connecting with children's interests. To do this:

1. Place a large sheet of paper or fabric on the floor and divide it into four or six squares.
2. Put an object in each square that represents a song or rhyme – for example, a toy bus to represent 'The Wheels on the Bus'.
3. Invite the children to pick up an object.

As they build their confidence, language and song repertoire, the choice of songs and rhymes can become more complex by using:

- a song to develop number
- a song to develop rhyme
- a song or chant linked to the seasons
- a hello or greeting song using all the languages in the group
- an object that invites a response, such as a small 'jumping' rabbit

The songs and stories can be shared with families, and vice versa: finding out about music and special songs from home can help settle young children.

Early art

There are many ways in which young children explore and represent their ideas through early art. These include two-dimensional (2D) activities, such as mark-making, drawing and painting, printing and collage. It also includes three-dimensional (3D) activities, such as sculpture, working with clay and model-making. Two or more of these activities can be combined, to evolve into a mixed or multi-media piece.

Very young children often make marks in spilt food or juice. They may also enjoy the physical sensations of drawing with a chunky crayon on bumpy cardboard or making shapes and patterns in the sand.

A convivial environment that encourages children to develop their drawing is beneficial. This involves taking time to listen to children's comments as they draw, and drawing alongside them. It is important to teach them specific skills – and support them to practise and develop these.

In the case study below, we see a fine example of observational drawing, inspired by the 'real art' of contemporary portraits.

Case Study

In a Reception class, the teacher shares with the children a range of contemporary portraits showing many cultures and ethnicities. They discuss what they see. She encourages the children to look at themselves in small mirrors and talk about the lines and shapes they see.

She then asks them to represent a soft outline of the shape of their face onto paper, sitting and drawing with them. Next, they add their features using pattern and shading. The children use what they have seen and talked about to add more detail to their drawings. To explore their drawing further, the children use postcards and oil pastels. The teacher demonstrates simple

(Continued)

methods of scribbling, smudging and blending. The following week, she prints off monochrome images of each child and suggests they might like to experiment with adding colour using pastels.

Projects such as this help children develop their abilities to see and observe in detail; to notice similarities and differences; to be aware of shapes, lines and patterns. These skills are relevant to many areas of everyday life and work. We see gardeners able to identify almost identical plants by noticing the minutest difference, and potters able to replicate virtually the same shape across a series of pots.

Early drama

Pretend play begins between 1 and 2 years. Toddlers and young children imitate behaviours they see around them. Examples of this might include putting teddy to bed or pretending to sip a hot cup of tea. At this stage, young children will benefit from plenty of familiar objects to explore and use in their play. A home-like space, representative of what children might find in their home, will be important. It may, for instance, contain cushions to represent chairs or a sofa; small baskets or saucepans with natural materials such as pinecones for food; and lengths of fabric for bedding.

As children move on to symbolic play, they use one thing to stand in for another. They may use a cardboard box for a car or a leaf for money. Developing an understanding of the use of symbol is essential for reading, writing and mathematics.

A curriculum that nurtures early drama will include opportunities for real-life experiences. This might be visiting the shops, a builder's yard or the doctors. These can then be extended through role play in which the children take the ideas and make them their own.

Imagination and imaginative play are enhanced through:

- exploring home experiences
- meeting and chatting with visitors who have particular jobs or skills
- a good selection of high-quality storybooks and poetry
- open-ended resources, such as: cardboard boxes, blocks, lengths of fabric, hats, scarves, belts, bags, pots, pans
- small objects like shells, clothes pegs and conkers, which will encourage children to develop their ideas further

Early drama involves story and characters. This is often the case with small-world play, where children may talk quietly to themselves, perhaps taking on the characters in their story. Socio-dramatic play involves a group acting out scenarios, negotiating rules and roles, problem-solving, and developing a story. Children who engage in frequent role play are more likely to be able to see another person's point of view, recognise that people think differently and develop a theory of mind.

Case Study

A group of 3- and 4-year-olds are engaged in a drama game inspired by the story *The Enormous Crocodile* (Dahl, 2016). With a large green cushion to represent the crocodile, the children chase back and forth, pretending to eat each other up! But the crocodile is caught instead. As you can imagine, the game can become noisy and energetic, with some children getting overwrought. The adults don't want to stop the game but need to find a creative way to refresh the play and offer a new direction.

The next morning, the children arrive to find that the crocodile is stuck in a swamp across the other side of the room. They begin a rescue mission. They use the blocks and planks to traverse the swamp. The crocodile is rescued, and the children start the game of chase all over again. One of the adults asks: 'Why is this crocodile chasing you? What does it want?' The children suggest that the crocodile is VERY hungry. They decide that the best thing to do is to make a shop selling crocodile food. They bake special crocodile biscuits to sell. A handmade book is created, using photographs of the game, and a simple repeating refrain, e.g. 'Snap! Snap! Snap!' This quickly becomes the favourite story for group times, and the adults organise copies of the book to be shared with parents.

Despite no first-hand experience of swamps or crocodiles (!) this dramatic play was hugely engaging. The story was allowed to evolve over time, appealing to both children and adults. It supported communication and vocabulary; physical skills; the ability to cooperate, negotiation skills, problem-solving skills and the capacity to work in a team.

In this social activity, the children had to interact with others so needed to use their social skills, given support when needed. It is also an emotional activity – many children encountered being scared. However, they were able to explore how to manage their feelings in a safe context.

Nurturing creativity

The Durham Commission Report on Creativity and Education (Durham University, 2021) recognises that fostering creativity and expressive arts and design can have huge benefits for children's resilience, wellbeing and life chances. It is not only the arts, but every curriculum area that has the potential for creative teaching and learning. We can also use Information and Communications Technology (ICT) to support creative learning.

For example, as part of their welcome to new children and families, one setting organised an online workshop. This involved families making dreamcatchers at home, using string, wool and recycled card. Parents and children could share their wishes, hopes and dreams as part of this creative project. Their dreamcatchers were then displayed in the setting.

The development of a creative curriculum

We need to ask: How do the creative parts of a curriculum develop? How can the art and design curriculum help?

A four-step process of creative development is proposed by Duffy (2006):

1.　Curiosity: what is this?
2.　Exploration: what can and does it do?
3.　Play: what can I do with this?
4.　Creativity: what can I create or invent?

Similarly, Craft et al. (2007) point out that creativity involves multiple skills and behaviours. As well as being curious, it includes 'being innovative, experimental and inventive'. The authors went on to coin the phrase 'possibility thinking'. The idea is that there is a shift in thinking from 'what is this, what does it do?' to 'what can I do with it?' They expand on this, saying that 'it involves finding and honing problems as well as solving them' (Craft et al., 2007, p. 2). The following example shows how Levi develops his creative thinking through a process of experimenting with blocks and designing an enclosure for his dinosaurs.

Case Study

Levi designs an enclosure for his dinosaurs. His key person, aware of his love of drawing, suggests he might like to sketch this. Levi chooses blue and green pencils to illustrate each dinosaur. He goes on to add lolly sticks, representing the towers of his building. He is delighted when the adult suggests they take photographs for his special book.

Levi's key person supports his language development by clearly describing what he is doing. This is particularly important as he is learning English as an additional language. Levi is also engaged with the development of his work - he can stand back from it and decide how to refine it. He goes back to improve his design by moving the towers closer together.

Levi's project is a clear illustration of the distinction between teaching creatively and teaching for creativity. Teaching creatively involves the adult being imaginative and creative themselves in order to make learning more interesting and effective. In the example above, this involved Levi's teacher organising an enticing play environment that reflected his interests.

Teaching for creativity involves encouraging children's own creative thinking. Knowing that Levi loves to draw, the adult suggests he does this. Photographing his drawing and construction validates Levi's work. It also connects these two creative activities.

Alongside high-quality art and design activities, adult interactions matter in cultivating children's creativity. These strategies include:

- sensitive suggestions and interventions
- well-timed questions
- modelling
- joining in with children's play

Being willing to get involved and scaffolding the process of children's creative thinking are essential. This is not to say that the result does not have value. It is part of the process. But if we focus primarily on what is produced, we overlook the significance of the steps taken to get there. The process constitutes the learning.

Expressive arts and design that reflect and celebrate the cultures of a diverse 21st century Britain

In 2021, the Department of Education reported that more than one in three of England's primary school children is from an ethnic minority (DfE, 2021b). Yet, the Creative Industries Council details that ethnically diverse communities are under-represented in the creative industries, with almost 2,000 people leaving the industries since 2009. 'This reduces the representation to just 5.4 per cent of the total workforce' (Creative Skillset, 2012, p. 4). The Expressive Arts and Design (EAD) curriculum must address this issue.

Firstly, think about how you might celebrate the skills and knowledge of the families and community. The following case study highlights this and the importance of taking time to build relationships.

—Case Study—

Four-year-old Maryam has recently started nursery. She arrives full of energy, eager to play outdoors with her friends. That morning, Maryam's mum shows her key person some photos of drawings that she has been doing at home. Maryam's key person follows up on this and takes some coloured chalks outdoors. The children draw and mark-make on the tarmac and paving stones. They agree that the stones make the best surface for drawing on. There are several confident English speakers in the group. This helps Maryam to develop her language and vocabulary. Her key person repeats and extends new words and phrases to describe the children's explorations. 'A red line, Maryam - look!' ... 'Sylvie is drawing a red line too.' Maryam adds several marks that appear to be Arabic script to one side of her drawing. The next day, Maryam's key person shows her mum a display of these images with the children's comments. Included in the display is a poster of Arabic symbols designed for children. Maryam's key person asks if her mum would like to help with the display, to add some handwritten words and phrases in Arabic script.

This example shows how a playful learning experience can grow from a child's interest and strengths. The key person's focus is on language acquisition and celebrating home languages. With a relaxed commentary, words and phrases are 're-cast' and repeated. The display showcases the children's drawings and writing, and draws on Maryam's family.

Ways to celebrate the skills and knowledge of families and community:

- Use home visits or the settling-in process to get to know families.
- Welcome the expertise that families bring: invite families to share their knowledge and skills or help develop a creative activity or project.
- Recognise individual children's identities and interests: at the start of each year, one school invites all the children to make a decorative handprint to celebrate their talents, interests and friendships. These are displayed like giant leaves on a welcome tree in the school foyer.

It is also important to consider how your setting shares its work with families. At the end of a project in the London Borough of Newham (McTavish, 2017), we invited families to join in with several celebrations. Short, illustrated leaflets were printed to share with families, so they could replicate some of the activities at home.

Drawing on the Curriculum Checklist for Anti-Racist Art and Design, created by the National Society for Education in Art and Design (NSEAD, 2021), here are some critical things to consider about your art and design offer:

- Does your curriculum include artists, makers and designers from a range of ethnically diverse communities?
- Do you include a broad range of art, craft and design?
- Do you proactively consider issues around gender, race, sexuality, disability and class in all your planning? How?
- Do you involve local artists and makers, or other arts-based communities? You might use a local artist's work to inspire an exploration of new media and materials or invite an artist to visit.
- Do you plan visits to galleries, museums, performances or other special outings? When you plan these, do you consider how this might represent your communities?
- Do you make links to your local community, its history and potential for art and design? For example, several settings based in an area renowned for ceramics developed a studio space to work with clay. Study visits were planned to see the local potteries, exposing the children to valuable, real-life experiences.

In addition to the points above and the many activities you include in the curriculum, the other essential aspect to consider is artistic display. This can be the work of children, artists or members of the community. It is important to consider the sorts of messages displays give. Display is not only about being aesthetically pleasing. Good displays are not a matter of either showcasing children's learning or representing the community. The two are inseparable.

Table 9.1 Art and design throughout the EYFS

	Birth to 3 years old	3- and 4-year-olds	4- and 5-year-olds: Reception
Attitudes and dispositions	Enjoy exploring objects, materials and malleable play.	In addition: Plan and think ahead about playing, exploring and sometimes making.	In addition: Reflect on what they are doing and creating; building on previous experiences and learning.
	Develop curiosity and creativity through the natural and made world, e.g. exploring leaves, conkers and shells to investigate colours and textures.	Reflect on choices: e.g. adults might say, 'I can see you've mixed two different types of green. Which colour do you think you might use?'	Collaborate with others, sharing skills, ideas and materials.
	Using scarves and ribbons to explore movement and music.	Keep trying when things are difficult; e.g. when the glue doesn't work, trying tape instead.	Develop stories in their imaginative play, and represent ideas through a wide variety of art including music, singing and dance.
Concepts and skills	Touch, grasp, mix, press, make marks.	In addition: compare, combine, manipulate	In addition: layer, transform, choreograph
	Use simple tools – crayons, brushes, scissors.	Use tools such as a holepunch, a fine brush, a large needle and thread.	Use a glue-gun or pottery turning wheel.
	Move and respond to music.	Explore and express ideas and feelings.	Represent ideas and thinking with a range of media and materials.
		Combine different media and materials, e.g. paint and collage.	Describe what they feel or see in response to an artwork, image or object.
Vocabulary	Soft, smooth, rough, sticky, pencil, chalk, crayon, paint, brush, scissors, tape, string, stapler, sculpture, painting, colour, dots, lines	In addition: prickly, media, materials, weaving, beautiful, imagine, shape, pattern, texture, two-tone, spin, jump, glide, tiptoe	In addition: mixed media/multi-media,
			form, space, balance,
			mood, atmosphere,
			names of the primary and secondary colours
			gallop, bounce, flow,
			symmetry, pointillism

Some aspects of art and design in the EYFS are outlined in Table 9.1. Children need a broad range of rich experiences and plenty of time to explore and use resources in their own way. They also need adults to teach them key skills and vocabulary. Both approaches will help them to become more independent, more able to put their ideas into action, more reflective and more evaluative of their own creativity and others'.

Conclusion

This chapter has offered a summary of key points to consider in creating an ambitious curriculum for expressive arts and design. As they grow in knowledge and expertise, children will gain many ways in which to express their ideas and thinking through the arts. We have seen how art presents valuable opportunities to celebrate the culture of children, families and the community. When adults join children on their artistic adventures, learning can be richer for all.

Reflective questions

1. Consider these three elements of the arts: practical, aesthetic and encounters with art. How well is this balanced in your art and design curriculum? Which element might you develop further?
2. In which ways might you draw on the knowledge and expertise of families to support an art and design activity or project?

10

Understanding assessment and curriculum

Jan Dubiel

Introduction

Creating opportunities and experiences for children to engage with our curriculum is at the heart of our work in the early years. Ensuring that we put this into action well drives the mass of decisions we take at both a strategic and day-to-day level. We build on children's individual needs as well as holding wider aspirations. We try to ensure that the curriculum is progressive, accumulative and appropriate. Many of the decisions we make require an effective approach to assessment, taking care to be authentic and accurate.

Putting the curriculum into action

To put the curriculum into action, we need to understand the nature, purpose and practice of assessment. We must recognise the key role of assessment, to be confident about:

- what elements of the curriculum we need to deliver
- how we can most effectively achieve this

Ofsted's definition of teaching in the early years identifies the role of assessment:

> Integral to teaching is how practitioners assess what children know, understand and can do as well as take advantage of their interests and dispositions to learning (characteristics of effective learning), and use the information to plan children's next steps in learning and monitor their progress.

(Ofsted, 2022)

Equally, the Statutory Framework for the Early Years Foundation Stage (EYFS) states:

> 2.1. Assessment plays an important part in helping parents, carers and practitioners to recognise children's progress, understand their needs, and to plan activities and support. Ongoing assessment (also known as formative assessment) is an integral part of the learning and development process. It involves practitioners knowing children's level of achievement and interests, and then to shape teaching and learning experiences for each child reflecting that knowledge. In their interactions with children, practitioners should respond to their own day-to-day observations about children's progress and observations that parents and carers share.

(DfE, 2021c, p. 18)

We could describe assessment as 'knowing the children that you work with so that you can support their learning and development'. Though this may sound simple, it belies greater complexities. In this chapter, I will explore these complexities. I will also articulate the role of assessment in relation to the curriculum.

It is worth clarifying that assessment is an ongoing, continual process. It is not a specific event. Our 'knowing of children' builds over time. Every activity, every observation, every moment of interaction enables us to refine and add to our understanding of each child. Really 'knowing the child' is distinct from the periodic collection of data.

This continual process of assessment checks:

- whether the child securely understands curriculum content
- whether the child has insecure knowledge and needs further support
- *how* the child is learning: engaging with new knowledge, skills and learning behaviours

Effective understanding and use of assessment is at the centre of effective practice.

In order to 'know the child' and work professionally with that information, we need to consider the specific elements of assessment. The following sequence of questions can help us to develop our understanding of the nature and purpose of assessment:

1. What information do we need?
2. How do we get the information?
3. How is that information used?
4. How is the information recorded and documented?

What information do we need?

Early years practitioners are responsible for supporting each child's learning and development. The question of 'what the child needs to learn' is, of course, highly contested, and shaped by the child's society and culture.

Practitioners need a pedagogical repertoire that consists of:

- direct teaching
- carefully considered interaction
- support
- challenge

The fusion of curriculum content (the 'what') with appropriate pedagogical approaches (the 'how') forms the core of our work as educators. To optimise this, we need to be clear about:

- the nature and content of the learning that will take place
- how children will consolidate and extend their learning
- how we will help children progress towards and achieve the planned outcomes in our curriculum

This is an important process. Educators needs to be clear about the information they need to achieve this. The EYFS sets out an overview of curriculum intentions. This is contained in the Educational Programmes and the Early Learning Goals for the end of the Reception year. *Development Matters* (DfE, 2021a), which is non-statutory, suggests the pathways for achieving those intentions. But the information practitioners need is more complex and intricate than this. Working with groups of children requires a deep knowledge and understanding of each individual child as a learner. It also requires wider understanding of the typical development of children's knowledge, skills and behaviours. This knowledge enables practitioners to understand the individual learning journeys that children take, and how best to support these. The principal purpose of assessment is to support each child's learning. We need to identify the most appropriate and significant information that we need.

We need to consider the child's personality, propensities and strengths as a learner. We need to think about what motivates and interests them, and conversely what demotivates them. This enables us to judge how well the content of the curriculum 'lands' with the child.

We need to consider:

- What specific interests motivate and engage the child in their learning?
- Are there specific resource areas (indoors or outdoors) that they gravitate towards?
- What is the child's level of development and attainment in the Prime Areas of the EYFS?
- What is the child's level of development and attainment in the Specific Areas of the EYFS?
- How secure are they in the Characteristics of Effective Learning?
- What types of interaction do they respond to?
    - Parallel adult presence and support?
    - Specific challenge and provocations?
- Do they typically engage in individual or group self-led activities?

How do we get the information?

Effective assessment requires accurate and authentic information. It must truly represent the information collected about the child. Invalid information (or data) is at best valueless and, at worst, misleading.

Authentic assessment ensures that perceptions of a child's learning, attainment and achievement are 'real'. It genuinely reflects what we know is important (rather than what is easy to measure).

The information we collect is important. It drives the decisions we make about how we support children's learning. Traditional approaches to assessment are often diluted versions of those used with older children. Such methods rely heavily on 'testing' to obtain information. Testing is considered to be objective and neutral.

A working definition of 'testing'

A *test-based assessment* is one in which a series of pre-set questions and/or activities are provided for a child to answer or respond to.

This may be achieved in several ways:

- by the child providing an oral answer
- by manipulating an object
- by pointing to an object or an image on a screen

An identical set of questions or activities is administered to each child in the group. For each question, there is a wrong or right answer or response. The child is scored accordingly. Each child gets a score, and the group is scored overall.

The problem with this practice in the early years is that it does not account for the nature of young children. Adults and older children understand what tests are about: that the aim is to get as many 'right answers' as possible. Young children do not know this. They do not know that the 'right answer' will have been decided. Nor do they know how to reach a 'right answer'. They often see the questions as an invitation to give a creative or individually perceived response. This may, or may not, provide the information being sought.

The tradition of observational assessment remains strong in early years education. This involves practitioners in observing children, primarily in self-led activities. Practitioners make a judgement about the child's level of development. They base this on the knowledge, skills and understanding the child demonstrates.

However, understanding and practice have evolved. We realise now that we need a more sophisticated approach to obtaining accurate information. 'Practitioner-led observational assessment' involves us in making accurate and meaningful judgements about children's attainment. We do this through observation and through interaction with the children. For example, we challenge children during their self-led activity, provoke responses and frame questions. This helps us to gain a clearer and more authentic picture of the child's capabilities. The child demonstrates how secure their learning is, by leading the activity. The practitioner can use their professional judgement, rather than just 'standing back'. That way, they can be confident of their conclusions.

What do we do with the information?

Supporting learning and development

Once we know that the information we have collected is accurate and authentic, we can focus on how we will use it.

Gathering assessment information enables us to understand and know the child. Then we can support, challenge and extend the child's learning and development. This process depends on our parallel understanding of the curriculum and how this progresses, in both sequence and depth.

Formative assessment has always been at the core of effective early years practice. As noted above, it is a key element of the Statutory Framework for the Early Years Foundation Stage. However, fusing this information with our knowledge of the curriculum is complex. It requires us to be both highly reflective and confidently intuitive about the decisions and actions that we take.

We will use much of this information during the multitude of day-to-day interactions that occur. We might instinctively respond to a comment a child makes, or to an observation of a behaviour or a communication. This is underpinned by our knowledge of the curriculum and our understanding of how children make progress. Additionally, it requires our intricate knowledge of each child. We need to understand their individual approach and how we can support or challenge their learning.

The influential REPEY (Researching Effective Pedagogy in the Early Years) study (Siraj-Blatchford et al., 2002) identifies 'individualised' assessment as a key route to quality outcomes for children. This approach relies on precise knowledge of the child. It also requires familiarity with progression in the curriculum:

> Our findings suggest that the most effective (excellent) settings ... achieve a balance between the opportunities provided for children to benefit from teacher initiated group work and the provision of freely chosen yet potentially instructive play activities. The evidence actually suggests that there is no one 'effective' pedagogy. Instead the effective pedagogue orchestrates pedagogy by making interventions (scaffolding, discussing, monitoring, allocating tasks), which are sensitive to the curriculum concept or skill being 'taught', taking into account the child's 'zone of proximal development', or at least that assumed in the particular social grouping.

> (Siraj-Blatchford et al., 2002, p. 43)

The REPEY research further identified the importance of learning that was initially child led, but then supported by an adult. This is described as 'child but adult extends' (Siraj-Blatchford et al., 2002, p. 54). As Figure 10.1 shows, an equal balance of activities which are child-initiated, adult-initiated, and initiated by the child but then extended by an adult, is most effective for children in the EYFS before the Reception year. The research suggests that this ensures the best outcomes for children. These approaches all need intuitive and responsive use of assessment knowledge, combined with an understanding of curriculum progression.

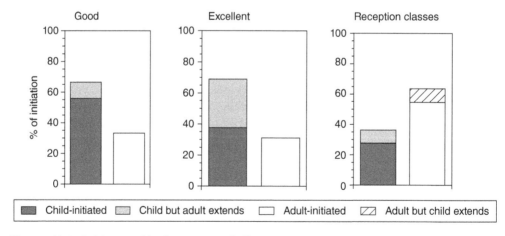

Figure 10.1 Initiation of high cognitive challenge activities within each setting type

(Siraj-Blatchford et al., 2002, p. 54)

Careful assessment is also vital in identifying specific aspects of learning that are insecure. Otherwise, these may prevent children from making sound progress. Figure 10.2 shows

Ofsted's model of learning, drawing on its curriculum research, which proposes a model of 'composites' made up of many 'component' parts (Ofsted, 2021). To use an analogy: children do not train for a big football game by playing lots of matches. Instead, they might train in fitness, ball skills like passing and shooting, and practise corners and other set-pieces. All that training helps children to develop the key skills they need to play football well: the 'components'. When a child can combine all of those 'components' fluently together, they can play effectively in the big match. Similarly, singing a large number of songs (composite) depends on an array of components:

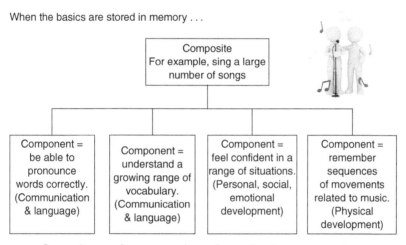

Composite: a performance made up of several parts or components

Figure 10.2 Composites and components

(Ofsted, 2021, Slide 14)

Careful analysis of children's activity can help us to recognise where children have not yet mastered a component they need. Accurate assessment can help us to identify specific knowledge, skills or behaviour to guide our interactions with children. This helps us to ensure that progress is secure and accumulative.

Summative assessment

The primary purpose of assessment is to provide us with accurate and meaningful information. This helps us to support children's learning effectively. As previously discussed, formative assessment is a powerful tool for improving teaching and learning. It is reactive and responsive to the child and the situation.

Summative assessment is also important. This is when we collect all the information – the data – together, to create a valuable overview of group and cohort progression. It can also help us to identify the impact that practice has had on learning and development. This serves two purposes.

It enables us to identify gaps or patterns in progress, particularly for specific groups of children. It also enables us to make a judgement about which aspects of the curriculum are most effective, and where we need to make improvements.

The delivery of the curriculum – in the widest sense – lies at the heart of what we do. We need to ensure that the curriculum has been delivered successfully.

Assessment data might be collected through home-grown or commercially produced systems. The information itself comes from practitioners' observational assessments, as described above. Summative assessment information is a by-product of the everyday approach to knowing children and supporting them. Summative assessment should not be a self-contained, standalone process in itself. Guidance like *Development Matters* might help to inform our judgements. But the information will originate from our evolving knowledge of the child.

It is worth exploring some of the challenges that this poses, including:

- the nature of child development, which is more like a series of overlapping waves than a clear sequence of steps
- the broad, interrelated nature of the early years curriculum

Summative assessment information provides a useful function. But it is dangerous to simplify assessment information so that it fits with a particular system or expectation. An appropriate curriculum for young children is holistic. It must include elements that are difficult to quantify in a simplistic way. Many of the most important elements of the EYFS are particularly challenging in this respect.

Understanding progress in this light is one such significant challenge.

The conventional view of progress in this context has, in the past, been to log the child's development against a statement or series of statements. For example, the previous EYFS Profile described children's attainment as 'emerging, expected or exceeding' in relation to each Early Learning Goal. Many other assessment systems followed that lead. They applied those three levels to the overlapping age-bands within the previous version of *Development Matters*. The intention was to show an authentic notion of progress, using the same statements that were intended to inform teaching and provision. The result was often confused and incoherent. What, for example, was the difference between 'exceeding 30–50 months' and 'emerging 40–60 months'? In some cases, assessment using the bands became a simplistic 'tick-list'.

The revised *Development Matters* has just three bands: Birth to 3, 3- and 4-year-olds, and Reception (4- and 5-year-olds). This might appear to reduce the ability to demonstrate progress. In fact, it provides a more appropriate opportunity to evaluate the impact of the curriculum and how secure the child's learning is.

Ofsted's discussion of learning and progress is a useful place to start in understanding this:

> Learning has been defined in cognitive psychology as an alteration in long-term memory: 'If nothing has altered in long-term memory nothing has been learned.' Progress, therefore, means knowing more (including knowing how to do more) and remembering more. When new knowledge and existing knowledge connect in learners'

minds, this gives rise to understanding. As learners develop unconscious competence and fluency, this will allow them to develop skills. Progress should not be defined by hitting the next data point. Rather, if learners attain within a well-sequenced, well-constructed curriculum, they are making progress.

(Ofsted, 2019b)

To understand how well the curriculum has been learnt, we need to find out how confidently and automatically the child uses the knowledge, skills and behaviours they have learnt. We cannot find this out through simple tick-lists: we need to view learning developmentally. Practitioner-led observational assessment enables us to make a more refined and meaningful judgement. This, in turn, will identify the best ways of supporting the child and describe the impact of teaching and provision.

We might use *Development Matters* to check whether a child has securely learnt the components they need to achieve a composite. An example is the composite of counting and using numbers fluently up to 5. The components are:

- Develop fast recognition of up to 3 objects, without having to count them individually ('subitising')
- Recite numbers past 5
- Say one number for each item in order: 1,2,3,4,5
- Know that the last number reached when counting a small set of objects tells you how many there are in total ('cardinal principle')
- Show 'finger numbers' up to 5
- Link numerals and amounts: for example, showing the right number of objects to match the numeral, up to 5

We might then assess the child's learning as follows:

- **'Entering'**: a child is not yet securely counting to 5. We need to offer more support so that the child becomes secure and fluent.
- **'Secure supported'** indicates that the statement describes the child who is secure in their counting, with support from an adult or in response to an adult provocation or request. The child has acquired the knowledge, but they are not yet using it independently. This provides us with the opportunity to create occasions within the setting that will enable the child to do this.
- **'Secure independent'** indicates that the child's understanding is secure. They can demonstrate this *without support or provocation from an adult*. The child can use their knowledge in the fluid and unconscious way that the Ofsted statement describes.

By reconceptualising our understanding of progress, we can illuminate the importance of 'deep' learning in the curriculum. This still allows us to generate useful data for the purposes described above.

How is the information recorded and documented?

Practitioner-led observational assessment:

- requires an intuitive professional confidence to tune into a child's learning
- enables us to understand how the curriculum is being embedded
- guides us in shaping appropriate and professionally considered responses
- helps us to support the child's continued development

We can also use this information to summarise individual attainment, and the attainment of groups of children. In this way, we can demonstrate progress and make ourselves accountable for the impact of the provision.

The 'knowing of children' remains core to effective EYFS practice. Using this information to ensure that children make secure progress continues to be its key purpose. This type of assessment is an essential part of effective practice. However, in some cases, the concept of assessment has become confused with a perceived need for physical 'evidence' of children's learning.

There are rich traditions of documenting children's learning and development. This helps practitioners to celebrate and understand the nature and trajectory of a child's progress. The renowned pre-schools of Reggio Emilia in Italy use documentation as a powerful way of framing their curriculum. They also use documentation to communicate the strong values that define their approach to childhood and pedagogy (Edwards et al., 2011). Margaret Carr's innovative work develops the concept of 'Learning Stories'. These support, celebrate and articulate children's development and success through pictorial and annotated documentation. Learning Stories can develop the professionalism of early childhood educators (Carr, 2001). These approaches build on a strong philosophy: the physical outcomes are an expression of this, and not merely a time-consuming activity.

Historically, during the development of the EYFS, there has sometimes been an over-reliance on physically recording evidence for the purpose of justification. Practitioners were wrongly told to gather multiple examples of 'evidence' to support their judgements for the EYFS Profile. Poorly managed moderation processes, in some areas, drove this. Commercial tracking systems encouraged practitioners to evidence their decisions of children's attainment against statements from *Development Matters*, using photographs or text. These misguided approaches separated assessment from a philosophy that celebrates learning and development. On occasions, it became an unwelcome and time-consuming additional dimension to the educator's role.

The 2021 EYFS acknowledges that paperwork, tracking data and digital recording of children's learning can lead to unnecessary workload. This is especially the case where practitioners feel that this is an expectation. In some cases, this culture has inadvertently interfered with interaction and effective teaching. Practitioners lose the momentum of powerful moments of dialogue as they reach for a means of recording the moment. The Statutory Framework for the EYFS has long been aware of this anomaly, and it clearly asserts that:

2.2. Assessment should not entail prolonged breaks from interaction with children, nor require excessive paperwork. When assessing whether an individual child is at the expected level of development, practitioners should draw on their knowledge of the child and their own expert professional judgement and should not be required to prove this through collection of physical evidence.

(DfE, 2021c, p. 18)

Assessing the child is part of the professional role of the practitioners. So is the interpretation of the assessment to indicate a particular level of development. External parties who wish to gain information about children's progress in the EYFS need to acknowledge that this information is complex. Any dialogue about this should begin with a conversation with the educators, not a review of documentation. The newly produced exemplification for the EYFS Profile (DfE, 2022) adopts this approach. It consists of educators talking about the children they work with, the observations and the conclusions they have drawn. They discuss how this describes each child's achievement and attainment in the context of the EYFS Profile.

Involving parents

As practitioners, we have expert, general knowledge about children's development. Parents are the experts in their own children. When practitioners and parents understand and trust each other, they can work collaboratively. This ensures the best outcomes for every child.

By sharing and discussing assessment information, we can explain the critical importance of early development to parents. This also creates an opportunity for us to learn from parents about the unique development of each child. This is true for ongoing formative assessment, and the two summative assessment checks: the Progress check at age 2 and the Early Years Foundation Stage Profile.

Most parents want to find out more about how children learn and how their brains develop. They are very likely to welcome this discussion.

The evidence tells us that the early home learning environment (HLE) is an important factor in children's success at school and in life. Practitioners in the early years are well placed to help parents understand their child's needs. We can support parents to enhance their child's development at home. This can have life-long benefits:

- The HLE is an important factor in the development of early speech, language and communication. This not only impacts on a child's development in the early years, but can persist until their GCSEs and A-Levels.
- The home learning environment is related to children's social and emotional development in the early years. The benefits continue until age 16.
- The quality of the HLE is as important to intellectual and cognitive development as parental factors, such as occupation and education. This suggests that what parents do with their child is just as important as who they are.

(DfE, 2018)

Conclusion: Principles of assessment in the early years

1. **Record what helps you to understand the child**. A child's learning and development can be complex and idiosyncratic. The nature of assessment is pivotal to understanding and then supporting and extending children's learning. For that reason, an authentic and accurate assessment is vital. On some occasions, it may be necessary to ensure that a child's activity is fully monitored to obtain an accurate picture. This may require some physical recording (writing an observation or photographing the child). The decision for this is the practitioner's alone, on the basis that it will support their professional knowledge.
2. **Record what is significant for an individual child**. When children make specific and notable advances in their development, you may want to note this as an important point in their journey. Again, the educator makes this decision. They will be able to decide what is or is not significant for the child.
3. **Record what you are going to forget**. In the intense ebb and flow of typical EYFS provision, a plethora of children's activity can overwhelm our memory. Brief moments of significance compete with each other and are then immediately overwhelmed by new ones. In this context, sometimes a brief aide memoire, a note to self, or a picture taken quickly, can capture the moment. This supports us to remember its significance later.

Reflective questions

Thinking about the purpose of documentation and recording in the EYFS:

1.   How can this support, rather than detract from practice?
2.   How can we make it a useful tool, rather than a hindrance?

11

Getting the curriculum right, so that every child can thrive in the early years

In this chapter, a range of authors consider how we can get the curriculum right in particular contexts. Tania Choudhury, Alex Hodgkiss and Julian Grenier consider how we can support young children learning English as an additional language. Lindsey Foster argues that young children with special educational needs and/or disabilities (SEND) have the right to access a broad, balanced and ambitious curriculum in the early years. Ed Vainker and Matilda Browne consider how we can ensure that the curriculum works for children who are disadvantaged. Finally, Sarah Porter explores outdoor environments as engaging and inspiring locations for learning.

Helping children who are learning English as an additional language to access the curriculum

Tania Choudhury, Alex Hodgkiss and Julian Grenier

English as an additional language

Speaking more than one language has lots of advantages for children. It is the norm in many countries around the world. Children will learn English from a strong foundation in their home language. It is important for you to encourage families to use their home language for linguistic as well as cultural reasons. Children learning English will typically go through a quiet phase when they do not say very much and may then use words in both languages in the same sentence. Talk to parents about what language they speak at home, try and learn a few key words and celebrate multilingualism in your setting.

(*Development Matters*, DfE, 2021a, p. 22)

Roughly one in every five children in an English school is learning English as an additional language (DfE, 2021b). In total, that means around 1.6 million children, a number that has roughly doubled in the last 15 years. England's rich diversity of language and culture is reflected in its population of children in early years settings and schools.

This section explores:

- What we know about learning English as an additional language (EAL)
- Typical stages of bilingual development
- Helping young children to learn English as an additional language

What we know about learning English as an additional language (EAL)

It is important to start off by noting that the term 'EAL' is broad. It simply means that a child is encountering a language at home other than English.

In other words, Adam – who has a fluently bilingual mother who speaks excellent English and Urdu at home – will be categorised as EAL. So will Fatemeh, who has just arrived as a refugee from Iran, chatting away in Farsi and knowing not a single word of English.

Research suggests that the most important consideration is a child's proficiency in English, not their EAL status. Proficiency in English takes time to develop. Many children arrive in early years settings without understanding or speaking much English. They will still be on their way to proficiency at the end of the Reception year. Proficiency in English is a strong predictor of later success in school, so it is important that we offer effective support to young children. This will help them to make friends, play and learn; and it will help them succeed later in school, too.

There are also two myths to challenge and some gaps in our understanding to be aware of. Perhaps the most important myth to challenge is the idea that young children will 'soak English up like sponges'. In fact, learning a new language is very hard work – for young children as much as for adults. It will not happen naturally because children are in a language-rich environment. We will have to think carefully about the support we give to children who are not yet proficient in English.

The second myth is the belief that children should switch to speaking English at home, once they start in an early years setting or in school. This advice is often handed out to parents. It can have serious and negative consequences for children (Hodgkiss, 2021). It can cut them off from wider family members: uncles, aunts and grandparents who speak the child's first language, but not English, for example. If the child's parents and other family members do not speak English well, the child might be left with no strong language models at all. In this type of 'subtractive bilingual environment', the child is unable to develop either language properly. This may affect their sense of belonging and emotional wellbeing. Advice of this kind may also imply that the child's first language is of a lower status than English. This perpetuates a wider racist narrative, that minority groups are inferior. It leaves parents feeling that the school perceives them and their culture in a negative way.

Typical stages of bilingual development

Research by Patton Tabors sets out the typical stages of learning English as an additional language:

1.   Children may start by continuing to use their home languages in the second-language situation. This is mostly likely to occur with younger children. For example, a 2-year-old Portuguese child kept saying 'la casa' to staff, during the first hour he spent in nursery without a parent. At pick-up time, his father explained that he was asking to go home.
2.   Children follow this with a non-verbal period. They collect information about English. They may use gesture to communicate.
3.   Children begin to 'go public' with their new knowledge. They may use individual words and phrases in English. Their speech may be imitative: for example, repeating the names of objects after an adult says them. They may use some formulaic English: for example, naming colours or counting. They may use some multi-word formulaic English, like 'help me' or 'don't like'.
4.   Children begin to develop productive use of English. They move beyond using just memorised chunks, creating original phrases. For example, they may say 'I want [and add a noun, like *bike*]'. Children may still sound like non-native speakers and may make mistakes with their grammar and vocabulary.

(Tabors, 1997, p. 39)

An excellent, free assessment tool from the Bell Foundation can help us to check children's development in English (Bell Foundation, 2019). Most children in the early years will be in Bands A and B. We can use these assessments when children move into Year 1, to ensure continued support for their English-learning needs.

At home, emerging evidence of the language use of young Bangladeshi-heritage children shows that:

•   Bengali/Sylheti use by parents was often motivated by the desire to strengthen and maintain relationships, and this was sometimes influenced by family members outside of the household (e.g. family members living abroad).
•   Children were sometimes a motivating factor for parents using English, particularly in cases where children preferred to speak English compared with Bengali/Sylheti.
•   Sometimes this was a cause of disappointment for parents, as despite their planned strategy to speak Bengali/Sylheti, their child responded in English.
•   Some parents felt that Bengali/Sylheti were valued in the UK, as the use of interpreters and literature from local authority and health services were available in Bangla.
•   Ultimately, the English language was the most valued in the UK as it is the national language, just as many described Bengali/Sylheti as being more highly valued in Bangladesh.

(Choudhury and Hodgkiss, 2021)

Helping young children to learn English as an additional language

Tabors's (1997) research is seminal. But it is important that we do not misunderstand it, and act as if our role is limited to observing how children move from one stage to the next in our 'language-rich environment'. The learning environment needs to include carefully thought-out opportunities for children to learn and use English.

We need to scaffold young children's use of English. We need to give them just enough help to communicate what they want to say, and gradually reduce our help so they become more independent.

We can scaffold English learning by:

- Using symbols and other visual aids, so children can point to what they want. If they indicate they want a turn on a bike, we can say the word 'bike' and then expand on this: 'you want a bike?'
- Commenting on children's play. We need to take care to give just a few key words, and not flood the child with English. At the sand tray, we might say 'you're digging in the sand'.
- Encouraging children to play with each other, even if they do not share a language. Children are inventive. They may use gesture, hold up real objects, and use some words, to understand each other.
- Structuring some situations and expecting children to join in, without making this high-pressure. For example:
  - singing songs or rhymes that are simple enough for children to learn some or all the words of
  - sharing simple books like *Where's Spot?* (Hill, 2013) and encouraging all children to say key words like 'dinner' and 'door'
  - sharing books like *We're Going on a Bear Hunt* (Rosen, 2000), so children can join in with the refrains
  - providing these books in home languages also ensures that the child quickly learns to make links between the two languages
  - using wordless picture books as a focus for conversation, encouraging children to point to details in the pictures and talk about what they notice; simple songs and rhymes will also help
  - sharing links of the books, songs and rhymes on YouTube so that children can practise at home, too
- Avoiding actions which reduce children's confidence. If a child says 'melon' instead of 'lemon', and we correct them by saying 'no, it's a lemon', that might put them off speaking in English next time. 'Testing' children by asking them multiple closed questions ('What colour is that? How many have you got?') is also unhelpful. Gently re-phrasing sentences when children make a mistake with the grammar or vocabulary is a better option. For example, when a child says, 'Give bike', we might say 'you want Ashraf to give you the bike'.

It is important not to assume that a child who only speaks a little English has a special need. They are most likely to be a typically developing bilingual child, rather than a child with a learning or language difficulty. They need lots of opportunities to hear and speak English with their peers. Practitioners sometimes refer to 'my EAL and SEND children' in one phrase, grouping both sets of children together. This is unhelpful.

Some children learning EAL may come from backgrounds which do not view children as conversational partners. Others may be refugees, experiencing trauma because of their relocation. Culturally sensitive discussions with parents are appropriate ways forward. After listening to the parent, we can offer support, guidance, or referral to a specialist agency. We need to be careful to listen to parents' own accounts of their family life, ethnicity, faith and culture, and guard against making assumptions.

It is important to look out for children learning EAL who might have a speech, language and communication delay or disorder. Ask parents about their child's use of their first language at home. We might look out to see if the child and parent chat together at the start or end of the session. If children are making little progress in both their home language, and in English, they will be severely disadvantaged. They need specialist help from a speech and language therapist. Using bilingual staff or an interpreter will help make this a rich assessment.

Young children are remarkably powerful learners, but we must not make the mistake of thinking that learning a new language is easy for them. We must support them as they learn English and watch out for those who are struggling. Children who are not progressing towards proficiency in English will find the Key Stage 1 curriculum very difficult.

Finally, it is important to consider some of the benefits of being multilingual. People who speak just one language are not able to engage in the range of learning, travel and culture that multilingual people take for granted. There may be cognitive advantages to multilingualism, too (Bialystok et al., 2012). For example, multilingual people may have a better understanding of how language works (metalinguistic awareness). They may find it easier to learn other modern foreign languages (Chalmers and Murphy, 2021). In our increasingly connected world, being multilingual is a great asset.

Reflective questions

1. How might you demonstrate to parents and children that multilingualism is an asset?
2. What will you do to make sure that all parents are involved in supporting their children's learning at home, not just fluent English speakers?

Helping children who have special educational needs and/ or disabilities (SEND) to access the curriculum

Lindsey Foster

It is a stark fact that children with SEND are, on average, 10–15 months behind other children by the end of the EYFS (Education Policy Institute, 2020, p. 21). We professionals in the early years must take this seriously. What happens during this period of life really matters.

According to the SEND Code of Practice, 'a child has special educational needs if they have significant learning difficulties in comparison to the majority of children of the same age or if they have a disability which prevents or hinders them from using educational facilities generally provided for children of the same age. Special Educational Provision is provision which is additional to or different from the educational provision made for children of the same age in mainstream schools' (DfE, 2015, p. 84). Many practitioners in the early years report seeing a rise in the number of children with SEND each year.

It is important, however, to remember that child development is not linear. Though a child may be identified as having SEND very early in life, they may no longer have the same needs later on. It is of upmost importance, then, that we identify any barriers that children may have as soon as possible. We can then put the right support in place for them. Every child must be given equal opportunities to progress.

We often ask questions such as 'How can we create an inclusive environment?' and 'How do we ensure that children with SEND access the curriculum?' However, it is more beneficial to ask, *'Are we doing enough to support children with SEND to access an ambitious curriculum that is broad and balanced?'*

In this chapter, I will explore what we mean by the term 'inclusion'; the importance of working with parents and external agencies; using formative assessment and how we can use audit tools to check how we are doing in our approach to inclusion.

What does inclusion mean?

The term 'inclusion' is widely used. We strive towards becoming more inclusive in our practice. It is worth stopping to ask what we mean by the terms *inclusion* and *inclusive practice*?

The Education Endowment Foundation's (EEF) guidance report *Special Educational Needs in Mainstream Schools* states that 'an inclusive school removes barriers to learning and participation, provides an education that is appropriate to pupils' needs, and promotes high standards and the fulfilment of potential for all pupils' (EEF, 2020b, p. 8).

A key factor here is distinguishing between having children with SEND present in the setting and helping every child to access an ambitious curriculum. In working towards the latter, the most important thing we can do first is to build a positive relationship with children and families. Practitioners can get to know the child's interests and fascinations before they are on roll. It is also the critical time for special educational needs to be identified. This enables liaison with external agencies already involved with the family, so that specific plans in place for the child can be followed up.

Case Study

Chris has Down syndrome. He cannot walk and has delayed communication and language. His parents have applied for a nursery place. The SENCO invites the family to visit. They can have a look around and ask questions. The key person arranges a home visit and starts getting to know them. In the meantime, the SENCO contacts the external agencies that are involved. The SENCO and key person discuss Chris's needs, arranging provision that is accessible. The key person, now familiar with his interests, plans activities that will absorb Chris on his first day.

The EEF guidance report on SEND states that 'effective teaching and learning requires positive relationships and interactions between teachers and pupils. Research has suggested that teachers' attitudes towards the inclusion of pupils with SEND are reflected in the quality of their interactions with pupils' (EEF, 2020b, p. 11).

One of Chris's identified barriers was that he was unable to walk. Enabling him to access a full curriculum, the nursery modified activities to his level, and sourced a walking frame and suitable chair. They also made sure no obstacles were in Chris's way when crawling.

Consequently, Chris's barrier did not stop him accessing the curriculum. His strong relationships with staff helped him to settle in well. Chris felt safe and was happy saying goodbye to his parents.

Chris was supported to make friends, modelling turn-taking and different ways of interacting. Practitioners supported Chris's communication by commenting on his play, using signs, gestures and objects. They also shared stories and songs.

Chris became a confident learner.

This is an example of inclusive practice. Chris did not have a separate programme. Rather, the setting made adaptations, enabling him to fully access the curriculum.

The value of working with parents

The SEND Code of Practice states that pupils, parents and carers must be actively involved in assessment and decision-making processes at all stages. The case study below shows how important it is to create positive relationships with the parents and child. It is crucial to listen to the parents' concerns and include their views in any plans: they have valuable insights into how well the child is doing outside the setting.

Parents of children with SEND are also on a learning journey. It can be difficult for parents to accept that their child has SEND, so it is important to offer support and guidance. This is delicate and needs careful handling.

─Case Study─

Working with Parents

When Tasmin started at nursery, she spoke a few single words. Her parents were worried about her communication and shared their concerns with the key person on the home visit. The key person reassured them and explained the support that they would provide for Tasmin. The SENCO also met with the parents and discussed their anxieties. She also arranged for an initial assessment with the speech and language therapist. After that, recommendations were made for both the parents and the nursery. A plan was designed for Tasmin and reviewed regularly with staff and parents. Tasmin attended 'Box Clever': a programme of social skills and intensive interaction interventions with the staff (Moroney, 2006, pp. 18-19). The speech therapist made a referral for further assessment of Tasmin's overall development. After 6 months, Tasmin was speaking more words and some short phrases. She was settling well and understood the routines better. She could sustain attention for a longer period. Tasmin's parents noticed her progress, reporting that she was speaking more at home and able to follow instructions.

The curriculum

The curriculum is a top-level plan of everything the early years setting wants the children to learn. As stated earlier, it is important to take account of children's interests as this helps to motivate children's learning.

Children with SEND are at risk of experiencing a narrower curriculum, together with more negative interactions with adults. The Researching Effective Pedagogy in the Early Years (REPEY) study found that children who were described by practitioners as 'struggling' to learn did not experience the same broad curriculum as the other children. They 'experienced double the amount of Personal and Social Education' (Siraj-Blatchford et al., 2002, p. 62). They also received 'the most behaviour management interactions from adults', whilst those children whose learning was described 'as expected' received 'more social talk and caring interactions from the adults in their settings' (Siraj-Blatchford et al., 2002, p. 64).

Therefore, it is important to 'scaffold' all children's learning: start from where the child is and offer help in small steps to enable them to become independent. 'Scaffolding up' means offering a child just enough help to access the curriculum. To help a child learn to use a knife, you might:

- Use hand over hand, holding the knife together as you move it to cut food
- Model: show the child how you cut with a knife, and then let them try
- Prompt: remind the child to press down and move the knife backwards and forwards to cut

With regular encouragement and repetition, the child will gradually learn to cut. You could use similar techniques to help a child play with blocks, make models with Duplo, or mix flour and water to make playdough. 'Scaffolding up' enables children to access the full curriculum. On the other hand, when the curriculum is narrowed and interactions are more negative, children with SEND do not have an equal chance to learn and thrive in the early years.

─Case Study─

Justin has a diagnosis of autism. He has limited language and communication, using sounds and gestures. He is very interested in cause-and-effect toys and the outdoors. Justin is self-directed, flitting from one activity to the next. His key person set a curricular goal for him to bake a bread roll. This was not something that Justin was initially interested in, but his key person thought it was important to be ambitious. Justin started by mixing two ingredients in a bowl. He did this with adult support, following a visual timetable. Every day Justin would spend time with an adult, having a go at the first step of the curricular goal. With lots of repetition, hand over hand support, modelling and prompting, Justin completed this step independently. He was very proud of his new skill and moved confidently on to the next step.

This is an example of inclusive practice where careful sequencing is used to build the child's learning over time.

If the 'differentiating down' model had been used, Justin would have missed the opportunity to bake a bread roll. It would have been seen as too difficult. Instead, Justin might have got involved in other areas of the provision, following his own lead. He might have missed important early learning in physical development, and understanding how substances change when you mix them together. This would *not* have been inclusive practice.

Scaffolding relies on effective formative assessment to get a precise understanding of where the child is at. The support stays in place for as long as they need it. For example, the practitioner may help a child at the snack table by using a core vocabulary board. When the child becomes able to use language to make their choice then that support is no longer needed.

The EEF guidance report on SEND (2020b) recommends that high-quality teaching supports all children including those with SEND. Some children will require specialist support. The non-statutory guidance *Development Matters* states: 'the observation checkpoints can help you to notice whether a child is at risk of falling behind. You can make all the difference by acting quickly. By monitoring a child's progress closely, you can make the right decisions about what sort of extra help is needed. Development Matters is not a long list of everything a child needs to know and do. It guides, but does not replace, your professional judgement' (DfE, 2021a, p. 5).

This reiterates the importance of knowing children well and building positive relationships with their families. When a child is struggling and at risk of falling behind, it is important to share this information with parents and team members. Plans can then be put in place to help the child overcome barriers.

The use of formative assessment

Using levels to label children is not good practice. They are often inaccurate. For example, a 4-year-old child with autism who is non-verbal could be assessed as 0–11 months for communication and language. This is not an accurate assessment. The child is a 4-year-old with an identified barrier in communication and language. This 4-year-old needs support and scaffolding, not an incorrect label. It is important not to place a ceiling on what they can achieve.

We should always follow the structured cycle of 'assess, plan, do, review'. Bearing in mind that children's development is not linear, this should be repeated regularly.

It is important continuously to reflect on:

- How inclusive is your setting?
- Are you continuously working towards further improvement?

One way of doing this is by using a structured observation rating scale: 'The Inclusive Classroom Profile' or ICP (Soukakou, 2012). This is designed to assess the quality of the provision for children with identified special educational needs and disabilities. There are 12 items in the profile. Most of them are assessed through making direct observations of approximately three hours.

These can be repeated throughout the year, enabling the setting to evaluate where they are doing well and where they can improve.

Reflective questions

1. Is our curriculum ambitious for all children with SEND?
2. How do we ensure that our provision is inclusive?

Helping children from disadvantaged backgrounds to access the curriculum

Ed Vainker and Matilda Browne

Ensuring that the curriculum works for all is the priority for any school or setting. The success of a curriculum is determined by how well it provides a positive experience for children who start the year furthest away from where we are aiming to take them. Over the last 10 years, we have sought to enable our children to flourish by working with their families and the wider community. As well as this, we work on refining the experience they have when they come to our school. We are convinced that a curriculum that serves our most disadvantaged children will also be a curriculum that helps every child to blossom.

We believe that parents play a critical role in ensuring that all children can access the curriculum.

This section explores:

- the importance of the first 1,001 days
- the value of an effective induction
- approaches to supporting disadvantaged children in the early years

Getting to the starting line – the first 1,001 days

The opportunity to help children from disadvantaged backgrounds to access the curriculum and thrive in school (and beyond) begins at conception. At Reach Academy Feltham, we have developed a 'cradle to career' model. This seeks to support parents and babies right from the start. We are currently working with more than 200 mothers and babies who have been referred to us for support.

Educators in the early years understand that public policy is far behind what we now know from science. The first thousand days are critical in ensuring that children flourish. However, that period is under-resourced, and parents face a postcode lottery in terms of their local offer.

Initially, our focus was on providing ante-natal education, based on the absence of this sort of support in Feltham. Over time, we have realised that what is critical in supporting parents and their children are positive, trusted relationships and fostering a sense of community. It is also crucial to hold parents in mind and notice what is going well in their parent–infant interactions. This helps parents to see their strengths and builds their confidence.

Case Study

Manisha and her husband moved to Feltham in 2019. They have two children: a 2-year-old boy, Shreyash, and a 3-month-old daughter, Saanvi. Manisha hasn't been able to go back to her work as a carer since the birth of their first child. She decided to stay home and take care of him due to his challenges and medical complications. Born prematurely, Shreyash used to cry all the time, frequently vomiting and sleeping poorly. As a first-time mother, with no local support network and no knowledge of how to deal with these challenges, Manisha found herself emotionally and physically exhausted, often on the brink of tears.

Health visitors referred her to the Reach Children's Hub because of its diverse perinatal offer. Following an in-depth induction, the Hub's Perinatal Lead and Manisha opted to access the intensive one-to-one intervention 'Baby Talk and Play'. At first, she was stressed because she didn't know how sessions would be, what to expect. She was also worried about how she would be perceived, especially because her efforts to get Shreyash to play with her and enjoy time together were giving no results. However, slowly and gradually, Debbie (who leads 'Baby Talk and Play') started guiding her and there was a lot of positive change. She comments that 'Manisha is more relaxed now and Shreyash is more connected to her. He never used to come and kiss and hug her. Well, maybe once in a blue moon. She used to go and kiss him, and he used to get irritated. But now, he's coming more often and he's playing with her.' 'It's a huge source of support,' says Manisha.

Because of his glue ear, Shreyash showed signs of speech and language delay. After discussing these issues with Debbie, we offered Manisha support with sign language and other helpful strategies to which her son now responds more frequently. Manisha comments,

'From the start, I started to implement the suggestions she gave me and from the very next day things started to change.' Manisha's determination and efforts showed clear signs of improvement, especially in the quality and amount of time spent with her children. For example, the play time increased from 1 minute to up to 20 minutes per play session, an enormous change.

In our experience, it is this sort of support that we have seen helps parents to help their children, regardless of background. We celebrate 'serve and return' interactions: a term that refers to carers being sensitive and responsive to their young child's signals and needs. Such positive interactions help build the healthy infant brain. Equally, they help with stress levels that have the potential to be toxic and impact negatively on the baby.

Starting to support parents at this very early stage is unusual. We are now working with schools around the country who are building their own 'cradle to career' models. Our schools and early years settings are anchor institutions in communities. We are trusted, embedded and universal, and can play a role in this critical period.

Inducting a new cohort into our settings

This focus on strong relationships with families remains a critical element of our work as we move into the EYFS. Supporting our disadvantaged students to access the curriculum begins with building a relationship of trust with parents and carers. This section explores how we build that trust, seek to develop a shared understanding and, ultimately, aim to build capacity in parents.

We take the induction of families very seriously. Whether moving into nursery or Reception, every child receives a home visit where we aim to build the relationship, share elements of our approach and take a detailed biography of the child. Home visits are key for learning from the parent or carer about their child. If we understand a child's context, we are more able to develop a curriculum to support them. We can try to ensure that we are reflecting their reality as well as pursuing a breadth of knowledge. This happens through a range of settling-in activities in the classroom, and opportunities throughout the summer to build confidence and familiarity with the staff and setting.

From there, we invest substantial resources in ensuring that parents have a clear understanding of the purpose of the EYFS – including the Prime Areas and the Characteristics of Effective Learning. We have found that parents sometimes have a narrow understanding of school readiness, so this is useful.

Case Study

Sylvia

Sylvia joined our 2s cohort in September 2021. When she joined, Anna, her mum explained that she was very advanced for her age. Sylvia is the youngest in a family of six siblings. Her attendance was poor. Eventually, we met Anna to discuss Sylvia. Anna explained that she did not see the need for nursery as Sylvia was a fluent speaker, knew all her numbers and was confident in talking about the world around her. All this was true. However, Sylvia had difficulty playing with other children, consistently leaning on adult support. She also struggled to tolerate delay. We thought it would be beneficial for Anna to gain a clearer understanding of the value of the early years. We spent time jointly observing Sylvia in play and talking about her strengths and areas of weakness. Through doing this, Anna felt more involved in the nursery, had a greater understanding of our curriculum and was ready to work in partnership to support Sylvia's outcomes.

The third priority is building parental capacity. We have seen a strong positive impact on children's outcomes from our work with parents. At Reach, this includes delivering the Family Links parenting programme which supports families with two areas that are priorities in our classrooms: clear communication and strong routines. The programme builds parental capacity and fosters further alignment between home and school.

In the classroom

We have the difficult job, as educators, to try and create a parity of experience in our classrooms, in turn supporting a parity of outcomes. This requires a balance between fostering children's interests and identifying the key skills and knowledge they need to engage in higher quality play and more meaningful experiences.

Both children presented in Table 11.1 are classic examples of those joining EYFS classrooms all over the country. The assessment information does not tell you a huge amount about each of them as a person. The information does, however, give you an idea of the language that they may arrive in the setting with; the skills that they may have honed; the experiences that they have had. We need a curriculum to challenge both these children. In the case of Child A, we need to provide access to the knowledge that Child B has collated through their lived experience.

Let's break down one of these experiences:

Table 11.1 Information about two children at Reach Academy Feltham from their home visit forms

	At home I enjoy	I have visited	I have been on a	I can/am learning to
Child A	watching TV playing video games	park	train	ride a bike
Child B	cooking/baking, drawing/painting, building things, reading stories, listening to music, watching television, dancing, feeding birds & animals	zoo, farm, aquarium, beach, central London (or another big city), museum, park	train, bus, boat, aeroplane	ride a bike, swim, use a climbing frame, catch a ball

Visiting a Zoo: this involves

- the journey there
- the entrance process
- the animals seen
- the habitats of the animals
- the noises the animals make
- their lunch
- the climbing frame they may have gone on
- the return journey
- recounting their experience, the following day

As educators of disadvantaged children, we need to break down these experiences so that all children can access this bank of knowledge and skills. In some cases, we might reproduce the experience. In other cases, our teaching and input will need to suffice.

Why? Because, for example, imagine these same two children listening to the story *Dear Zoo* (Campbell, 2010), an EYFS classic. Unless the teacher understands the curriculum and has proactively planned to close these gaps, Child B will get a lot more out of it than Child A. The gap, consequently, widens. It is for this reason that adult interactions in play are so important.

In our setting, we discuss children's learning as a diet tailored to the needs of the specific child. Some children may need further:

- instruction in play
- adult interaction
- focus on key vocabulary
- introduction to the new elements of the experience
- teaching of important knowledge

What we are not saying is that Child A will not learn from Child B and vice versa; of course they will. But because we have a responsibility for ensuring the progress of *all* children, we cannot rely on happenstance. We must be intentional in everything we do to ensure that no child is left behind.

Through this intentionality in the classroom, along with creative, proactive work to support parents and the wider community, we can ensure that all children are able to access the curriculum and flourish. All regardless of their background.

Reflective questions

1. Why is getting to know the children we work with so important when it comes to curriculum?
2. How can we ensure a curriculum that is not based on what most children already know or have experienced?

Valuing outdoor learning

Sarah Porter

I grew up in a town and then a village. I was incredibly lucky to be able to roam through woods and fields and walk to the village on my own. I remember crossing streams, building dams, making dens and arriving home to tell my parents all about it. My memories of exploring the world around me are vivid. They make me who I am and have helped to form my values as an educator.

Most of my teaching career has been in towns and cities. One of the most exciting parts of this has been learning with children and families outdoors. Whether in a built-up urban environment or a rural one, children can get outside to explore their natural surroundings.

Early in my career, I worked in a setting with an amazing baby room. They could explore freely, crawling out of the room into the garden. If babies and young children are to learn the difference between earth and grass, they need to see and touch it. It is never too early for direct interaction with the physical world.

Exploring nature and physical development

Friedrich Froebel, the 19th century German educator, developed a set of underlying principles for his kindergartens. One of these was *engaging with nature* and a strong emphasis on the importance of outdoor play. This has inspired the tradition of the nursery garden. Froebel describes how nothing is as important as the 'conjoint study of nature' (Froebel, 1912, p. 101).

There is a key difference between learning outdoors and taking learning outside. Learning outdoors means engaging with the environment and developing a relationship to it. Taking learning outside is a matter of doing outside what is usually done inside – for instance, sitting at a desk mark-making.

There are many ways for children to relate to their outdoor environment. Adults and children can go for a walk, observing and talking about nature. Babies may point at something that catches their eye – a bird, a dog. Adults will name what they see.

Toddlers begin to test their physical abilities outdoors. They try out different surfaces, noticing how different surfaces have different properties that require particular skills. They will work out how to keep their balance on grass, paving slabs and slopes.

Case Study

Recently, I rang a parent to tell them their child got a minor bump on her head when playing on the monkey bars. The parent said that every day her daughter came home talking about 'trying to be as good as her friend'. She was doing her best to achieve this. The parent understood how important this goal was to her and that it meant challenging herself and taking risks. Her main concern was that her little bump didn't stop her from trying. Regular climbing, swinging and running support gross motor development.

Children also begin to focus on tiny objects when spending time outdoors. They find small pebbles, ladybirds, daisies, blades of grass. Reaching out for and picking these up support their fine motor skills.

The interconnected curriculum

The EYFS states that 'all areas of learning and development are important and interconnected' (DfE, 2021c, p. 7). This seems particularly true of learning outside.

A child stirring a pot of soil and water in the mud kitchen may add some leaves falling off the trees. The pebbles and sticks they collect to add to the pot will be different sizes and shapes. They may look up at the trees and notice the wind blowing the branches. It will be more meaningful if an interested practitioner joins in, talking about how our seasons work and how the wind behaves.

Outdoor activities often enable deeply involved learning.

Case Study

I watched a curious 3-year-old spend an entire morning devising a system of gutters and pipes. Fully absorbed, he was attempting to link them together to run water into the sandpit. Although the system fell apart several times, he persisted. In the end, he was able to pour water down the pipes and watch it travel along the gutter into the sandpit.

This child was an active learner, following his interests and with a project in mind. He persisted in his aim, not deterred by setbacks. He was learning about the natural materials which make the world around him. He was discovering how they behave and can change.

Gardening

Through gardening children experience the cycles of life and death, growth and decay.

(Tovey, 2016, p. 65)

Gardening outside is a very different prospect to growing seeds inside. Inside gardening is valuable, though not as rich. When digging over a raised bed outside, children come across worms, spiders and beetles. They get to know the names of the creatures they find and talk about them. Conversations are endless.

Planting seeds, bulbs and vegetables is a sustained activity. They need to water and check on their plants several days a week. Some may predict what might happen and test it out. The links between time and nature become apparent. Children recognise that growing is a process with its own timeline. Growing cannot be rushed.

Gardening can also provide a connection between home and school. I was planting seeds with some 2-year-olds last spring. One child was keen and planted several pots of seeds. She whispered something to me. My Bengali-speaking colleague translated this as 'Grandma'. When I asked her mum, she said her daughter regularly helped her grandma in the garden. This child was keen to share that gardening was an important part of her home life.

Observing cycles of growth in the garden can lead to an understanding of where food comes from. Children can eat the salad, tomatoes and potatoes they planted: they see that food has origins. The yams and okra they see at the market are the end products of a long process.

Life and death

Tovey describes how being outside can lead to children observing 'life and death' (Tovey, 2016, p. 65).

Last summer, a beautiful starling flew into a glass door in the nursery and died instantly. The site supervisor picked it up and asked us if the children would like to see it. The children were engrossed by this beautiful bird, asking lots of questions.

Children are often reflective about death, wanting to understand what has happened. For example, they asked if the bird could still see and fly. We always let families know if we have such discussions in case the children have questions they want to pursue at home.

Death is integral to learning about the cycle of life. Children are captivated by the arrival of frogspawn in our pond and the community one. Frogs tend to spawn on a sunny spring day and the children are often able to see it. The pond is full of noisy frogs. Clusters of spawn follow this. The children see what happens as the spawn develops into tadpoles, froglets then frogs. It sparks a lot of questions and sophisticated conversations. Children often want to represent their learning through drawing or making models.

Sensory learning

Being outside provides a wealth of sensory experiences. Splashing in puddles is fun, but also enables children to learn about how water behaves. They also see how it feels and what effects they have on it.

Simply planting a few pots of herbs can provide a range of smells. Coming up with words to describe these smells extends their language skills.

Feeling the smoothness of pebbles and the prickles of plants attunes children to natural textures. Finding words for what they feel like and comparing them to other objects elaborate their use of language.

In urban environments, there are moments of wonder that adults and children can enjoy. They can smell an East London bluebell wood and see the colours of a red admiral butterfly.

Managing very little outdoor space

Learning outside can be challenging in a setting with little outside space or none. However, nurseries and childminders can be creative, even on a tight budget.

Babies and toddlers find a walk around the block interesting, especially on a rainy day. They watch rainwater run down a drain, stamp through puddles and listen to its sounds.

One small setting made connections with a nearby community garden. The children went there to plant and care for their plants. The daily walk also gave them a chance to notice their local environment.

A childminder linked to our setting had a friend with an allotment. She took the children to observe the seasonal changes on the allotment.

Even a tiny nursery garden or a childminder's patio can have a small mud kitchen!

Working with parents

Most parents will be happy that their child is learning about the outdoors. Some may struggle, worrying they will get dirty, cold or sick. They may be anxious that they will hurt themselves or get lost. It is important to listen to parents' concerns and try to reassure them.

Explaining the learning that goes on outside is often encouraging. Sharing how you plan and assess risks is also important. Parents usually feel more confident if they come along one day and see for themselves. Sharing photos and videos can also help gain parents' trust. Talking to parents about their own memories of outdoor learning can be useful too. Helping parents to buy or borrow appropriate clothing to keep their child warm and dry can also make them feel more assured.

The locality and further afield: Forest and Beach Schools

Babies are aware of their immediate family and their home. As they develop, they become more aware of the wider world. They get to know nursery staff, familiar shops and routes in their community.

Early years settings can give *all* children opportunities to explore their local community. We can visit parks and community gardens, inviting families along too.

Forest School is a powerful way for children to access local wooded areas. They climb trees, collect conkers, saw branches, make dens and sit around a fire. All these things, and more, contribute to their understanding of the world around them. Forest School can help develop their confidence and social, physical and communication skills.

For some children, this is a totally new thing. They may feel wary due to the lack of familiarity. The clear structure of Forest School, the expertise of trained leaders and regular visits will help them to feel safe. It is important that Forest School is inclusive: *all* children must be part of it, irrespective of mobility or ability.

In my setting, Forest School has piqued the interest of several educators. Some are so excited at the prospect of learning about their environment with children that they train as Forest School leaders.

Beach School is a very particular experience. A beach presents a unique landscape and skyline. This may be entirely new to many children; others may have only visited a crowded beach in the summer. A beach in winter has a different feel. You hear birds and have a clear view out to sea. You have more space to find seaweed, shells and sea creatures. You can make large patterns in the sand.

During our beach visits, I have watched children fully absorbed in the environment. They develop their own games, dig, throw stones into the sea and collect objects. One day we were taken aback by the high tide, so had to stay on the promenade. The children were completely enthralled by the power of the waves crashing on the wall.

To sum up, the excitement and joy of the outdoors are something that all children must be given the chance to engage with. This will open up a whole new world to them. No one should miss out on this.

Reflective questions

1. Can you think of three specific ways in which you support children and families with learning about the natural world around them?
2. Can you think of one outdoor learning experience for children that really stands out for you? What are the reasons for this?

To be effective, the curriculum must be suitable for every child. That means ensuring that we understand the different learning needs and strengths of all the children. We also need to bear in mind that many young children learn best when they are outdoors.

Historically, many of the children learning English as an additional language, children with SEND and children from disadvantaged backgrounds have missed out on crucial early learning. They have not been able to access the curriculum, or make sound progress through it. Once children fall behind, it is very hard for them to catch up. As Professor Iram Siraj argues in the Foreword, 'the life-course trajectories of all future learning are set early, and rarely change during primary and secondary education. It is much easier to change trajectories in the early years.'

12

Vertically integrated curriculum design: Secure foundations for children's future learning

Jemima Rhys-Evans and Cassie Buchanan

Introduction

Early years practice is polarised. The same applies to curriculum design. These polarisations include: knowledge vs skills; child-centred vs adult-directed; direct instruction vs enquiry learning; observation vs interaction; and core knowledge vs emotional nurture.

At Charles Dickens Primary School, we have tried to pick a path through these difficulties to design an enriching curriculum framework – one that inspires our children now and prepares them for future learning.

We have attempted to move away from an *'either or'* model and towards a *'both, and'* approach. We adapt our practice depending on the time of day, the children in front of us and the learning goals we are pursuing. We have a broad 'pedagogical repertoire' (Grenier, 2019).

This is mirrored in our approach to curriculum. We have a clear, taught curriculum with an unswerving focus on three areas:

- personal, social and emotional development (PSED)
- literacy
- maths

If early foundations are not laid in these subjects, we run the risk of widening gaps as children progress through school. Alongside this, we have the environmental curriculum using resources, activities and support for children's:

- social and communication skills
- ability to self-regulate
- stamina and curiosity

This curriculum is not, and is unlikely ever to be, a finished product. In this chapter, we will discuss why vertical integration of the curriculum is important and how we have attempted to achieve it. We will share some of the evidence we use to inform our approach.

Context

Charles Dickens Primary and Nursery School is in Borough, South London. The early years provision consists of a 2-year-old unit, a nursery and two Reception classes.

The school community reflects the diversity of our local area: some of the poorest postcodes next to some of the most affluent. The percentage of children eligible for extra funding for disadvantage hovers between 35 and 40%. We are multi-cultural, with almost every corner of the world represented. Over 70% of families speak a language other than English in the home and are often first-generation migrants to the UK.

We began to evaluate our curriculum when we expanded from 1.5- to 2-form entry in 2015. Prior to that, we had mixed-year-group classes and operated on a 2-year rolling curriculum. This presented a huge challenge to the sequencing of knowledge and skills, and to teachers being sure that new learning was building on secure foundations.

As we started this work, we became more aware of the lack of coherence between Early Years and Key Stage 1. Though our outcomes were in line with, or above, national averages, we continued to see children struggle with the Year 1 curriculum. Something needed to change.

Values

At about the same time, we started working on our school values. This arose following a Peer Review visit from some of our partner schools. There was a sense that all our staff 'sort-of knew' what the values of the school were. We 'kind of knew' what we felt to be important. However, this had not been clearly articulated, beyond the fact that we had great expectations for all children.

Following a year-long consultation process, we distilled our values into three core principles. These gave us a clear framework to shape and inform our curriculum:

- *Academic excellence*: ensuring strong outcomes at every phase and stage
- *Creativity*: fostering curiosity about the world and tools for self-expression
- *Social intelligence*: developing active citizens in the school community and wider world

The revised Early Years Foundation Stage

We started to review our provision through two lenses: the school values and the wider curriculum challenges of the whole school.

The arrival of the new Statutory Framework for the Early Years Foundation Stage (EYFS) (DfE, 2021c) brought a third dimension to incorporate. It prompted us to reflect on the challenges and opportunities that it offered and how these aligned with our practice. In particular, it made us ask: how we could we better prepare *all* children for Year 1, especially those in more challenging circumstances?

Our evaluation and development of the EYFS curriculum have been influenced by:

- our contextual changes and their impact on the whole-school curriculum
- the clear articulation of our values, leading to better shared understanding
- changes to the National Curriculum, increasing the level of challenge in Year 1
- the revised EYFS framework, empowering us to do less but to do it better

Old questions emerged. What was the right balance of child-led and adult-led learning? Should we allow children to pursue their own fascinations or intervene to help broaden their horizons? One the one hand, advocates of Froebel argue for play-based learning with targeted adult guidance. On the other, proponents of Montessori champion structured learning opportunities. And thirdly, some of our EYFS team, with experience teaching in Key Stage 1, recognise the benefits of integrating direct instruction into the daily timetable.

A two-stranded curriculum started to emerge. The first strand is the *taught curriculum*, delivered through short, adult-led sessions. The second strand is the *environmental curriculum*, delivered through carefully designed play opportunities. This synthesis highlights the strengths of each approach at different times and for different children. The needs of each individual child should drive each aspect of the curriculum, as well as adult-led involvement.

We intend that children reaching Year 1 will be well equipped. The curriculum promotes progression across all subject areas into Year 1 more effectively. It is a vertically integrated curriculum.

Vertically integrated curriculum

In *Principled Curriculum Design*, Dylan Wiliam identifies vertical integration of the curriculum as one of the seven principles of curriculum design. He explains: 'it needs to be clear how material taught at one point in time builds on materials taught earlier and feeds into what is to be taught later' (Wiliam, 2013, p. 28).

Christine Counsell uses the analogy of curriculum as a racecourse or running track (from the Latin *currere*, meaning to run or proceed): 'Curriculum is content structured over time … it points to the curriculum as continuous. Not just a sequence or a chronology, it's much more like a narrative. Curriculum is content structured as narrative over time' (Counsell, 2018).

For this narrative to make sense, it needs to be carefully sequenced so that the foundations are securely laid for the next stage of learning. However, we must not be so busy thinking about the next that we neglect the now. Each element of the curriculum must have both a short-term and a long-term function (Counsell, 2018) so that we can answer both questions:

- Why is this particular piece of learning important now?
- How will it contribute to future learning?

The curriculum in Reception and Year 1 must be fully understood by practitioners. They need a shared understanding of the 'now' and 'next' of each element of the curriculum. Without this, teams may operate in isolation, resulting in a lack of coherency.

Gaps and overlaps

In the past, we did not prioritise this coherence and sequencing across phases. This was problematic for two reasons. Firstly, it resulted in gaps in children's core knowledge. This might be less important for *cumulative* subjects such as history where the learning is revisited in different contexts over time. However, it poses a huge challenge for the more *hierarchical* subjects such as phonics and maths where new learning is dependent on secure prior knowledge. In these subjects, gaps at the end of Reception tend to widen in Year 1, particularly for disadvantaged children (FFT Datalab, 2019).

Using time efficiently: Avoiding duplication

Though we would not tolerate duplications anywhere else in the curriculum, in Reception and Key Stage 1 it seems to be acceptable – for example, teaching the properties of 2D shapes in both.

This is not to undermine or underestimate the value of *overlearning* through revisiting core concepts and skills. Julian Grenier writes about this in his blog post, '5 things to reflect on in the EYFS':

> To become good at using scissors, you have to practise over and over again. This is sometimes called 'overlearning'. You can't call a child skilled at using scissors just because they can cut paper. They need to keep practising, even though in one way they have already mastered all the skills ... (Grenier, 2019)

The key difference here is the *intentionality* of overlearning. Revisiting important parts of learning to embed understanding is a powerful learning tool. It prepares foundations strong enough to support new learning. Conversely, accidental repeated learning takes up valuable curriculum time.

Vertical integration in practice: Responsive teaching vs planned curriculum

We defined our curriculum goals: the non-negotiables that children need to be ready for Year 1. We then wanted to design learning activities that would help children reach those goals. We also wanted to 'start with children's experiences in their family and immediate environment, so that learning is meaningful' (Grenier, 2020, p. 27).

The key point here is that these two aims are not incompatible. The curriculum can *start* with children's life experiences and interests but *must* move beyond them.

Tackling gaps between some boys and some girls

Like many schools, we once fell into the trap of widening the writing gap between boys and some girls. This happened because we allowed reluctant writers to avoid fine motor activities in the continuous provision.

Save the Children's *The Lost Boys* report states that 'the available evidence suggests the gender gap in the Early Years shows itself predominantly in:

- boys participating less in the type of activities and games, such as storytelling and nursery rhymes, that support language and literacy development at home, pre-school and school.
- boys being less likely to acquire the characteristics that will one day help them to learn to read and write – such as motivation, self-regulation, confidence and engagement.'

(Save the Children, 2016, p. 5)

We want our curriculum to be responsive to children's early life experiences, their prior knowledge and their interests. This does not necessarily mean that the curriculum needs to change. Rather, our curricular contexts need to be flexible.

─Case Study─

We observed that a group of children were eagerly mark-making when taking orders and writing menus in the class café. When we began our new topic of polar exploration, we replaced the café with a travel agency. This led to a dramatic drop in writing activities for the group of target children. Consequently, we repurposed the role-play area as an ice-cream parlour, allowing the children to continue with their new-found joy of purposeful writing, while still pursuing our new topic. The context for learning had changed, but the core learning goals remained the same.

Balancing child-led and adult-led learning

At Charles Dickens, we aim to balance short taught inputs with plenty of time for child-led and play-based learning. To keep the inputs short, we stripped back the curriculum. Trying to cover too much overwhelms both children and adults.

We thought carefully about what we wanted children *to know* and *be able to do* before Year 1. Alongside this, we considered the time it would take for *all* children to be secure in this learning. Children learn at different speeds, some needing more adult-led support than others. That is not to say they should do 'more maths', for example. Rather, they need to do activities and skills that will enable them to *access* maths. This might be listening to and talking about stories involving number.

A mastery approach

> Depth in early learning is more important than covering lots of things in a superficial way.
>
> (*Development Matters*, DfE, 2021a, p. 9)

We reduced the amount of content in the taught curriculum. This allowed more time for us to get to grips with it. We wanted to allow the children to immerse themselves in the learning and to secure key concepts before moving on. The Education Endowment Foundation's *Improving Mathematics in the Early Years and Key Stage 1* guidance report recommends that 'Practitioners should be aware that developing a secure grasp of early mathematical ideas takes time' (EEF, 2020a, p. 6).

This is equally true in other areas of the curriculum, such as phonics and early reading. The EEF's guidance report *Preparing for Literacy* emphasises the importance of securing the foundations for phonics through 'storytelling, activities to develop letter and sound knowledge, and singing and rhyming activities' (EEF, 2018b, p. 6). In all, we have slowed down. Instead of moving children quickly through their phonics, we ensure that solid foundations are laid *for all*.

This mastery approach is particularly important in subjects such as maths and phonics where new learning must sit on secure foundations. Ofsted's 2019 School Inspection Update found:

> There are serious consequences for pupils when a curriculum is not sequenced or designed effectively. Gaps in pupils' knowledge accumulate as they become layered on top of one another in a curriculum sequence. This accumulation of gaps, known as dysfluency, limits pupils' ability to acquire the complex skills that depend on them, and may even prevent them entirely from gaining those skills. This problem is sometimes called 'cumulative dysfluency'.
>
> (Ofsted, 2019c, p. 6)

It is also important for children's personal, social and emotional development (PSED). A child cannot start to build relationships with their peers if they are unable to separate from their parents at the classroom door. They can't understand the needs of others until they become familiar with their own.

It was important for us to map out the key skills for these three hierarchical subjects: PSED, literacy and maths.

The mastery approach permits us to do less, but to do it better. We could say that we have one curriculum for formally taught content and one for child-led, play-based learning.

The taught curriculum: Hierarchical subjects

Table 12.1 gives an overview of the goals of the taught curriculum in Reception. The streamlined content allows us to feel confident in children securing knowledge in these subjects before moving on to new learning.

Children have daily taught sessions for PSED, literacy and maths. We use Department for Education accredited commercial schemes for maths and phonics to ensure progression into Year 1: 'Maths — No Problem!' and 'Floppy's Phonics'. For PSED, we have developed our own whole-school Wellbeing Curriculum (www.wellbeingschool.com). This was initially derived from the RULER approach, a social and emotional learning programme originating from Yale University (www.rulerapproach.org). In nursery and Reception, this is supplemented with content from the Think Equal programme (https://thinkequal.org): a social and emotional learning programme with a focus on equality, diversity and anti-discrimination. The team have found this particularly useful to develop a shared language around anti-racism and anti-sexism and it has helped them to have the confidence to engage in difficult conversations. This has

Autumn	Spring	Summer
I can settle in and become a confident, independent learner		
• I separate confidently from my parent at the start of the session and engage in the day's learning • I independently explore activities in the continuous provision with sustained attention • I play alongside friends • I play collaboratively • I take part in learning in small groups • I can focus during carpet sessions for up to 15 minutes	• I respond positively to challenge • I learn collaboratively • I can complete focused activities in a small group	• I persevere with difficulties • I make comments about my learning and play in my Special Books and show pleasure/pride in what I have done • I talk about and reflect on my learning
I can read a red book		
• I can read with an adult for 10 minutes • I know phase 2 sounds • I can blend phase 2 sounds	• I know phase 3 sounds • I am reading a pink book	• I know phase 4 sounds • I am reading a red book
I know my numbers to 20		
• I can count to 10, forwards and backwards • I can write the numbers to 10 • I can count objects to 10	• I can count to 20, forwards and backwards • I can count objects to 20	• I know my number bonds within 10 • I can write the numbers to 20
I can talk about people		
• I can talk about people in my family • I can talk about people in other countries	• I can talk about people from the past • I can talk about people in the community	• I can talk about people from the past • I can talk about people in my family and community • I can talk about people in other countries
I can write a fairy tale		
• I can use a pencil • I can write my name • I can write some of the letters of the alphabet	• I can write all the letters of the alphabet • I have developed a comfortable and stable pencil grip	• I can communicate some ideas in writing • I am beginning to link words together into phrases and sentences
I can grow a sunflower		
• I can talk about different living things, including myself, and their habitats	• I can describe different states of water and how they move	• I can explain the role of water in keeping plants and animals alive • I know that plants grow from seeds
I can perform a gymnastics routine		
• I can stand on one leg	• I can do a forward roll	• I can catch a gymnastics ball
I can create a self-portrait		
• I can mix some colours and paint an object	• I can draw an original artwork inspired by Marc Chagall	• I can sculpt a free-standing clay sculpture

complemented ongoing work to ensure that the resources and books are diverse and that practitioners avoid stereotypical attitudes.

Bold Beginnings (Ofsted, 2017) found that maths was not generally as well taught as phonics in Reception. It is worth, therefore, giving additional consideration to the mathematics curriculum. You can find further information about maths in the early years in Chapter 7 of this book.

Charles Dickens has been using the 'Maths — No Problem!' mastery scheme in Years 1 to 6 for several years. This year, the publishers have extended the programme to include Reception. Our head of mathematics, Themistocles Bakas, reflects on our progress with the new scheme so far:

> There is a strong focus on mastery, on the learning and practising of core mathematical principles through play. By mastering these core principles, children are as well-prepared as possible to access the Year 1 curriculum from day 1. Each lesson is a small step, recalling and then building on the previous day's learning. These core principles are then built upon in Year 1 seamlessly. In part, this is facilitated by the use of the programme from Reception all the way to Year 6. This ensures that the language, use of concrete resources and visual representations are consistent across EYFS to the end of Key Stage 2.

> Crucially, although there is a strong focus on numeracy, this doesn't detract from the importance of play-based learning. This ensures the fostering of positive attitudes and interest in maths.

Children who need extra help in these areas of learning receive it within the context of the enabling environment. Children are not extracted from play to do more 'lessons'. Instead, their learning may take the form of more adult support within their play. This might be help with turn-taking, understanding social cues, counting and extending their vocabulary.

The taught curriculum: Cumulative subjects

Other areas of the curriculum tend to be more *cumulative*: key concepts are revisited in different contexts as a child journeys through school. It is often the concepts and vocabulary rather than the contexts themselves which constitute the core learning.

That they may be easier to catch up on, does not mean that these subjects are any less important. They offer abundant opportunities to celebrate children's diverse families and backgrounds and challenge stereotypical attitudes.

Science

At Charles Dickens, we have what may well be the smallest Forest School in the country. Though little, its impact is mighty! All children in our early years provision have at least one session of Forest School per week. They might tend the plants; listen to stories around the fire;

make art from natural materials; build dens. Forest School provides a different context for children to communicate, develop vocabulary, socialise and self-regulate.

It also sows the seeds for their understanding of the natural world. Children from our nursery provision will arrive in Reception with basic knowledge: how plants grow, how they can provide us with food, the names of some plants. This knowledge is extended and enriched in Reception. By the time they reach Year 1, they are more than ready to benefit from the science curriculum.

Humanities

Table 12.2 shows the progression of children's knowledge over time in humanities subjects.

From Year 1, humanities subjects are taught in discrete lessons: history, geography and RE. In Reception, we introduce children to what we mean by these different subjects.

In history, children talk about events in their lives and those of their parents and grandparents. They start to understand that there is a past and stories from before they were alive. As they talk about their own families and pasts, their language and sense of identity are strengthened.

Just as talking about the past introduces children to history, taking about places introduces them to geography. We want them to understand that there are different places and that people lead different lives in these places.

A link school in Nairobi gives us the opportunity to find out about the lives of children living in Kenya. Importantly, we get to find out about the lives of real people. We are not working on the basis of a stereotype. Kenyans are not all the same!

Rather, the children learn about the diversity of Kenyan life: hot and cold, urban and rural, seasides and mountains, modern and traditional, lions and football.

Similarly, we do the groundwork for understanding different religions by exploring various festivals. The dominant religions in the school are Islam and Christianity. We secure children's understanding of these religions before looking at Judaism, Sikhism, Hinduism, Buddhism and atheism. By Year 6 children can draw on their depth of knowledge and engage in comparative religion studies.

The proximal function of this learning is to understand what is meant in Year 1 by history, geography and RE.

Expressive arts

One of the school's core values is creativity. This is lived and breathed by the high status given to the creative arts. For example, every child, from the 2-year-olds to Year 6, is taught every year by specialist art, music and dance teachers.

Table 12.2 Humanities learning in Reception and Key Stage 1 at Charles Dickens Primary School

	Autumn 1	Autumn 2	Spring 1	Spring 2	Summer 1	Summer 2
Year R	**Past and Present** Immediate family **People, Culture and Communities** Kenya	**Past and Present** Grandparents and recent past – where am I from? **People, Culture and Communities** Diwali and Nativity	**Past and Present** Dinosaurs **People, Culture and Communities** China	**Past and Present** Early humans – cavemen **People, Culture and Communities** Roles and jobs – design a town **People, Culture and Communities** Easter	**Past and Present** Knights and castles **People, Culture and Communities** Maps and the local area – what is a map?	**Past and Present** The local area past and present – The River Thames **People, Culture and Communities** World map – world travel – a sense of the world
Year 1	**Geography** Our local area **Islam** What does it mean to be a Muslim?	**History** Dinosaurs **Christianity** What does God look like in Christianity?	**Geography** Shanghai **Islam** What does God look like in Islam?	**History** The History of Flight **Christianity** What is the meaning of Easter?	**History** Gunpowder, Fleabites & Flame **Islam** What is the hajj?	**Geography** The Seaside **Christianity** What does it mean to be a Christian?
Year 2	**History** The Stone Age **Islam** What is the Qur'an and why is it still read today?	**Christianity** What is the meaning of Christmas?	**Geography** The UK **Islam** Why is Muhammad so important to Muslims?	**Christianity** What is the Bible and why is it still read today?	**History** Ancient Egypt **Islam** What happens inside a mosque?	**Christianity** Who were the people of the Old Testament?

Art

Skills are plotted out for every year group to ensure progression in drawing, painting and 3D art. Due care is given to ensure that children explore a diverse range of works. This includes artists past and present, artists of colour, female artists, and artists from other under-represented groups.

Care is also taken to match artists to year groups, according to the reproducibility of their work. Nursery children learn about Matisse, for example, as they can emulate his work by tearing or cutting paper.

Music

The same is true of the music curriculum. The proximal functions feed into phonics and literacy. The emphasis in music on listening, rhythm and rhyme are precursors for reading and language composition. Remember that 'singing and rhyming activities develop phonological awareness' (EEF, 2018b).

Working with subject leaders

Subject leaders focus on both specialist knowledge and the big picture to ensure the curriculum is vertically aligned. They help plan lessons that will ensure children are ready for the Year 1 curriculum while the early years educators ensure that children's learning is accurately pitched and relevant for the children in their classes.

This is the taught curriculum. PSED, literacy and maths are taught every day. Other subjects are taught in one short session per week. For the rest of their time in school, children are engaged in self-directed, play-based learning. It is in this play that children learn the behaviours that will support their learning as they move through school, the most important of these being self-regulation and communication.

The environmental curriculum

We have thought long and hard about how to harness the power of play-based learning to develop self-regulation and communication skills. Careful thought goes into the curation of activities, zones and resources that will engage children, deepen and extend their learning, and foster their imaginations.

In this rich context, the best thing the adult can often do is to take a step back. This gives children the freedom to learn from each other, negotiate their play and problem solve. They cannot do this if we are hovering.

When adults get out of the way, the nursery setting highlights peer teaching. Two- to 4-year-olds move freely about. Older children lead the play and scaffold the language and social interactions with deftness.

The role of the adult, in general, is to *observe* so that they can:

1. Step in to support children with resources or resolving conflict.
2. Evaluate the impact of the taught curriculum. Is it being practised and secured by the children? Are adaptations to the curriculum or the environment needed?
3. Identify children who need further support.

As well as observing, this is a time when adults can focus on those children who need further support. They can:

*   share stories and model play
*   sit alongside children and scaffold language
*   pick an activity linked to a child's interests such as a jigsaw – this will help them to develop their learning as well as 'stick' at the task

This focus on teaching children to persist with difficult tasks, make decisions independently and work things out for themselves is based on research that shows self-regulation is important for both academic attainment and wellbeing in later life (Schoon et al., 2015).

Conclusion

The Effective Provision of Pre-School Education Project found that the advantages for a child's development of attending a particularly effective pre-school centre persist up to age 7. Two key findings were:

*   'Centres which put particular emphasis on literacy, maths, science/environment and children's "diversity" promoted better outcomes for children in their subsequent attainment, especially in reading and mathematics at age 5.'
*   '[S]ettings strong on the intellectual aspects of the curriculum tended to be strong on the social/behavioural side as well'.

(Sylva et al., 2004, p. 4)

By balancing the taught, adult-led curriculum with child-led exploration, we aim to harness the immense potential of both. Through being purposeful in what we teach directly and in the way we support child-led play, we ensure that every child has the opportunity to master the knowledge necessary for future success.

Reflective questions

1. What role do subject leaders play in supporting the curriculum in early years?
2. How does the planned curriculum flex to consider children's experiences and interests?

13

An evidence-based curriculum: Using the Early Years Toolkit to inform curriculum design

Melissa Prendergast

Introduction

Designing a curriculum for our settings may feel both exciting and daunting! It might feel like a huge responsibility to think of all the things we want children to learn and experience. On the other hand, we could relish the opportunity to decide what is best for our particular cohort and community. This chapter aims to guide you towards evidence-based resources that will help guide your decision-making. Our starting point is to ensure that our curriculum content meets the requirements of the educational programmes set out in the Statutory Framework for the Early Years Foundation Stage (EYFS) (DfE, 2021c).

Development Matters (DfE, 2021a) provides us with robust evidence-informed guidance and examples of best practice to help shape our curriculum. It helps our curriculum design by supporting reflections on breadth and progression, but it isn't a curriculum plan. Importantly, it does not represent the boundary of what is expected. Such decisions lie with practitioners and settings.

Our curriculum must:

- be ambitions
- promote equality and tackle discrimination
- have early language at its heart
- build on our expert knowledge of our children, families and local communities

It is vital that we know about the strengths of children, families and the community, and the challenges facing them, when creating and implementing a curriculum.

It is important that we move away from an assessment-driven curriculum, where the Early Learning Goals dictate what we teach.

Taking all that into account, we are still left with some big decisions. How do we decide what is most important? Are there aspects that will have a bigger impact on children's later education and life chances? Are there things that we have always done or things we always wished we could do?

Designing a curriculum requires *informed* professional conversations to explore these questions. We must be mindful about where we are drawing our information from. Not all sources of information or pieces of evidence are of equal quality. We must always aim to view educational approaches and claims with a critical lens. For more support on identifying the best evidence, the Institute for Effective Education (IEE) has produced a useful publication, the *Engaging with Evidence Guide* (IEE, 2019).

The IEE (2019) recommends three sources of evidence as being the most helpful and reliable when deciding which approach to use:

- robust experiments
- systematic reviews
- meta-analysis

Experiments are useful because they will tell us if a particular approach works. Systematic reviews give an overview of the evidence from research studies on a particular topic. Meta-analysis uses the numerical results from lots of studies and combines them together to give a measure of impact on outcomes.

A barrier for many of us when being research-informed is time. It takes time to read and digest research evidence and even more time to keep up to date with it. The Education Endowment Foundation (EEF) aims to address this problem.

The EEF is an independent charity which focuses its work on breaking the link between family income and educational achievement. It aims to support teachers, practitioners and educational leaders to close the disadvantage gap and raise attainment by using the best available evidence. One aspect of this support is evidence synthesis, where a summary is created of all the best educational evidence available in the UK and internationally. This is then presented in the form of a Teaching and Learning Toolkit for schools and the Early Years Toolkit for the EYFS.

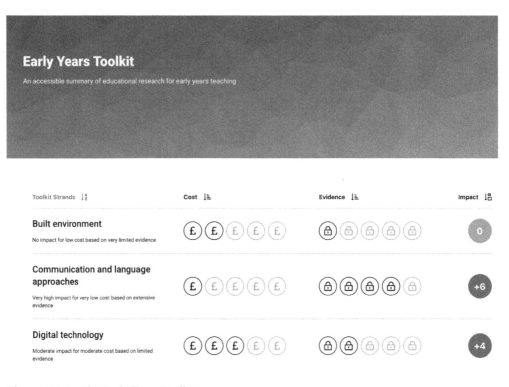

Figure 13.1 The Early Years Toolkit

What is the Early Years Toolkit?

The Early Years Toolkit (EEF, 2018) is a web-based summary of educational research, presented in a clear and easy to digest format and regularly updated. It was created by the EEF as the early years counterpart to the Teaching and Learning Toolkit. The Toolkit aims to help us make decisions about how best to use our resources to improve outcomes for all children, especially disadvantaged children. The EEF sees the Toolkit as a way to bridge the gap between educational research about what is beneficial and what actually happens in settings day to day.

The Early Years Toolkit is based on over 1,500 high-quality educational research studies. These studies provide data about what happens when particular approaches are used in early years settings around the world. The evidence is a synthesis of existing meta-analyses and quantitative systematic reviews. This means we can feel confident that the evidence base is robust.

The evidence is grouped into 12 key topics or strands. Each strand is given a summary rating in three categories: its average impact on attainment, the strength of the evidence supporting it and its cost (Figure 13.1). The Toolkit is updated regularly as new evidence emerges, making it a live and powerful resource.

Yet, we mustn't be swept away by the power and clarity of the Toolkit. The EEF cautions against seeing it as a definitive set of approaches that will improve outcomes in every setting.

We must instead see it as high-quality information about what has worked and what has not worked in other settings. It tells us *what has worked* but not *what works*, a subtle but vital distinction. We *can* use this evidence to suggest what is likely to be successful – a 'best bet'.

How can we use this research and evidence to inform professional conversations?

To make best use of this evidence, we need to add in our professional expertise. Since the evidence does not provide definitive answers, applying our professional knowledge and experience alongside the evidence allows us to decide if it will work in our setting and how. As the CEO of the EEF, Professor Becky Francis, says:

> Evidence does not provide easy solutions, but evidence-informed improvement is a process that has integrity and holds greater promise than any alternative.

> (Francis, 2020)

Our settings and contexts are unique. We know the particular circumstances in our settings, the unique features of the cohort, the barriers to learning and the issues facing the families we work with. An approach that might have a significant impact on outcomes in one setting will need considerable adjustments to have the same impact in another. Our professional knowledge is as powerful and important as the evidence. Drawing on our professional expertise allows us to take the information in the Toolkit and use it to make 'evidence-informed' decisions about what is likely to work best in our context. This quotation from Dylan Wiliam frames our professional conversations:

> In education, 'what works?' is not the right question because everything works somewhere and nothing works everywhere, so what's interesting, what's important in education is: 'Under what conditions does this work?'

> (Wiliam, 2009)

Engaging with research and evidence also presents us with other opportunities – the chance to give our educational practices a spring clean! We can check if our current work is backed up by research evidence. We can move away from approaches that do not have a positive impact on children's outcomes. This is especially useful when examining assumptions and ideas about early years practice that might be outdated. Education seems to be a field where outdated or unevidenced strategies persist unchallenged. Or, even when successfully challenged, they are not removed from everyone's practice.

 Take, for example, the idea of 'learning styles', which first appeared in the 1950s. This is the theory that we all have a preferred style of learning and when matched with a style of teaching, our learning is more effective and efficient. Do you remember wondering if you were a visual, auditory or kinaesthetic learner? Well, there is no robust evidence to show that this theory has a positive impact on outcomes at all. In fact, the EEF argues that it could actually have a detrimental effect on children's progress by restricting the activities they take part in and hampering the belief that effort leads to success (EEF, 2021b). This is a myth that has been successfully challenged (Newton and Salvi, 2020), yet remains a widespread belief.

In the early years, there are pervasive theories about how to teach early mathematics. One is based on the idea that maths is everywhere and that a high-quality enabling environment is full of opportunities to play mathematically. Through sensitive interactions during children's play, practitioners can turn those opportunities into moments when mathematics can be taught. The second theory is that with a dedicated maths area full of mathematical objects and equipment, children will independently engage in hands-on exploratory play and learn mathematical concepts. There are problems with both these theories, especially when applied as solitary strategies. Clements and Sarama highlight that myths about early education abound:

> Many beliefs people hold about early maths have a grain of truth in them, but as a whole are not true – they are largely myths. But the myths persist, and many harm children.

> (Clements and Sarama, 2018, p. 71)

In their 2018 paper, 'Myths of Early Math', Douglas Clements and Julie Sarama address these two theories about the teaching of early mathematics. They agree there is evidence to suggest that teachable moments, when done well, can be successful: but as the sole strategy they are inadequate. They argue that it requires a high degree of skill, subject knowledge and dedicated time to use this approach. They argue that it is unrealistic for any teacher to spot and act upon teachable moments for multiple children, consistently, over a whole year. When it comes to hands-on exploratory play, they see manipulatives and building blocks as having a positive impact on children's mathematical experiences. However, they cite the National Mathematics Advisory Panel (2008), who suggest that this is insufficient on its own. They argue that education should never be solely child-initiated or teacher-directed. Interactions with adults are key, small groups being particularly effective. They suggest that the fact that mathematical knowledge builds, with concepts and skills connected and sequenced, means that incidental learning through independent exploratory play cannot be supportive. It is through intentional mathematical activities, with planned teaching, that children can successfully learn mathematical concepts. These myths emphasise the need for a hybrid pedagogy. Children need all types of learning. Effective mathematical teaching must involve opportunities to explore maths in play, direct teaching in small groups and using opportunities throughout the day to highlight naturally occurring maths. Clements and Sarama conclude:

> … avoiding the myths and listening to the findings of research and the wisdom of expert practice will serve both teachers and children well.

> (Clements and Sarama, 2018, p. 71)

The EEF guidance report *Improving Mathematics in the Early Years and Key Stage 1* (EEF, 2020a) reviewed the best international research and consulted experts to arrive at five key recommendations for effective practice. These recommendations echo the features of effective mathematical teaching highlighted by Clements and Sarama (2018).

Sometimes having a spring clean of our beliefs, assumptions and approaches is just what is needed! We often need to stop doing something in order to use other, more impactful approaches. Being engaged with research allows us to sharpen our focus and gain insight into what might work.

Making the most of the Early Years Toolkit

Delving into the evidence summaries in the Toolkit may confirm some of what we already know. There might also be some evidence that surprises us! Before starting, it is important to take time to understand how to interpret the Toolkit.

Each strand is rated across three categories (see Figure 13.1). The first is cost and is a measure of the average cost of delivering the approach. The second measure is a rating of evidence strength, the padlocks representing the robustness of the evidence. The third is the average impact on attainment over an academic year. This measure shows the average number of additional months of progress made by children who received the intervention, compared to similar children who did not.

To get the most out of the Toolkit, consider the following three tips (adapted from EEF *Teaching and Learning/Early Years Toolkit Guide*, 2021c).

1. **Look carefully at the implementation cost, evidence strength and impact all together**

The strength of the evidence matters. For example, at first glance the approach of 'Play-based learning' looks very positive with 5 months' additional progress. However, the evidence security rating is one 'padlock', meaning that there is 'very limited evidence' (Figure 13.2). That does not mean that play-based learning is under-researched or doubtful. Rather, it points to the difficulty of evidencing the benefits of play in a secure way. The strongest evidence would come from a trial in which some young children accessed play-based learning, and another group, matched for similar characteristics, did not have any planned time for play in their early years setting. This would be impossible to achieve in England because the EYFS makes play-based approaches to learning a legal requirement. The best choices we can make around the use of play-based pedagogy will draw on both our understanding of the evidence and our professional knowledge and experience. The Toolkit can support our decisions. It should not dictate them.

Figure 13.2 Play-based learning

The cost-effectiveness of an approach must also be considered. Take, for instance, providing nursery places from a younger age, so children have two years of early years education before starting school. The impact is high at 6 months' additional progress, but the costs are estimated as being very high (Figure 13.3).

Figure 13.3   Earlier starting age

2.   Read the Toolkit entry for the strand in detail

Here we find details about the approach, what it costs and what impact you might expect. We also find information on the individual studies that the summary is based on. This allows us to think 'behind the average'. These details can really matter when we are thinking about implementing an approach in our own setting.

3.   Look at the other EEF resources which can be used alongside the Toolkit

The Toolkit is a fantastic starting point for becoming evidence informed. To find out more about how an approach has been applied, the EEF evaluation reports present detailed information. Their guidance reports provide comprehensive recommendations on how to apply approaches in practice.

Key findings in the Early Years Toolkit

One of the strands that the Toolkit highlights as being key in early years is 'Communication and language approaches'. Here the impact is high with extensive evidence and low cost (Figure 13.4).

Figure 13.4   Communication and language approaches

Communication and language approaches

When we look in more detail, this approach refers to strategies that promote spoken language and verbal interaction. The studies included in the evidence base have used a wide variety of strategies, but all with the same aim of explicitly supporting communication. The synthesis of this evidence shows that *all* children seemed to benefit. Some studies show a slightly higher impact for children from disadvantaged backgrounds. There was a notable difference in the effectiveness of some of the approaches compared to others. Strategies involving books and techniques like dialogic reading were especially effective. The importance of professional development and support for staff to implement strategies was a key finding in most of the studies. The evidence base also seemed to indicate that employing more than one strategy to support communication and language was more effective than relying on just one approach.

This robust evidence validates putting communication and language at the heart of any early years curriculum.

Implementation and professional judgement

When adopting an approach from the Early Years Toolkit, it is important to think carefully about the principles of implementation. There is a section in each Toolkit strand page called 'How could you implement in your setting?' Here there are a set of key questions to prompt the preparation and planning required to adopt that new approach.

Implementing a change as big as a new curriculum into our settings is a challenge. It is worth, then, delving deeply into the details of implementation. Careful and deliberate planning will support the process. It doesn't matter how robust the evidence for an approach is in theory; what matters is how it is translated into day-to-day practice.

The EEF's guidance report *Putting Evidence to Work – A School's Guide to Implementation* (2019) is an incredibly useful document that will guide you through this change. The implementation process outlined has been summarised into what we affectionately call the 'cake diagram' at East London Research School (Figure 13.5). Each phase of implementation is explained in more detail in Table 13.1, at the end of this chapter.

Implementation process

Four foundational principles of the guidance report are:

- treat implementation as a process, not an event
- plan and execute change in stages: do not try to change everything at once
- review existing practices: stop doing things which do not improve children's learning or experience in the EYFS
- do fewer things better

Those four principles run through Table 13.1, which suggests some of the key questions you might ask yourself before you start to make any changes, and to guide planning and evaluation.

Table 13.1 Phases of implementation

The 'explore' phase:	Considerations
• Evaluate your provision using your knowledge of the evidence together with your professional judgement • Identify a key priority for change	• Which aspect of your planned curriculum is a priority? • Is there a problem you need to address? • Is it a real problem or just a hunch? You need to use a robust process of gathering and interpreting data to inform this decision. Investigating the Early Years Toolkit to inform our curriculum design is also part of the explore phase. You are starting to make evidence-informed decisions about what to implement. The final aspect of 'explore' is to examine if your chosen approach will work? How likely is it to meet your needs? Will the time and effort costs outweigh any potential benefit?
The 'prepare' phase:	Considerations
• Pause: rushed implementation can lead to failure • Check that your team is ready, willing and able to make the intended change	• Have you spent enough time listening to staff to understand the problem you want to tackle? • Does everyone agree it is a problem? The 'prepare' phase of implementation is an intensive stage that requires as much time as you can spare to get it right. The first step is to create a clear and detailed plan. This could take the form of a whole curriculum plan or it could be a plan for an individual approach from the Toolkit that you have decided to implement as part of the curriculum. The key is being very specific and thinking about what it will look like in reality. You need to plan and deliver training to develop a shared understanding of the change. You need to be clear about what implementation will look like every day 'on the ground' – what will staff be doing differently? Planning ongoing support and training for staff is important, not just a one-off event.

The 'deliver' phase	Considerations
• Monitor how the change is going and listen to your team • Make intelligent adaptations where appropriate	• Are you checking that the intended changes are happening 'on the ground' every day? • Are you encouraging staff to use the new practices, and modelling them for those who still need help? • Are you checking carefully that staff are given enough help to implement the changes you planned? This is a tricky phase that will require continuous reflection and adaptation to manage difficulties in a positive, adaptive and progressive way. This should help you to keep practitioners motivated and committed to adopting the change faithfully. Continuing professional development and adding support in the form of coaching or mentoring will aid the transfer of conceptual knowledge. In turn, this will lead to changed practice when working with children. Once the core aspects of the approach are established, it may be valuable for practitioners to use their professional judgement to make intelligent adaptations. However, you need to take care that these do not undermine the crucial, evidence-informed aspects of the new approach. It is important not to rush into making changes to your plan: check that you have given staff enough support with anything that is not working yet.
The sustain phase	Considerations
• Continue to support staff Check that changes continue to have a positive impact on children's experience of the EYFS and their learning	• Is the approach securely embedded? • Are you making sure that new staff are trained and supported in the approach? The fourth stage of the implementation process is 'sustain'. This can occur in earnest once we are confident the new approach is having a positive impact on children's experience of the EYFS and their learning. During this phase, we work on supporting staff to make the change permanent whilst continuing to support and praise its use. The final step is to plan to sustain the approach over time.

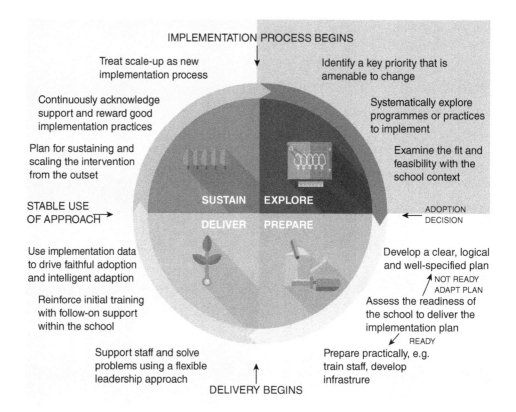

Figure 13.5   Implementation process

Conclusion

Until recently, early years practitioners have not been able to access a high-quality, user-friendly summary of educational research. As a result, we have often taken decisions without having the best possible information at our fingertips. We might have invested large sums of money in improving the physical environment of our setting, indoors or outside. Yet the evidence suggests we would gain more impact if we focused on improving the quality of our interactions with children, to boost children's early communication.

Ultimately, the decisions we make come down to our own professional judgement. The Toolkit is a useful resource to help us challenge our assumptions and work with the best available evidence. It can help us to make sound decisions to benefit the children we work with.

Reflective questions

1. Are there beneficial approaches summarised in the Toolkit that could form part of your new curriculum?
2. Which approach feels the most important for your specific context?

14

Professional development: Ensuring staff have the knowledge, skills and confidence they need

Siobhan Campbell

Introduction

Who amongst us does not want to be able to do our job in the best way possible and have the greatest impact on the lives of the children we work with? We engage in professional development to increase our capacity to do this. It is necessary to ask, however, how much of the time we invest in this is worthwhile?

I have been fortunate as a primary school teacher and leader to benefit from substantial investment in my professional development. I recognise this is not the case for us all. Some of it has been fantastic and remains memorable 10 years later. Much of it was interesting in the moment, but quickly forgotten.

We often feel comfortable with the 'easy to action' tips we gather from colleagues and the publications we read. But where is the evidence for these tips and tricks we pick up along the way? What is the point of them unless they lead to improvement in our practice, to better outcomes?

There is a need to place evidence at the forefront of professional development. The activities in which we invest time, energy and financial resources should have a great impact on our children. They should help us to provide high-quality provision, improve outcomes and narrow the disadvantage gap.

Over the years, I have been responsible for designing and delivering professional development programmes. The following information from the Education Endowment Foundation's (EEF) guidance report *Effective Professional Development* provides food for thought:

> A third of teachers in England typically take part in professional development at least once a week but only 38% of teachers surveyed in October 2018 agreed that 'time and resource allocated to professional development are used in ways that enhance teachers' instructional capabilities'. Moreover, substantially fewer classroom teachers (29%) agreed with this statement compared to headteachers (73%).
>
> (EEF, 2021a, p. 5)

So, what is it that makes some professional development more 'lasting' than others? How can we make informed choices about the professional development we invest in?

No single programme or form of professional development works in the same way in all contexts. How, then, can we adapt resources to optimally suit our particular context?

Challenges of professional development for early years educators

Somewhat uniquely within the stages of education, early years teams are comprised of a range of educators. The evidence review for the Fostering Effective Early Learning (FEEL) study notes:

> Educators often have different understandings and experiences, and different qualifications and roles within their schools and settings. Given these differences, they may benefit from different approaches to professional development and different content in the professional development.
>
> (Siraj et al., 2016, p. 22)

This variation in starting points matters less in forms of professional development such as coaching. Here we can make individual adjustments according to content. However, this variation makes a real difference when we look at the impact of larger scale professional development programmes.

> The FEEL study advocates team working and collaboration, and includes different styles and processes for learning as one way of supporting learner diversity and allowing educators to develop and change at their own pace.
>
> (Siraj et al., 2016, p. 22)

A significant constraint affecting quality professional development in the EYFS is longer opening hours and shift work. Once again, team working and collaboration as a form of professional development is a fruitful way around this. This means good practice can be developed 'live' when shifts overlap. In other words, it can go on with practitioners on the nursery floor. In phases other than early years, a barrier to such effectiveness is that professional development often takes place outside the classroom. This is less likely to translate into practice.

Case Study

The nature of shift work in the early years means that getting people together can be tricky. Here are some examples of creative solutions to this.

In the London South Teaching School Hub, a project with early years staff uses a model of 'learn it, see it, try it'. Settings work together to pool their experience and expertise. Staff attend short, evidence-based initial training, around one and a half hours long.

Examples of things the group looks at:

- the balance between interacting and interfering
- how to individualise planning

Initial input is followed up with the opportunity to observe it in practice. Staff then make an action plan of the aspects they want to develop. And the cycle repeats.

This model allows settings to share expertise at no extra cost. It avoids buying it in and sending people out to attend courses. It also enables application within the setting, making it more likely that improvements will be sustained.

Scheduling such sessions is specific to each setting. It is important to consult staff on the best times for them and their team. In some places, to get people together, staff agree to stay after work or have a later start on another day. Sometimes staff take 'time back' at quieter times of the week/term/year. Bringing a group of staff together requires flexibility.

Case Study

A creative project is running at School 360 in the London Borough of Newham. The school is looking at their interactions with children in the early years.

(Continued)

Staff have a tablet set up on a tripod, ready to record. They choose an interaction they want to capture for 15 minutes. The recording is then shared in a group reflection. More experienced practitioners can scaffold any reflections made, looking at aspects of the evidence base. Co-headteacher, Sarah Seleznyov, emphasises the importance of staff feeling confident to be open with colleagues for this to be successful. For example, strong practitioners go first, modelling the approach and nobody is forced to take part if they feel uncomfortable. This particular method allows the staff to have agency.

The Education Endowment Foundation's guidance report: *Effective Professional Development*

The report draws on the best available evidence for designing and adapting professional development. We can use it to increase the likelihood of our professional development being of the highest possible quality.

It is always important to define what we mean by professional development. We can draw on the evidence review for the Fostering Effective Early Learning (FEEL) study, which defines professional development as follows:

> Professional development applies to a range of activities which attempt to increase the knowledge, skills, and/or attitudes of ECEC (Early Childhood Education and Care) educators working with young children and their families/carers. Ultimately, through supporting educators and their practice, the long-term aim of professional development is to enhance the children's personal, social, behavioural and cognitive outcomes.
>
> (Siraj et al., 2016, p. 21)

The EEF guidance report describes it as:

> … structured and facilitated activity for teachers intended to increase their teaching ability.
>
> (EEF, 2021a, p. 7)

In both cases, it is about improving our knowledge, skills and practice. The FEEL study underlines the longer-term point of this as improving outcomes for children.

Mechanisms

The EEF guidance encourages us to think of 'mechanisms' or 'core building blocks'. These are aspects of professional development that are both observable and replicable.

The EEF has determined 14 mechanisms divided into four key areas (Figure 14.1).

EFFECTIVE PROFESSIONAL DEVELOPMENT
The mechanisms of PD

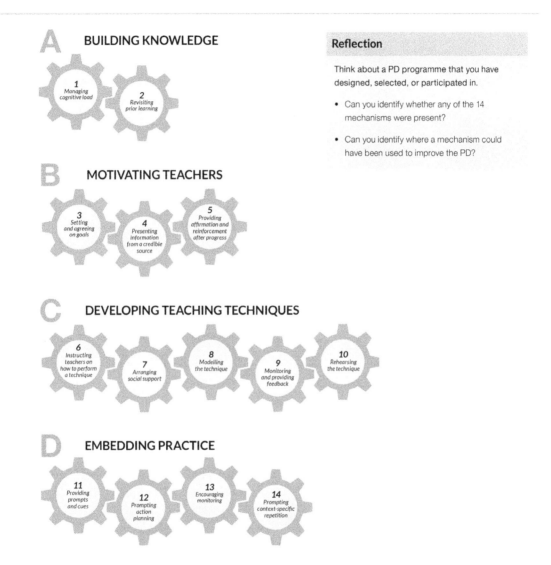

Reflection

Think about a PD programme that you have designed, selected, or participated in.

- Can you identify whether any of the 14 mechanisms were present?

- Can you identify where a mechanism could have been used to improve the PD?

Figure 14.1 Mechanisms for effective professional development

The evidence shows us that effective professional development has a 'balanced design'. This means including a mechanism from each of the four areas.

Reflecting on these mechanisms and a 'balanced design' helps explain why some professional development has a more positive impact than others.

When we look at Figure 14.2, the perils of an unbalanced design are laid out. Looking at the first row: a programme that does not allow for practice to be embedded will most likely result in people reverting to old habits after a period of time.

Building knowledge	Motivating teachers	Developing teaching techniques	Embedding practice	Likely outcome
✓	✓	✓		If embedding practice is missing, a teacher may understand the content, be motivated to improve, and have the techniques to do so but—after a period of time—may revert to old habits.
✓	✓			When developing techniques and embedding practice are absent, this could lead to the 'knowing, doing gap'. Here, a teacher may be fully aware of what they need to do and be motivated to do it; unfortunately, they do not know how to do so, nor do they have the tools to deliver.
✓				Here teachers may have effectively built the knowledge but lack the motivation and skills to implement.
	✓	✓	✓	In this instance, while teacher motivation and implementation may be present, they may have misunderstood and misapplied the initial knowledge.
✓	✓	✓	✓	Where professional development features a mechanism from each group, it may be more likely to be effective.

Figure 14.2   Ensuring a balanced professional development design

The FEEL study's evidence review identifies a set of features present in successful professional development (Siraj et al., 2016, p. 23). These include: content, process and affect. There is notable consistency across the EEF's mechanisms and the FEEL study's features:

- Content is similar to the mechanisms in 'Building knowledge'.
- Process is similar to the mechanisms in 'Developing teaching techniques' and 'Embedding practice'.
- Affect is similar to the mechanisms in the 'Motivating teachers' group.

When adapting or designing our professional development, there are always trade-offs when considering how many mechanisms to use. These include considerations about funding and time. The best bet is to use as many mechanisms as possible and at least one mechanism from each group.

The EEF's guidance *Putting Evidence to Work – A School's Guide to Implementation* (EEF, 2019) reminds us that effective professional development requires initial training *and* high-quality follow-up coaching. A common mistake is to only deliver the initial training.

Content matters

When we look at mechanisms, we focus on 'how' we carry out professional development. Yet it is equally important to keep in mind strong content. We do, after all, want to make sure the right things stick!

In answer to the question 'Why use evidence?', Professor Becky Francis, CEO of the EEF, says:

> Evidence does not provide easy solutions, but evidence-informed improvement is a process that has integrity and holds greater promise than any alternative.
>
> (Francis, 2020)

The EEF's Early Years Toolkit (EEF, 2018a) is an excellent starting point for the evidence. Chapter 13 provides an in-depth summary of how it works. The Toolkit is not designed to tell us what *will* work, but to give us a solid starting point. It gives the 'best bets' based on what has and hasn't worked. It is not a substitute for professional judgement, but when combined with in-house expertise, settings have the best possible chance of maximising impact for their children.

Adult learning and the challenge of behaviour change

The professional culture of our settings really matters. None of us will be surprised to learn that our working environment affects how well we do our work. Kraft and Papay describe this as follows:

> Teachers working in more supportive professional environments improve their effectiveness more over time than teachers working in less supportive contexts. On average, teachers working in schools at the 75th percentile of professional environment ratings improved 38% more than teachers in schools at the 25th percentile after ten years.
>
> (Kraft and Papay, 2014, p. 476)

Kraft and Papay (2014, p. 479) outline how we can promote improvement at a faster rate by establishing the following three ingredients:

- collaboration with colleagues
- receiving meaningful feedback on our practice
- recognition of our efforts

When these ingredients are present, staff are more likely to thrive.

The EEF's *Effective Professional Development* report (2021a) draws on evidence of human behaviour to support its guidance. For example, if we know that setting goals can positively change human behaviour in athletics or health, it is likely that it will do the same for us.

It can, however, be hard for us to change small habits, let alone make big shifts in our practice or introduce a continuous trickle of changes. The importance of hand washing in hospitals is a commonly used example of the difficulty of making changes. It is worth thinking about why this is the case. Hand washing is a straightforward action and there is widespread consensus that it is beneficial. It can even save lives. Yet its implementation in hospitals is inconsistent.

We need to think more carefully about what support is required to achieve widespread and consistent changes in behaviour. Staff training alone has evidently not led to sustained change in hospitals.

A combination of the following help achieve long-term change (Wilson et al., 2011):

• eliciting peer pressure
• the importance of role models
• incorporating 'opinion leaders'
• culture-changing interventions

Wilson et al. point out other factors that *may* influence behaviour change in staff, including:

• staff turnover
• gaps in our knowledge
• insufficient training
• unclear communications
• changing priorities
• competing demands
• competing practitioner and leader beliefs

These points show how much the culture of a professional environment and focusing on fewer priorities really matter. If we recognise the weak spots in our settings, we can work on them. We will then have a much firmer foundation for any professional development we pursue.

The EAST framework from the Behavioural Insights Team (Service et al., 2015) offers an understanding of how to encourage the desired behaviours. They suggest making them easy, attractive, social and timely:

• *Easy* is all about simplifying the message. By making something come across straightforwardly, we make it more likely to be adopted.
• *Attractive* is about attracting attention to what we are aiming for. This could be in how we present what we are doing. It could also include designing rewards systems for maximum effect.

- *Social* is about using the power of networks, encouraging commitment to others and setting up a group to lead by example.
- *Timely* is about encouraging behaviour changes people are most likely to be receptive to.

You will notice that these align with a number of the mechanisms identified by the Education Endowment Foundation.

It is pretty common for we human beings to resist change! Consequently, we may (sometimes inadvertently) block the potential impact of professional development. *Switch: How to Change Things When Change is Hard* (Chip and Heath, 2011) describes three ways to help reluctant people change their behaviour:

1. Grow your people: People must believe they are able to make a change. How can you make them believe they are capable of behaving differently?
2. Shrink the change: Don't make a task feel too big. Celebrate small wins and milestones that are within reach and meaningful.
3. Find the feeling: Motivate the elephant. Engage people's emotional side and get elephants on the right side through collaboration. You must motivate a person to become interested in your problem. Make people feel something.

(Chip and Heath, 2011, p. 123)

Implementation

It can be tempting to think that 'the more training input, the better'. However, many reviews of professional development have failed to find evidence that more is better. Instead of focusing on the amount of professional development, we should focus on the balanced design of it with reference to mechanisms and their effective *implementation*.

Effective implementation enables teachers to see what it would look like in their work with children. The EEF's *Effective Professional Development report* (2021a) is most useful when we consider it within their larger framework for effective implementation. It is helpful to revisit the EEF's 'cake diagram' (Figure 14.3) in the light of this chapter. At each phase, we need to consider how we are going to support implementation through effective professional development for our teams.

Explore

In this phase, we explore the key priorities of our setting. This determines our focus for professional development: it must be closely linked to whole-school improvement and priorities. It is not a stand-alone programme.

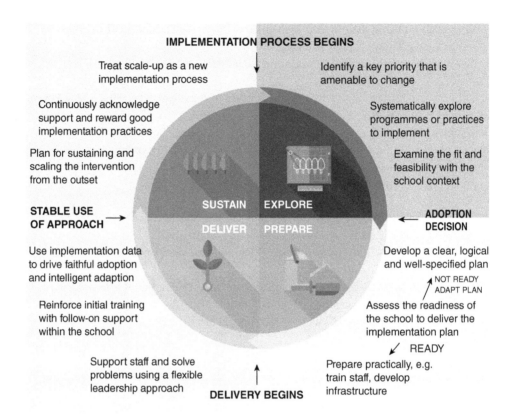

Figure 14.3   Implementation process

Prepare

In this phase, we introduce new skills, knowledge and strategies with explicit training.

Deliver

In this phase, we reinforce initial training with follow-on coaching. This is designed to support staff and solve any problems that arise.

Sustain

In this phase, we acknowledge and reward good practice. We may scale up or enhance the practice and plan to sustain and scale what we are doing.

Conclusion

Effective implementation also relies on our sensitivity to the bandwidth of our colleagues. If we are asking them to give energy to something new or to explore something more deeply, we need to think about how they can fit this in. What can we do less, or streamline? Is what we are implementing at the heart of our core strategy? Or is it an 'extra' thing that risks diluting our work overall? If it is not at the heart of our core strategy, we need to ask whether we are working on the right thing. Or, indeed, whether we need to review our overall strategy regarding professional development.

Reflective questions

1. Where do you look for advice or information for improving teaching and learning in your setting?
2. What are the barriers to the use of evidence in early years settings?
3. Think of some professional development that had a strong, long-term impact on your practice. What made it stand out from other professional development?
4. When staff attend external professional development, who ensures they put learning into practice once back at school? From where do they get support to embed and sustain their learning?
5. Think about a professional development programme that you have designed, selected or participated in. Can you identify whether any of the 14 mechanisms were present? Can you identify where a mechanism could have been used to improve professional development?
6. What are the top three barriers in your context for changing behaviour? How might you overcome these?

Afterword

Alison Peacock

I have been asked to share some thoughts here about why I believe the first phase of children's learning 0–5 years is of such vital importance. Working with our youngest children is both a joy and a huge responsibility. As adults, whether parents, carers or educators, it is our role to provide a safe, nurturing environment that is nonetheless challenging, that inspires curiosity, provokes questions and encourages recall and reflection. We want our children to experience open-ended opportunities for play, enquiry, to build and express their imagination and to fully develop physically. Early years settings in the world-renowned Reggio Emilia, Italy, recognise the importance of providing a beautiful environment both indoors and outdoors. An environment designed for optimal children's learning rather than for adult convenience is crucial. The joy of Forest School sessions, for example, is clearly illustrated in Chapter 11.

There are so many aspects to early childhood education discussed within this book, but one of the most important areas is that of language development. Children need language to think. They need language to express needs, wants and opinions. From their very earliest days, the desire to communicate is strong and with this the need to be heard, to be offered patient listening with intent. Dialogue is key. Back-and-forth interactions between infant and adult build the beginnings of powerful meaning-making which is at the heart of conversation. Early literacy must always be understood through the power of talk and through physical gesture. Expression of ideas embodied through movement is fundamental and is one of the reasons that extended carpet time for young children can be counterproductive. As we emerged from the first lockdown and children returned to full-time school, a parent reported that her child had returned home complaining 'School isn't "bendy" enough'. From this child's perspective, the routines and strictures of the classroom were just too rigid compared with the freedom of home. We need to consider how flexible our early years provision is and whether routines are in place for the convenience of adults or truly to support the learning of children.

This book is full of inspiring examples and wise advice about how to support early childhood education, offering a fulfilling curriculum that is fully inclusive and embraces the needs of each individual child. The world should be a wonderful, endlessly fascinating place for children. Working alongside children to help them make sense of new experiences and to draw connections between those experiences is to introduce and consolidate learning. However, children will learn more when guided and supported by an educator who is knowledgeable, who can ask and answer questions and extend the child's thinking. Self-styled discovery is not enough alone but, as with most things in life, there is a balance to be found. Motivation to explore, to wonder, to play and discover are all important starting points for learning. In this book, we consider knowledge and understanding of the world, with many prompts for how to embed this within the everyday experience of an early years setting.

Within our day care, nurseries and Foundation Stage classes, the role and expertise of teachers and early years colleagues is of fundamental importance. Intuitive, caring, emotionally supportive teaching is vital but the development of intellectual cognitive skills alongside social and emotional development is key. Our children need to work with adults who are themselves life-long learners, committed to finding out all they can about how best to support children's development. The skills of early years educators should never be underestimated. Nurture alongside intellectual challenge is essential for flourishing. One without the other is not conducive to the learner's wellbeing. This is why I agree with Siobhan Campbell about the vital need for professional learning across the entire early years workforce. Colleagues need to move beyond intuition towards professional dialogue and reflection. In many settings, this is best achieved through key workers regularly talking together not only about what children are observed to be doing but ways in which their learning can be scaffolded to achieve further challenge and success. There can be no substitute for adult subject knowledge and rich language skill. Additionally, engaging with books like this one, attending conferences and webinars, becoming a member of the Chartered College of Teaching, all provide the means to extend and develop professional skills.

The future world for our children is in peril. Engagement from the earliest days with the United Nations Sustainable Development Goals should be a priority. As we saw in Chapter 8, children are often highly motivated by social action initiatives within their community and should not be underestimated in terms of what might be achieved as a collective. We have only to think of the leadership roles and activities taken on with skill by many Year 2 children who have reached the 'top' of their infant school setting. High expectations within a supportive 'can-do' environment lead to impressive achievement.

Finally, it is so important that our early years settings offer a rich, welcoming environment for all where every child sees a reflection of themselves and of their home circumstances. We need to ensure that all staff learn to see diversity and difference as strengths. Children constantly take their cues from the comments and behaviours of trusted adults, which is why equalities training and awareness-raising should be warmly embraced. Similarly, actions that may lead to the labelling of children should be resisted. We must avoid a deficit model of education at all costs. The last thing any child needs is to be stifled or restricted in their development by well-meaning adults who wish to avoid risk-taking. Our children need to understand that learning has no limits, that everyone is special and that their future is full of possibility.

Professor Dame Alison Peacock is the Chief Executive Officer of the Chartered College of Teaching

References

Abrams, D., Swift, H. and Houston, D. (2018) *Research Report 119: Developing a National Barometer of Prejudice and Discrimination in Britain*. Available at: www.equalityhumanrights.com/sites/default/files/national-barometer-of-prejudice-and-discrimination-in-britain.pdf (Accessed 5 April 2022).

All Party Parliamentary Group (APPG) on Social Mobility (2019) *Closing the Regional Attainment Gap*. Available at: www.suttontrust.com/wp-content/uploads/2019/12/APPG-2019.pdf (Accessed 5 April 2022).

Allen, R. and Thomson, D. (2016) 'Changing the subject: How are the EBacc and Attainment 8 reforms changing results?' Available at: www.suttontrust.com/our-research/changing-the-subject (Accessed 5 April 2022).

Anno, M. (1986) *Anno's Counting Book*. London: HarperCollins.

Athey, C. (1991) *Extending Thought in Young Children: A Parent–Teacher Partnership*. London: Sage.

Barrett, M., Lyons, E. and Bourchier-Sutton, A. (2006) 'Children's knowledge of countries', in Spencer, C. and Blades, M. (eds) *Children and Their Environments*. Cambridge: Cambridge University Press, pp. 57–72.

Beck, I.L., McKeown, M.G. and Kucan, L. (2013) *Bringing Words to Life: Robust Vocabulary Instruction*. London: The Guilford Press.

Bell Foundation (2019) 'EAL assessment framework for schools: Primary'. Available at: www.bell-foundation.org.uk/resources/detail/assessment-framework-eyfs (Accessed 5 April 2022).

Bernard, C. (2022) *Intersectionality for Social Workers: An Introduction to Theory and Practice*. Abingdon: Routledge.

Bialystok, E., Craik, F.I. and Luk, G. (2012) 'Bilingualism: Consequences for mind and brain', *Trends in Cognitive Sciences*, 16(4), 240–50.

Bonetti, S. (2019) *The Early Years Workforce in England: A Comparative Analysis Using the Labour Force Survey*. Available at: https://epi.org.uk/publications-and-research/the-early-years-workforce-in-england (Accessed 5 April 2022).

Bromley, N. (2014) *Open Very Carefully – A Book With a Bite!* London: Nosy Crow Ltd.

Bronfenbrenner, U. (1977) 'Toward an experimental ecology of human development', *American Psychologist*, 32(7), 513–31.

Burke, N. (2018) *Musical Development Matters*. Available at: https://early-education.org.uk/wp-content/uploads/2021/12/Musical-Development-Matters-ONLINE.pdf (Accessed 5 April 2022).

Cain, K. (2010) *Reading Development and Difficulties*. Chichester: BPS Blackwell.

Campbell, R. (2010) *Dear Zoo*. London: Macmillan Children's Books.

Carle, E. (1997) *Brown Bear, Brown Bear, What Do You See?* London: Puffin.

Carr, M. (2001) *Assessment in Early Childhood Settings: Learning Stories*. London: Sage.

Center on the Developing Child (2011) 'Building the brain's "air traffic control" system: How early experiences shape the development of executive function'. Available at: https://developingchild.

harvard.edu/wp-content/uploads/2011/05/How-Early-Experiences-Shape-the-Development-of-Executive-Function.pdf (Accessed 5 April 2022).

Chalmers, H. and Murphy, V. (2021) 'Multilingual learners, linguistic pluralism and implications for education and research', in Ernesto, M. and Woore, R. (eds) *Debates in Second Language Education*. Abingdon: Routledge, pp. 66–88.

Child Poverty Action Group (CPAG) (2021) 'Child poverty facts and figures'. Available at: https://cpag.org.uk/child-poverty/child-poverty-facts-and-figures (Accessed 5 April 2022).

Children Act (1989) Available at: www.legislation.gov.uk/ukpga/1989/41/contents (Accessed 5 April 2022).

Chip, H. and Heath, D. (2011) *Switch: How to Change Things When Change is Hard*. London: Random House Business Books.

Choudhury, T. and Hodgkiss, A. (2021) 'How do young Bangladeshi and Sylheti-speaking children talk and play at home? An update on an ongoing research project'. Available at: https://research-school.org.uk/eastlondon/news/how-do-young-bangladeshi-and-sylheti-speaking-children-talk-and-play-at-home-an-update-on-an-ongoing-research-project (Accessed 5 April 2022).

Clark, A. (2010) *Transforming Children's Spaces: Children's and Adults' Participation in Designing Learning Environments*. Abingdon: Routledge.

Clements, D.H. and Sarama, J. (2014) *Learning and Teaching Early Math: The Learning Trajectories Approach*. Abingdon: Routledge.

Clements, D.H. and Sarama, J. (2017) 'Play, Mathematics, and False Dichotomies'. Available at: https://dreme.stanford.edu/news/play-mathematics-and-false-dichotomies (Accessed 5 April 2022).

Clements, D.H. and Sarama, J. (2018) 'Myths of early math'. Available at: https://eric.ed.gov /?id=EJ1199517 (Accessed 5 April 2022).

Clements, D.H. and Sarama, J. (2021) *Learning and Teaching Early Math: The Learning Trajectories Approach* (3rd edn). Abingdon: Routledge.

Cooke, G. and Lawton, K. (2008) *For Love or Money: Pay, Progression and Professionalisation of the 'Early Years' Workforce*. London: Institute for Public Policy Research.

Cooper, H. (1999) *Pumpkin Soup*. London: Corgi Childrens.

Counsell, C. (2018) 'Senior curriculum leadership 1: The indirect manifestation of knowl-edge – (A) curriculum as narrative'. Available at: https://thedignityofthethingblog.wordpress.com/2018/04/07/senior-curriculum-leadership-1-the-indirect-manifestation-of-knowl-edge-a-curriculum-as-narrative (Accessed 5 April 2022).

Craft, A., Cremin, T., Burnard, P. and Chappell, K. (2007) 'Developing creative learning through possibility thinking with children aged 3–7', in Craft, A., Cremin, T. and Burnard, P. (eds) *Creative Learning 3–11 and How We Document it*. London: Trentham Books.

Creative Skillset (2012) 'Employment census of the creative media industries'. Available at: www.screenskills.com/media/1552/2012_employment_census_of_the_creative_media_industries.pdf (Accessed 5 April 2022).

Dahl, R. (2016) *The Enormous Crocodile*. London: Puffin.

Dale, P. (1990) *Ten in the Bed*. London: Walker Books.

Department for Education (DfE) (2009) *Building Futures: Believing in Children. A Focus on Provision for Black Children in the Early Years Foundation Stage*. Available at: https://dera.ioe.ac.uk/8958/7/ey_bca_bldfuture0000809_Redacted.pdf (Accessed 5 April 2022).

Department for Education (DfE) (2015) *SEND Code of Practice*. Available at: https://assets.publishing.service.gov.uk/government/uploads/system/uploads/attachment_data/file/398815/SEND_Code_of_Practice_January_2015.pdf (Accessed 5 April 2022).

Department for Education (DfE) (2018) *Improving the Home Learning Environment*. Available at: https://assets.publishing.service.gov.uk/government/uploads/system/uploads/attachment_data/file/919363/Improving_the_home_learning_environment.pdf (Accessed 5 April 2022).

Department for Education (DfE) (2021a) *Development Matters: Non-statutory Curriculum Guidance for the Early Years Foundation Stage*. Available at: www.gov.uk/government/publications/development-matters--2 (Accessed 5 April 2022).

Department for Education (DfE) (2021b) 'Schools, pupils and their characteristics: January 2021'. Available at: www.gov.uk/government/statistics/schools-pupils-and-their-characteristics-january-2021 (Accessed 5 April 2022).

Department for Education (DfE) (2021c) *Statutory Framework for the Early Years Foundation Stage*. Available at: www.gov.uk/government/publications/early-years-foundation-stage-framework--2 (Accessed 5 April 2022).

Department for Education (DfE) (2022) 'Early years foundation stage: Exemplification materials'. Available at: www.gov.uk/guidance/early-years-foundation-stage-exemplification-materials (Accessed 5 April 2022).

Department for Education and Skills (DfES) (2002) *Birth to Three Matters*. London: DfES.

Dickinson, D.K., McCabe, A. and Sprague, K. (2003) 'Teacher Rating of Oral Language and Literacy (TROLL)', *The Reading Teacher*, 56(6), 554–64.

Douglas, H. (2007) *Containment and Reciprocity: Integrating Psychoanalytic Theory and Child Development Research for Work with Children*. Abingdon: Routledge.

Duffy, B. (2006) *Supporting Creativity and Imagination in the Early Years* (2nd edn). Maidenhead: Open University Press.

Durham University (2021) *Durham Commission on Creativity and Education – Second Report 2021*. Available at: www.dur.ac.uk/resources/creativitycommission/DurhamCommissionsecondreport-21April.pdf (Accessed 5 April 2022).

Dweck, C.S. (2007) 'The perils and promises of praise', *Ascd*, 65(2), 34–9.

Early Education (2012) *Development Matters in the Early Years Foundation Stage (EYFS)*. Available at: https://dera.ioe.ac.uk/14042/7/development%20matters%20in%20the%20early%20years%20foundation%20stage_Redacted.pdf (Accessed 5 April 2022).

Early Years Alliance (2018) 'Moving right from the start'. Available at: www.eyalliance.org.uk/moving-right-start (Accessed 5 April 2022).

Early Years Coalition (2021) *Birth to 5 Matters: Guidance by the Sector, for the Sector*. Available at: https://birthto5matters.org.uk (Accessed 5 April 2022).

Education Endowment Foundation (EEF) (2018a) 'Early Years Toolkit'. Available at: https://educationendowmentfoundation.org.uk/education-evidence/early-years-toolkit (Accessed 5 April 2022).

Education Endowment Foundation (EEF) (2018b) *Preparing for Literacy: Improving Communication, Language and Literacy in the Early Years*. Guidance Report. Available at: https://educationendowmentfoundation.org.uk/education-evidence/guidance-reports/literacy-early-years (Accessed 5 April 2022).

Education Endowment Foundation (EEF) (2019) *Putting Evidence to Work: A School's Guide to Implementation.* Available at: https://educationendowmentfoundation.org.uk/education-evidence/guidance-reports/implementation (Accessed 5 April 2022).

Education Endowment Foundation (EEF) (2020a) *Improving Mathematics in the Early Years and Key Stage 1: Guidance Report.* Available at: https://educationendowmentfoundation.org.uk/education-evidence/guidance-reports/early-maths (Accessed 5 April 2022).

Education Endowment Foundation (EEF) (2020b) *Special Educational Needs in Mainstream School: Guidance Report.* Available at: https://educationendowmentfoundation.org.uk/education-evidence/guidance-reports/send (Accessed 5 April 2022).

Education Endowment Foundation (EEF) (2021a) *Effective Professional Development: Guidance Report.* Available at: https://educationendowmentfoundation.org.uk/education-evidence/guidance-reports/effective-professional-development (Accessed 5 April 2022).

Education Endowment Foundation (EEF) (2021b) 'Learning styles'. Available at: https://educationendowmentfoundation.org.uk/education-evidence/teaching-learning-toolkit/learning-styles (Accessed 5 April 2022).

Education Endowment Foundation (EEF) (2021c) *Teaching and Learning/Early Years Toolkit Guide.* Available at: https://d2tic4wvo1iusb.cloudfront.net/documents/toolkit/EEF-Toolkit-guide.pdf?v=1643636419 (Accessed 5 April 2022).

Education Policy Institute (2020) *Education in England: Annual Report.* London: EPI.

Edwards, C., Gandini, L. and Forman, G. (eds) (2011) *The Hundred Languages of Children: The Reggio Emilia Experience in Transformation.* Westport, CT: Praeger Publishers.

Eglington, K.A. (2003) *Art in the Early Years.* London: Routledge.

Elfer, P. (2015) 'Positive relationships: Emotion – mixed feelings'. Available at: www.nurseryworld.co.uk/features/article/positive-relationships-emotion-mixed-feelings (Accessed 5 April 2022).

Elfer, P. (2018) *Developing Close, Thoughtful Attention to Children and Families in the Early Years Pedagogy.* Available at: https://eyhub.co.uk/wp-content/uploads/2021/04/Work-Discussion-Evaluation-Final-Report-to-Froebel-Trust-30-April-2018-2.pdf (Accessed 5 April 2022).

Ehlert, L. (2014) *Leaf Man.* London: Clarion Books.

Epstein, A. (2007) *The Intentional Teacher: Choosing the Best Strategies for Young Children's Learning.* Washington, DC: National Association for the Education of Young Children.

Epstein, D. (1993) 'Too small to notice? Constructions of childhood and discourses of "race" in predominantly white contexts', *Curriculum Studies*, 1(3), 317–34.

Equality Act (2010) Available at: www.legislation.gov.uk/ukpga/2010/15/contents (Accessed 5 April 2022).

Fawcett Society (2020) *Unlimited Potential – The Final Report of the Commission on Gender Stereotypes in Early Childhood.* Available at: www.fawcettsociety.org.uk/unlimited-potential-the-final-report-of-the-commission-on-gender-stereotypes-in-early-childhood (Accessed 5 April 2022).

Fischer Family Trust (FFT) Datalab (2019) 'How attainment gaps emerge from Foundation Stage to Key Stage 4'. Available at: https://ffteducationdatalab.org.uk/2019/10/how-attainment-gaps-emerge-from-foundation-stage-to-key-stage-4-part-one (Accessed 5 April 2022).

Fleer, M. (2021) 'Conceptual playworlds: The role of imagination in play and learning', *Early Years*, 41(4), 353–364.

Foorman, B., Beyler, N., Borradaile, K., Coyne, M., Denton, C.A., Dimino, J., Furgeson, J., Hayes, L., Henke, J., Justice, L. and Keating, B. (2016) *Foundational Skills to Support Reading for*

Understanding in Kindergarten through 3rd Grade: Educator's Practice Guide (NCEE 2016-4008). Washington, DC: National Center for Education Evaluation and Regional Assistance (NCEE), Institute of Education Sciences, US Department of Education.

Francis, B. (2020) 'Why superficial compliance with research is dangerous'. Available at: www. tes.com/magazine/archive/why-superficial-compliance-research-dangerous (Accessed 5 April 2022).

Froebel, F. (1912) *Froebel's Chief Writings on Education*. London: Edward Arnold.

Frye, D., Baroody, A., Burchinal, M., Carver, S., Jordan, N. and McDowell, J. (2013) *Teaching Math to Young Children: A Practice Guide* (NCEE 2014-4005). Washington, DC: National Center for Education Evaluation and Regional Assistance (NCEE), Institute of Education Sciences, US Department of Education.

Gelman, R. and Gallistel, C.R. (1986) *The Child's Understanding of Number*. Cambridge, MA: Harvard University Press.

Gifford, S., Gripton, C., Williams, H.J., Lancaster, A., Bates, K.E., Williams, A.Y., Gilligan-Lee, K., Borthwick, A. and Farran, E.K. (2022) *Spatial Reasoning in Early Childhood*. Available at: https:// psyarxiv.com/jnwpu (Accessed 5 April 2022).

Gilmore, C., Gobel, S. and Inglis, M. (2018) *An Introduction to Mathematical Cognition*. Abingdon: Routledge.

Goldschmied, E. and Jackson, S. (1993) *People Under Three: Young Children in Day Care*. London: Routledge.

Gopnik, A., Meltzoff, A.N. and Kuhl, P.K. (1999) *The Scientist in the Crib: Minds, Brains, and How Children Learn*. New York: William Morrow.

Goswami, U. (2015) 'Children's cognitive development and learning', in *Cambridge Primary Review Trust*. Available at: https://cprtrust.org.uk/wp-content/uploads/2015/02/COMPLETE-REPORT-Goswami-Childrens-Cognitive-Development-and-Learning.pdf (Accessed 5 April 2022).

Greater London Authority (2021) '3.1m children in England going to schools in areas with toxic air'. Available at: www.london.gov.uk/press-releases/mayoral/31m-kids-going-to-schools-in-are-as-with-toxic-air (Accessed 5 April 2022).

Grenier, J. (2019) '5 things to reflect on in the EYFS'. Available at: http://juliangrenier.blogspot. com/2019/09/5-things-to-reflect-on-in-eyfs.html (Accessed 5 April 2022).

Grenier, J. (2020) *Working with the Revised Early Years Foundation Stage: Principles into Practice*. London: Sheringham Nursery School and Children's Centre.

Grimmer, T. (2021) *Developing a Loving Pedagogy in the Early Years: How Love Fits with Professional Practice*. Abingdon: Routledge.

Hill, E. (2013) *Where's Spot?* London: Puffin.

Hodgkiss, A. (2021) 'Home language learning: What factors matter, and how do we support families?', *EAL Journal E-Issue*, 14, 78–82.

Hurd, A. and McQueen, D. (2010) *Wellcomm: A Speech and Language Toolkit for the Early Years*. Brentford: GL Assessment.

Institute for Effective Education (IEE) (2019) *Engaging with Evidence Guide*. York: IEE.

Jabadao (2009) 'More of me'. Available at: www.jabadao.org/post/more-of-me (Accessed 5 April 2022).

John, K. (2012) 'Supervision, part 2: Achieving effectiveness'. Available at: www.nurseryworld. co.uk/features/article/supervision-part-2-achieving-effectiveness (Accessed 5 April 2022).

Justice, L. and Ezell, H. (2004) 'Print referencing: An emergent literacy enhancement strategy and its clinical applications', *Language, Speech, and Hearing Services in Schools*, 35(2), 185–93.

Kelly, D.J., Quinn, P.C., Slater, A.M., Lee, K., Gibson, A., Smith, M., Ge, L. and Pascalis, O. (2005) 'Three-month-olds, but not newborns, prefer own-race faces', *Developmental Science*, 8(6), F31–6.

Kraft, M.A. and Papay, J.P. (2014) 'Can professional environments in schools promote teacher development? Explaining heterogeneity in returns to teaching experience', *Educational Evaluation and Policy Analysis*, 36(4), 476–500.

Lane, J. (2008) *Young Children and Racial Justice: Taking Action for Racial Equality in the Early Years – Understanding the Past, Thinking about the Present, Planning for the Future.* London: National Children's Bureau.

Law, J., Theakston, A., Gascoigne, M., Dockrell, J., McKean, C. and Charlton, J. (2017) *Early Language Development: Needs, Provision and Intervention for Preschool Children from Socioeconomically Disadvantaged Backgrounds.* Available at: https://educationendowment-foundation.org.uk/education-evidence/evidence-reviews/early-language (Accessed 5 April 2022).

Lumsden, E. (2021) 'Rethinking early childhood services – change from within'. Available at: www.nurseryworld.co.uk/news/article/rethinking-early-childhood-services-change-from-within (Accessed 5 April 2022).

Marmot, M. (2020a) *Build Back Fairer: The Marmot Covid-19 Review.* Available at: www.health.org.uk/publications/build-back-fairer-the-covid-19-marmot-review (Accessed 5 April 2022).

Marmot, M. (2020b) 'Health equity in England: The Marmot review 10 years on', *BMJ*, 368.

McMillan, M. (1930) *The Nursery School.* London: J.M. Dent & Sons Ltd.

McTavish, A. (2017) *The Creative Thinking and Learning Project.* Available at: www.annimctavish.uk/book/creative-thinking-and-learning-project (Accessed 5 April 2022).

Millar, R. (2004) 'The role of practical work in the teaching and learning of science', *Commissioned paper, Committee on High School Science Laboratories: Role and Vision.* Washington, DC: National Academy of Sciences, p. 308.

Ministry of Education and Culture, Finland (2016) 'Joy, play and doing together; recommendations for physical activity in early childhood'. Available at: https://julkaisut.valtioneuvosto.fi/handle/10024/78924 (Accessed 5 April 2022).

Moroney, N. (2006) 'Box clever: Improving children's talking through play', *Bulletin of the Royal College of Speech & Language Therapists*, 650, 18–19.

National Mathematics Advisory Panel (2008) *Foundations for Success: The Final Report of the National Mathematics Advisory Panel.* Washington, DC: US Department of Education.

National Society for Education in Art and Design (NSEAD) (2021) 'Anti-racist Art Education (ARAE) curriculum checklist'. Available at: www.nsead.org/resources/curriculum/arae-curriculum-checklist (Accessed 5 April 2022).

Nelinger, A., Album, J., Haynes, A. and Rosan, C. (2021) *Their Challenges are Our Challenges – A Summary Report of the Experiences Facing Nursery Workers in the UK in 2020.* London: Anna Freud National Centre for Children and Families.

New Zealand Education Evaluation Centre/Te Ihuwaka (2021) *Science in the Early Years.* Available at: https://ero.govt.nz/sites/default/files/2021-04/Science%20in%20the%20Early%20Years%20Early%20Childhood%20and%20Years%201%20to%204.pdf (Accessed 5 April 2022).

New Zealand Education Review Office/Te Tari Arotake Mātauranga (2016) *Early Mathematics: A Guide for Improving Teaching and Learning.* Available at: https://ero.govt.nz/our-research/early-mathematics-a-guide-for-improving-teaching-and-learning (Accessed 5 April 2022).

Newton, P.M. and Salvi, A. (2020) 'How common is belief in the learning styles neuromyth, and does it matter? A pragmatic systematic review', *Frontiers in Education*, 5, 602451.

Obama, B. (2012) 'Address to the National Geographic Bee'. Available at: https://geographyeducation.org/2012/09/06/president-obama-on-geography-education (Accessed 5 April 2022).

Office for Standards in Education (Ofsted) (2017) *Bold Beginnings: The Reception Curriculum in a Sample of Good and Outstanding Primary Schools*. Available at: https://assets.publishing.service.gov.uk/government/uploads/system/uploads/attachment_data/file/663560/28933_Ofsted_-_Early_Years_Curriculum_Report_-_Accessible.pdf (Accessed 5 April 2022).

Office for Standards in Education (Ofsted) (2019a) *Education Inspection Framework: Overview of Research*. Available at: https://assets.publishing.service.gov.uk/government/uploads/system/uploads/attachment_data/file/963625/Research_for_EIF_framework_updated_references_22_Feb_2021.pdf (Accessed 5 April 2022).

Office for Standards in Education (Ofsted) (2019b) *Education Inspection Framework 2019: Inspecting the Substance of Education*. Available at: www.gov.uk/government/consultations/education-inspection-framework-2019-inspecting-the-substance-of-education/education-inspection-framework-2019-inspecting-the-substance-of-education (Accessed 5 April 2022).

Office for Standards in Education (Ofsted) (2019c) 'School inspection update'. Available at: https://assets.publishing.service.gov.uk/government/uploads/system/uploads/attachment_data/file/772056/School_inspection_update_-_January_2019_Special_Edition_180119.pdf (Accessed 5 April 2022).

Office for Standards in Education (Ofsted) (2021) 'Ofsted and the EYFS reforms'. Available at: www.foundationyears.org.uk/wp-content/uploads/2021/03/LED-events-March-2021-Ofsted.pdf (Accessed 5 April 2022).

Office for Standards in Education (Ofsted) (2022) 'Early years inspection handbook for Ofsted-registered provision'. Available at: www.gov.uk/government/publications/early-years-inspection-handbook-eif/early-years-inspection-handbook-for-ofsted-registered-provision-for-september-2021 (Accessed 5 April 2022).

Office for National Statistics (2021) 'Gender pay gap in the UK: 2021'. Available at: www.ons.gov.uk/employmentandlabourmarket/peopleinwork/earningsandworkinghours/bulletins/genderpaygapintheuk/2021 (Accessed 5 April 2022).

Osgood, J. (2011) 'Contested constructions of professionalism within the nursery', in Miller, L. and Cable, C. (eds) *Professionalization, Leadership and Management in the Early Years*. London: Sage.

Ouellette, G. and Sénéchal, M. (2017) 'Invented spelling in kindergarten as a predictor of reading and spelling in Grade 1: A new pathway to literacy, or just the same road, less known?', *Developmental Psychology*, 53(1), 77–88.

Philip, S. and Gaggiotti, L. (2020) *I Really Want to Shout!* London: Templar.

Phillips, A. (2019) 'Attention seeking'. Available at: www.londonreviewbookshop.co.uk/podcasts-video/video/adam-phillips-and-devorah-baum-attention-seeking (Accessed 5 April 2022).

Price, D. and Tayler, K. (2015) *LGBT Diversity and Inclusion in Early Years Education*. Abingdon: Routledge.

Qualifications and Curriculum Authority (QCA) (2000) *Curriculum Guidance for the Foundation Stage*. Sudbury: QCA.

Rathman, P. (2012) *Good Night, Gorilla*. London: Story House Egmont.

Raver, C.C., Blair, C. and Willoughby, M. (2013) 'Poverty as a predictor of 4-year-olds' executive function: New perspectives on models of differential susceptibility', *Developmental Psychology*, 49(2), 292–304.

Rosen, M. (2000) *We're Going on a Bear Hunt.* London: Walker Books.

Rowe, D.W. and Wilson, S.J. (2015) 'The development of a descriptive measure of early childhood writing: Results from the Write Start! writing assessment', *Journal of Literacy Research*, 47(2), 245–292.

Rustin, M. (2008) *Work Discussion: Implications for Research and Policy.* London: Karnac Books.

Save the Children (2016) *The Lost Boys: How Boys are Falling Behind in Their Early Years.* Available at: www.savethechildren.org.uk/content/dam/global/reports/the_lost_boys_report.pdf (Accessed 5 April 2022).

Scaife, J. and Inskipp, F. (2001) *Supervision in the Mental Health Professions: A Practitioner's Guide.* Hove: Psychology Press.

Schoon, I., Nasim, B., Sehmi, R. and Cook, R. (2015) *The impact of early life skills on later outcomes.* Available at: https://discovery.ucl.ac.uk/id/eprint/10051902/1/Schoon_2015%20The%20 Impact%20of%20Early%20Life%20Skills%20on%20Later%20Outcomes_%20Sept%20fin2015. pdf (Accessed 5 April 2022).

Service, O., Hallsworth, M., Halpern, D., Algate, F., Gallagher, R., Nguyen, S., Ruda, S. and Sanders, M. (2015) *EAST: Four Simple Ways to Apply Behavioural Insights.* Available at: www. bi.team/publications/east-four-simple-ways-to-apply-behavioural-insights (Accessed 5 April 2022).

Simpson, D., Loughran, S., Lumsden, E., Mazzocco, P., McDowall Clark, R. and Winterbottom, C. (2018) 'Talking heresy about "quality" early childhood education and care for children in poverty', *Journal of Poverty and Social Justice*, 26(1), 3–18.

Simpson, D., Loughran, S., Lumsden, E., McDowall Clark, R. and Winterbottom, C. (2017) '"Seen but not heard": Practitioners work with poverty and the organising out of disadvantaged children's voices and participation in the early years', *European Early Childhood Education Research Journal*, 25(2), 177–88.

Simpson, D., Lumsden, E. and McDowall Clark, R. (2015) 'Pre-school practitioners, child poverty and social justice', *International Journal of Sociology and Social Policy*, 35(5/6), 325–39.

Siraj, I., Kingston, D., Neilsen-Hewett, C., Howard, S., Melhuish, E., de Rosnay, M., Duursma, E. and Luu, B. (2016) 'Fostering effective early learning: A review of the current international evidence considering quality in early childhood education and care programmes in delivery, pedagogy and child outcomes'. Available at: https://ro.uow.edu.au/sspapers/4287 (Accessed 5 April 2022).

Siraj-Blatchford, I. (2009) 'Conceptualising progression in the pedagogy of play and sustained shared thinking in early childhood education: A Vygotskian perspective'. Available at: https:// ro.uow.edu.au/sspapers/1224 (Accessed 5 April 2022).

Siraj-Blatchford, I., Muttock, S., Sylva, K., Gilden, R. and Bell, D. (2002) *Researching Effective Pedagogy in the Early Years.* Available at: https://dera.ioe.ac.uk/4650/1/RR356.pdf (Accessed 5 April 2022).

Siraj-Blatchford, I., Taggart, B., Sylva, K., Sammons, P. and Melhuish, E. (2008) 'Towards the transformation of practice in early childhood education: The effective provision of pre-school education (EPPE) project', *Cambridge Journal of Education*, 38(1), 23–36.

Skene, K., O'Farrelly, C.M., Byrne, E.M., Kirby, N., Stevens, E.C. and Ramchandani, P.G. (2022) 'Can guidance during play enhance children's learning and development in educational contexts? A systematic review and meta-analysis'. Available at: https://srcd.onlinelibrary.wiley. com/doi/full/10.1111/cdev.13730 (Accessed 5 April 2022).

Soukakou, E.P. (2012) *Inclusive Classroom Profile (ICP)*. Baltimore, MD: Brookes Publishing.

Sylva, K., Melhuish, E., Sammons, P., Siraj-Blatchford, I. and Taggart, B. (2004) *The Effective Provision of Pre-School Education (EPPE) Project: Final Report – A Longitudinal Study Funded by the DfES 1997–2004*. Available at: https://discovery.ucl.ac.uk/id/eprint/10005309/1/sylva2004EP-PEfinal.pdf (Accessed 5 April 2022).

Sylva, K., Siraj-Blatchford, I. and Taggart, B. (2003) *Assessing Quality in the Early Years: Early Childhood Environment Rating Scale – Extension (ECERS-E), Four Curricular Subscales*. London: Trentham Books.

Tabors, P. (1997) *One Child, Two Languages*. Baltimore, MD: Brookes Publishing.

Tedam, P. (2015) 'Understanding diversity', in Waller, T. and Davies, G. (eds) *An Introduction to Early Childhood* (3rd edn). London: Sage, pp. 90–109.

Tedam, P. (2020) *Anti-oppressive Social Work Practice*. London: Sage.

The Early Math Collaborative, Erikson Institute (2014) *Big Ideas of Early Mathematics: What Teachers of Young Children Need to Know*. Hoboken, NJ: Pearson.

Thompson, N. (2021) *Anti-discriminatory Practice* (7th edn). London: Red Globe Press.

Tickell, C. (2011) *The Early Years: Foundations for Life, Health and Learning – An Independent Report on the Early Years Foundation Stage to Her Majesty's Government*. Available at: https://assets.publishing.service.gov.uk/government/uploads/system/uploads/attachment_data/file/180919/DfE-00177-2011.pdf (Accessed 5 April 2022).

Tovey, H. (2016) *Bringing the Froebel Approach to Your Early Years Practice*. London: Taylor and Francis.

Tremblay, R. (2002) 'Prevention of injury by early socialization of aggressive behavior', *Injury Prevention*, 8(suppl. 4), iv17–iv21.

United Nations (2016) 'The 17 goals'. Available at: https://sdgs.un.org/goals (Accessed 5 April 2022).

United Nations Children's Fund (UNICEF) (2019) 'A summary of the UN Convention on the Rights of the Child'. Available at: www.unicef.org.uk/rights-respecting-schools/wp-content/uploads/sites/4/2017/01/Summary-of-the-UNCRC.pdf (Accessed 5 April 2022).

Venkadasalam, V.P. and Ganea, P.A. (2018) 'Do objects of different weight fall at the same time? Updating naive beliefs about free-falling objects from fictional and informational books in young children', *Journal of Cognition and Development*, 19(2), 165–81.

White, E.B. (2014) *Charlotte's Web*. London: Puffin Classics.

White, J. (2013) *Playing and Learning Outdoors: Making Provision for High Quality Experiences in the Outdoor Environment with Children 3–7*. Abingdon: Routledge.

Whitebread, D., Anderson, H., Coltman, P., Page, C., Pasternak, D.P. and Mehta, S. (2005) 'Developing independent learning in the early years', *Education 3-13*, 33(1), 40–50.

Wigfield, J. and Guthrie, A. (2000) 'Engagement and motivation in reading', in Kamil, M., Mosenthal, P., Pearson, D. and Barr, R. (eds) *Handbook of Reading Research* (3rd edn). New York: Longman.

Wiliam, D. (2009) 'Assessment for learning: Why, what and how?' *(Inaugural Professorial Lecture)*. London: Institute of Education.

Wiliam, D. (2013) *Principled Curriculum Design*. Available at: https://webcontent.ssatuk.co.uk/wp-content/uploads/2013/09/Dylan-Wiliam-Principled-curriculum-design-chapter-1.pdf (Accessed 5 April 2022).

Wilson, S., Jacob, C.J. and Powell, D. (2011) 'Behavior-change interventions to improve hand-hygiene practice: A review of alternatives to education', *Critical Public Health*, 21(1), 119–27.

World Health Organization (WHO) (2018) *Nurturing Care for Early Childhood Development: A Framework for Helping Children Survive and Thrive to Transform Health and Human Potential*. Available at: https://apps.who.int/iris/bitstream/handle/10665/272603/9789241514064-eng.pdf (Accessed 5 April 2022).

Index